Wit

HAPPENS

Wit HAPPENS

Global Jewish Humor

Edited by JENNIFER CAPLAN,
JARROD TANNY & AVINOAM PATT

Wayne State University Press
Detroit

ISBN 9780814352595 (paperback)
ISBN 9780814352588 (hardcover)
ISBN 9780814352601 (ebook)

Library of Congress Control Number: 2025945080

Cover design by Nathaniel Roy Design.

Grateful acknowledgment is made to the Charles and Hannah Block Fund for Jewish Studies for the generous support of the publication of this volume.

Wayne State University Press rests on Waawiyaataanong, also referred to as Detroit, the ancestral and contemporary homeland of the Three Fires Confederacy. These sovereign lands were granted by the Ojibwe, Odawa, Potawatomi, and Wyandot Nations, in 1807, through the Treaty of Detroit. Wayne State University Press affirms Indigenous sovereignty and honors all tribes with a connection to Detroit. With our Native neighbors, the press works to advance educational equity and promote a better future for the earth and all people.

Wayne State University Press
Leonard N. Simons Building
4809 Woodward Avenue
Detroit, Michigan 48201-1309

Visit us online at wsupress.wayne.edu.

CONTENTS

ACKNOWLEDGMENTS

No book is written in a vacuum, but an edited collection such as this one comes with such an extensive list of people to thank that there is no way we could list everyone. There are, however, some people we want to be sure we acknowledge. First of all, we would like to thank everyone involved in the original conference that gave birth to this collection. It ran from February 28 through March 1, 2020, so among everyone else, we need to thank the airline industry for not shutting down until the following week so that the conference could even happen. The conference, called "No Respect: Jewish Humor Around the World," took place at the University of North Carolina Wilmington (UNCW) and was primarily funded and supported by the Charles and Hannah Block Fund for Jewish Studies and the Department of History. The Block Fund also provided subvention support for the publication of this volume, for which we are very grateful. Many of the participants in that conference are also represented in this volume, but the volume also contains some new friends we made along the way and some colleagues at the conference were not able to contribute, so we thank all those who have been part of this project, from 2020 to now.

We would like to thank the faculty and staff in the Department of History at UNCW who helped make our 2020 conference a smashing success. As department chair, Lynn Mollenauer, with the terrific assistance of Andrea Massey Boney and Meaghan Wright, oversaw much of the logistics involving the hotel, campus space, and coordination with the university. We would also like to thank the Taft Research Center at the University of Cincinnati for the funding support for this publication.

Jenny says, "Thank you to Jarrod and Avi for helping to direct this often lumbering but always navigable ship. I need to thank my friends and family for understanding when I was too stressed about looming deadlines to be much fun, even when they didn't understand exactly what the book was about (Thanks, Dad, for once saying, 'What do you mean Jewish humor beyond the Ashkenazi bubble? There aren't any Sephardic comedians!' and proving to me that the book was, in fact, as necessary as we thought it was!)."

Jarrod says, "First and foremost I would like to thank my coeditors, Jenny and Avi. Jenny organized this conference with me from the idea's very inception in 2018, otherwise known as 2 PPE (pre-pandemic era). Having Avi join the team gave us the necessary push to see the transformation of a collection of essays into a published collection of essays. At UNCW, I would like to thank my colleagues for their participation in the conference and the attendant events. In addition to Lynn, Meaghan, and Andrea, I would like to thank David Houpt, Michael Seidman, and Venkat Dhulipala for chairing the conference panels. Thank you to Jeanne Persuit and the Department of Communication Studies student production team (Austin Chandler, Hannah Lewis, Luccas Souza Cruz, and Maddie Peterson), who made the programs for the initial conference. I would also like to thank my parents for their tireless support. And, of course, I thank my children, Sarah and Max, who are now adults and vaguely more aware of this book's existence than they were of my first book, published when they were five."

Avi adds: "Special thanks to Jenny and Jarrod for inviting me to join you as a coeditor of this volume. If a camel is a horse designed by committee, then an edited volume can sometimes end up being a dead horse. After five years and many rounds of editing, I am glad to see our horse trotting into the world. Thanks to both of you for your good nature and collaborative spirit. And a special thanks to our authors for your wonderful contributions. The students in my Jewish humor classes at the University of Hartford, the University of Connecticut, and now New York University have always challenged me to think about Jewish humor in new ways and to understand how humor works differently for different audiences. I hope that some of the insights gleaned from this volume will make their way into future classroom conversations and not just be fodder for future routines. I am grateful as always to my family for your continued support and to my children, Maya, Alex, and Micah, all aspiring comedians in their own minds. Many thanks to the staff of Wayne State University Press, who are masters of the edited horse."

INTRODUCTION

Wit Happens: Global Jewish Humor

Jennifer Caplan, Jarrod Tanny, and Avinoam Patt

"Let's talk about something more cheerful. Have you any news of the cholera in Odessa?" asked Tevye the Dairyman. We can do one better. Let's talk about the corona in Carolina. Are you interested in that, Pan Sholem Aleichem?[1] No joke. COVID-19 nearly shut down our global Jewish humors conference, meticulously planned for March 2020. And while the event transpired and our participants escaped the impending plague to the shelters of home and family by a hair, the worldwide catastrophe almost dealt a fatal blow to this edited volume drawn from our conference proceedings. We write these opening words nearly five years later, in January 2025, probably close to the record of elapsed time between conference and book. If only we had actually set out to achieve this record!

It is ironic—or, worse, it undermines the purpose of this volume—that we begin with a classic line from the canonical text of Sholem Aleichem's "shtetl humor" reinvented with a vengeance for a Jewish comedy conference in twenty-first-century Wilmington, North Carolina. But how could we resist such an opening? How could we miss the opportunity to perpetuate the stereotype that, as Sarah Blacher Cohen succinctly put it decades ago, the Jews are "the butt of a cruel joke,"[2] and no matter how miserable our misfortune, we feel a burning compulsion to kvetch about our fate.

Of course, neither cholera nor corona is exclusively a Jewish experience. Nor is their use as a starting point for a sardonic tale of "Jewish luck" true of all Jewish communities. The chapters in this volume are a testament to the diversity of Jewish humor, a global phenomenon, all too often dominated by the east European Ashkenazi experience: flight from the land of pogroms, persecution, and cholera to a more prosperous America, where Jewish success is nevertheless haunted by the ghosts of the Pale of Settlement. So we continue to do as we imagine our ancestors to have done. We joke.

Jewish humor is a popular subject for scholars and readers alike. Most of the scholarship stays within the "Ashkenazi bubble," focusing on humor from eastern Europe, North America, and in some cases Israel. Scholars have traditionally argued that the experience of the shtetl, and the antisemitic violence common in them during the eighteenth and nineteenth centuries, created the mentality that allowed "Jewish humor" to develop.[3] There are several historical reasons why the United States became the center of gravity for Jewish cultural production, and therefore Jewish humor in the twentieth century. The Holocaust, of course, is one reason, but anti-Jewish (and anti-religious) efforts in the USSR contributed as well. Furthermore, while Jewish life was developing in the new state of Israel, it was a life beset by the problems of building a new nation, establishing an economy and government, and struggling against hostile neighbors. Jews in the United States, however, were becoming upwardly mobile and increasingly comfortable, and that comfort allowed them to produce art, including humor, at an unprecedented rate. The sheer quantity of American Jewish humor has overshadowed the reality that there is not just one "Jewish humor" but many "Jewish humors."

Additionally, while some scholarship has attempted to move beyond the linear "shtetl to America" narrative, this approach can suffer from the problems inherent in trying to analyze humor across space and time.[4] Scholars who have attempted to show that (Ashkenazi) Jewish humor has its roots in the Bible and the Talmud (see, e.g., Hershey Friedman's *God Laughed: Sources of Jewish Humor* and Michael Wex's *Born to Kvetch*) fail to explain why it only carried over to the Ashkenazi Yiddish experience and not to Sephardic Jews. While there is a relationship between the Talmud and Jewish humor, Wex, much like Friedman, projects an Ashkenazi bubble model onto the past. "Like so much of Jewish culture, kvetching has its roots in the Bible, which devotes a great deal of time to the nonstop grumbling of the Israelites, who find fault with everything under the sun. They kvetch about their problems and they kvetch about the solution." As

Wex concludes, "Judaism in general and Yiddish in particular place an unusual emphasis on complaint."[5]

In *Jewish Comedy: A Serious History*, Jeremy Dauber makes a valiant attempt to connect Jewish humor across time and cultural spaces. Yet his book is organized thematically, with each chapter progressing from the Bible to the twenty-first century. This leads to a flattening of history, and his analysis is not sufficiently grounded in the specific context of its times. In short, the tendency in the historical literature has been to assume, on the basis of Yiddish humor and the humor created by Jewish immigrants to America, that it is possible to search for the origins of Jewish humor in the Bible and Talmud by reading backward based on the Ashkenazi experience, without fully explaining how and in what forms Jewish humor might have developed in other parts of the Jewish world.

Humor is often hyper-localized, depending not only on the structures of language but also on shared cultural references and touchstones.[6] *Wit Happens* is novel in its approach insofar as it demonstrates that Jewish humor is a much broader category than existing literature has acknowledged. One of our interventions into the standard canon is to provide special focus and attention to Israeli humor. Part of the standard narrative argues that Jewish humor is a diaspora phenomenon, created in the crucible of the loss of European Jewry. The corollary of that idea is that because Israel is the opposite of the diaspora there is a dearth of Israeli humor.[7] As Telushkin asserts in *Jewish Humor*, "There is not a great deal of humor being created in Israel, and most of what exists is not very funny, at least to non-Israelis. Because people in power are able to deal with their problems directly, they have no need to settle for the personal gratification of a sharp put-down or witticism."[8] Not only has this idea proven demonstrably false as more and more Israeli humorists have left their mark on film, television, and literature, but Israeli Jewish culture is much more globally diverse than American Jewish culture, and this diversity further undercuts the idea that "Jewish humor" is a uniquely Ashkenazi phenomenon.[9] In fact, in many respects Mizrachi Jews have been at the forefront of the Israeli stand-up and sketch comedy scene, observing, critiquing, and poking fun at the Ashkenazi elite.

Wit Happens, therefore, seeks to explore the range of Jewish humors not only across time but, more importantly, across space. This volume will argue that we should not persist in thinking of Jewish humor as the unique legacy of the journey from eastern Europe to the United States. The canonization of American Jewish humor as the singular "Jewish humor" has relegated other Jewish humors—Sephardic humor, Israeli humor, post-Holocaust European Jewish humor, Soviet Jewish humor, and so forth—to the margins.[10] They are either ignored or viewed as imitations or interpretations of the American Jewish model. Rather than contest the importance of American Jewish comedy, the chapters in this volume will challenge and complicate its alleged hegemony. The chapters will all examine how the time and the place in which a humorist is working impact the humor created. There may be some lines that we can draw that connect Jewish humors from different parts of the world, but the primary focus of the volume is to highlight what sets the various humors apart. Our volume will look at the varieties of modern Jewish humor around the world with several questions in mind: To what extent can one speak of "Jewish humor" as a global phenomenon with shared attributes? Given that American Jewish humor has received so much scholarly attention (much of it justified), to what extent is this "American model" of Jewish humor applicable to other communities and why? This includes places of immigration like Canada, Australia, and South Africa, which are often thought to have mirrored American patterns but have in fact been subject to their own regional forces; Old World communities, such as France, which have in recent decades witnessed an influx of Jews from the former USSR and non-European lands; the former USSR, where Jews migrated from the Pale of Settlement to Moscow and crafted Soviet comedy with a Yiddish inflection, much as New York Jews did in Hollywood, but endured a half century of state-sponsored antisemitism testing their cultural resilience;[11] and Israel, the Jewish state, which promotes itself as the negation of the Jewish exilic condition that purportedly undergirded Jewish humor in previous centuries.

This volume is needed, especially at this moment in history. Jews remain a global people, even though most Jews live in the United States or Israel. But even within those two spaces there are Jewish subcultures from around the globe, and the growing number of Jews from backgrounds that are not traditionally Jewish (e.g., African American, Latinx, East Asian, and Jews by choice) means it is past time to highlight the complexity and transnationality of Jewish identity.

The chapters in this volume analyze Jewish humor within this global context. Rather than present a unilateral trajectory of Jewish humor migrating from the shtetl to New York, Hollywood, and beyond, these chapters argue for the importance of analyzing the development of Jewish humor across space and time. What can we learn from situating contemporary Jewish humor in conversation with ancient sources? How might we understand American Jewish humor differently by comparing its development to Jewish humor in North Africa, India, Germany, or Montreal? How do issues of audience and translation affect the reception of Holocaust humor in Israel, America, Japan, or France? Such are the analytical questions raised by juxtaposing the chapters in this volume as part of a global conversation on Jewish humor.

Although much of the humor under discussion transcends a simple timeline, the book is organized following a roughly chronological approach. This allows us to demonstrate not only the change in Jewish humor over time but also the increasingly globalized reach of Jewish humor. In his chapter on Mel Brooks, Mark Leuchter analyzes *Blazing Saddles* with a prophetic lens, asking whether the relationship presented by Brooks between his protagonists Sheriff Bart (Cleavon Little) and the Waco Kid (Gene Wilder) is in fact part of a much longer Jewish comedic trope of satirizing the *'am ha'aretz* (or the people of the land) with biblical origins. In situating such an analysis of the prophet Mel Brooks within a much longer Jewish literary milieu, Leuchter widens the lens beyond the specific American context (and even beyond a Jewish-Gentile Yiddish context) to examine the origins of Jewish humor from a biblical perspective. Ber Kotlerman examines the translation of another urtext of Jewish humor, Sholem Aleichem's *Tevye*, in its journey from the written page to Broadway, before analyzing the relationship between Sholem Aleichem's work and that of Charlie Chaplin. In a fascinating examination of Chaplin's Tramp and Sholem Aleichem's Menachem Mendl and other characters, Kotlerman notes certain parallels between the styles of the two comic geniuses, as well as Sholem Aleichem's admiration for the Little Tramp. (Chaplin as a non-Jewish Jew appears later in this volume, through Jonathan Abel's analysis of his reception in Japan.)

Like Leuchter's chapter on Mel Brooks in this volume, Lauren Brooks also reads an American Jewish comedy text backward, in this case through a fascinating analysis of *Seinfeld* and Kafka. Brooks demonstrates an intriguing antiauthoritarian parallel between the works and specifically their comic relation to authority; in this way, Brooks makes a case for a serious rereading of Kafka, specifically through the lens of global Jewish humor. As we move beyond World War II and into the mid-twentieth century, Grace Kessler Overbeke's work on Jean Carroll, America's first Jewish female stand-up comedian, helps shine proper attention on an overlooked first lady of stand-up comedy. In her chapter, Overbeke also argues that the specific context of Carroll's routines at charitable events to benefit Jewish Zionist organizations and domestic Jewish institutions expressed a Jewish identity that had been stunted by assimilatory pressure in midcentury United States. By performing in Jewish contexts, Carroll performed Jewish humor, even if her jokes may not have been perceived as specifically "Jewish." Ariane Santerre presents the case of Jewish French writer Romain Gary, whose 1967 novel *La Danse de Gengis Cohn* introduces his eponymous character, an outrageous Yiddish cabaret comedian who, after having been executed during the Holocaust, spends his time in modern Germany as a dybbuk, haunting the consciousness of the ex-SS officer responsible for his death. Santerre analyzes Gary's provocative humor, finding connections between the Yiddish and French cultural traditions at the root of his comedic creativity. Jarrod Tanny makes a case for a distinctive form of Montreal Jewish humor through the works of Mordecai Richler, arguing that the writer's "sardonic pluck is the product of the unique social, cultural, and political landscape of Montreal, a historically cosmopolitan city and a site where competing nationalisms have clashed, much like Odessa of the late nineteenth and early twentieth centuries." Tanny demonstrates the degree to which geography and local politics can inform the development of unique types of Jewish humor, which must be examined in their specific context, whether Odessa, Montreal, New York, Los Angeles, or Chicago.

Turning to the late twentieth and early twenty-first centuries, Jonathan Abel, in his chapter on Holocaust humor in Japan, and specifically the case of Kobayashi Kentaro and the controversy around a 1990s Holocaust skit that saw him removed as director of the opening ceremony at the 2020 Tokyo Olympics, examines the "Jewish" in Jewish humor: How does Jewish humor function in a place with relatively few Jews? How might humor be perceived as Jewish without Jews? As Abel argues, Jewish humor in the Japanese context becomes a universal humor "desired by the global public to evoke our collective self-centered feeling of victimhood and outcastness, our shared sense of not belonging, having been scapegoated, as well as our responsibility for making others feel as though they don't belong, for scapegoating others." If Jewish humor can play Jewishly in a place where there are no Jews, then we really must consider its implications as a global phenomenon. Jennifer Caplan analyzes the work of Joann Sfar, a graphic novelist born to an Ashkenazi Jewish mother and an Algerian Sephardic father. While born and raised in France, Sfar was heavily influenced by the legacy of Francophone colonization of North Africa. Caplan's analysis of *The Rabbi's Cat* complicates standard definitions of what constitutes "Jewish humor" using the form of the graphic novel to emphasize absurdism and the experience of a colonized other rather than the standard Jewish humor tropes of wordplay, immigration, and antisemitism. As Caplan suggests, Sfar's work argues for the possibility of Jewish "humors" unique to specific cultural, geographic, and linguistic regions where Jews have lived.

The most recent Jewish humor relies heavily on satire, sketch comedy, and stand-up comedy. Liat Steir-Livny argues that the Israeli satirical mainstay *Eretz Nehederet* (*It's a Wonderful Country*) has played a central role in making Holocaust humor and satire part of mainstream Israeli television through its now twenty-year run (2003–present). Steir-Livny demonstrates that the show's numerous Holocaust skits have legitimized Holocaust humor in the eyes of the public, first by using humor and satire to criticize forms of Holocaust commemoration in Israel and second by using Holocaust humor, satire, and parody to draw attention to other burning issues in Israeli culture. Avinoam Patt analyzes a more recent arrival to the Israeli sketch comedy scene, *HaYehudim Ba'im* (*The Jews Are Coming*), a satirical TV show devoted to sketches that target the entire history of the Jewish people from biblical times to the 1990s through a humorous lens, including sketches on World War II and the Holocaust. Patt argues that the show effectively returns the Shoah, or Holocaust, to the broader scope of Jewish history, using the Holocaust as a prism for critiques of Israeli society, trivialization of the memory of the Holocaust, and contemporary memorial practices. *The Jews Are Coming* not only integrates Israeli humor into the best traditions of Jewish humor but also uses humor to do what it does best: to demonstrate that nothing is sacred or off-limits. The show's creators, Natalie Marcus and Asaf Beiser, suggest we can ask questions about every aspect of Jewish history, even the Holocaust.

Marat Grinberg analyzes the central and intricate role played by Jews in Soviet comedy in the 1960s–1980s through the film *The Humorist*, directed by Michael Idov and released in 2019. Grinberg shows how Idov's film foregrounds Jewishness in Soviet comedy and reveals its relevance for post-Soviet Russian politics and crises. Set in pre-Perestroika Soviet 1980s, the film is also a critique of Putin's Russia and, as Grinberg argues, "ultimately seems to suggest that to be a Jew is to tell jokes and to perennially do so from behind bars if this Jew chooses to remain in Russia." Finally, Daniel Heifetz analyzes the comedy of Samson Koletkar, a California-based comedian who was born into the Bene Israel community in Mumbai. Through an analysis of Koletkar's stand-up routines, the author demonstrates how Koletkar uses humor to render skepticism about his Indian Jewish identity innocuously absurd even as it makes Indian Jewish identity legible for American audiences.

One of the perennial questions asked by scholars of Jewish humor is why the Jews have become inextricably linked with comedy. There is widespread agreement today that this association is a modern Western phenomenon. With emancipation, Jews entered European civil society but in many respects remained on the margins, prompting many, perhaps beginning with Heinrich Heine, to question and mock the communities that continued to view them with suspicion after centuries of exclusion.[12] In twentieth-century America, the rise of mass entertainment furnished the Jews with the opportunity to populate these new cultural industries as a pathway to integration and social mobility.[13] The "funny Jew" became a stereotype, one who makes you laugh through self-deprecation, ironic observations, perpetual alienation, and linguistic manipulation. Our volume has problematized such attributes of the proverbial "funny Jew" by showcasing the global variety of Jewish humors. But are Jews considered intrinsically funny in these non-Ashkenazi non-Western cultural spaces? There is no simple answer to this question, given Jews' disparate sociological and political landscapes. Yet the worldwide hegemony of American culture in the second half of the twentieth century entailed the dissemination of American stereotypes. Perhaps the American "funny Jew" now has a global familiarity he would have lacked a century ago. We hope that our collection of chapters will inspire scholars to explore this subject further. We see this collection not as the conclusion of a conversation but as the opening salvo of what we hope becomes a robust and thriving discourse on Jewish humor in *all* spaces, not just Ashkenazi ones.

An analysis of Jewish humor worldwide challenges the idea that it is exclusively an American Jewish phenomenon. A recurring theme in this collection is that Jewish humor remains firmly rooted in the perspective of the outsider—that of the minority who, as Groucho Marx quipped, is ambivalent about "belonging to the club" or of Heinrich Heine, who admitted that "baptism is a matter of indifference to me," converted to Lutheranism for social advancement, and threatened to "turn Catholic out of spite, and hang myself." The global Jewish humorists featured here often draw on their outsider, minority, or immigrant status to critique majority cultures, maintain a sense of distance (and thereby preserve a distinct identity), and use humor as a way to navigate the minority experience. If this holds true, a global comparative approach moves us beyond the "Ashkenormative" framework and toward a more comprehensive theory of global Jewish humor. What, then, unites the humorists explored in this volume? Figures such as Mel Brooks, Sholem Aleichem, Kafka and Seinfeld, Jean Carroll, Romain Gary, Mordecai Richler, Chaplin in Japan, Joann Sfar, Michael Idov, Samson Koletkar, and the Israeli creators of *The Jews Are Coming* and *Eretz Nehederet* all share a common thread: They are global Jewish outsiders, each with at least one foot firmly planted "outside the club." By examining their work, we can begin to trace the global routes of Jewish humor. We know there is much more to say about the subject. We are excited about, and look forward to, where these conversations take the study of global Jewish humor.

*   *   *

So we have come full circle, and perhaps we should ask in closing what Tevye the Dairyman, the archetypal Jew of shtetl humor, and Samson Koletkar, who fashions himself as an exotic and improbable Jew, might say to each other. Would Tevye ask Koletkar for some cheerful news about the bubonic plague in India? Would Koletkar try to one-up Tevye and quip, "Funny, you don't look Jewish"? Perhaps. Koletkar would likely tell Tevye that God never answers him and that he should bring Vishnu, Rama, and Krishna into the conversation. Tevye would undoubtedly be lost by that point but would nevertheless invite Koletkar and his "friends" Vishnu, Rama, and Krishna to his daughter's wedding, where they could dance "Hava Nagilla" together and maybe, just maybe, find a prospective South Asian match for one of his other daughters. They should all be so lucky.

Notes

1 Sholem Aleichem, "Hodl," in *Tevye the Dairyman and the Railroad Stories*, trans. Hillel Halkin (New York: Schocken Books, 1987), 69.

2 Sarah Blacher Cohen, ed., *Jewish Wry: Essays on Jewish Humor* (Bloomington: Indiana University Press, 1987), 2. See also Michael Wex, *Born to Kvetch: Yiddish Language and Culture in All Its Moods* (New York: St. Martin's Press, 2005).

3 Lawrence Epstein, *The Haunted Smile: The Story of Jewish Comedians in America* (New York: PublicAffairs, 2001), is but one classic example of the shtetl-to-America humor narrative. Other examples of this standard approach include Ruth Wisse, *No Joke: Making Jewish Humor* (Princeton: Princeton University Press, 2013); Joseph Telushkin, *Jewish Humor: What the Best Jewish Jokes Say About the Jews* (New York: W. Morrow, 1992); and Sarah Blacher Cohen, *Jewish Wry*, just to name a few.

4 See, for instance, Jeremy Dauber, *Jewish Comedy: A Serious History* (New York: W. W. Norton, 2017). Dauber's book adopts a thematic approach with each chapter covering antiquity through modernity across the world.

5 Wex, *Born to Kvetch*, 3–4.

6 See Jennifer Caplan, *Funny, You Don't Look Funny: Judaism and Humor from the Silent Generation to Millennials* (Detroit: Wayne State University Press, 2023), for an approach that attempts to keep Jewish humor situated in its own place, time, and cultural milieu.

7 Telushkin, for example, titles his chapter on Israeli humor in *Jewish Humor* "Why Are There So Few Funny Israeli Jokes?" He argues that "there is not a great deal of humor being created in Israel, and most of what exists is not very funny, at least not to non-Israelis." Wisse debunks this notion in her chapter "Hebrew Homeland" in *No Joke*.

8 Telushkin, *Jewish Humor*, 173.

9 On Israeli Humor, see, for example Avner Ziv, ed., *Jewish Humor* (Tel Aviv: Papyrus Publishing House at Tel-Aviv University, 1986); Eyal Zandberg, "Critical Laughter: Humor, Popular Culture and Israeli Holocaust Commemoration," *Media, Culture & Society* 28, no. 4 (2006): 561–79; Liat Steir-Livny, "Beyond the Chamber Quintet: Holocaust Humor on Israeli TV in the 2000s," in *Israeli Television: Global Contexts, Local Visions*, ed. Miri Talmon and Yael Levi (New York: Routledge, 2021), 235–46; and Avinoam Patt, "Yad Vashem You So Fine: The Place of the Shoah in Contemporary Israeli and American Comedy," in *Laughter After: Humor and the Holocaust*, ed. David Slucki, Gabriel N. Finder, and Avinoam Patt (Detroit: Wayne State University Press, 2020), 261–84.

10 *Laughter After*, edited by Slucki, Finder, and Patt, is one attempt to seriously explore the boundaries of Holocaust humor in varying times and national contexts.

11 On the Jews from Odessa who shaped Soviet culture, see Jarrod Tanny, *City of Rogues and Schnorrers: Russia's Jews and the Myth of Old Odessa* (Bloomington: Indiana University Press, 2011). On cultural resilience under Soviet control, see also Marat Grinberg, *The Soviet Jewish Bookshelf: Jewish Culture and Identity Between the Lines* (Waltham, MA: Brandeis University Press, 2023), who demonstrates that despite governmental constraints, Soviet Jewry produced a vibrant culture through what he calls "reading practices." On Soviet Jewish Humor, see David A. Harris and Izrail Rabinovich, *The Jokes of Oppression: The Humor of Soviet Jews* (Northwale, NJ: Jason Aronson, 1988).

12 See, for example, Blacher Cohen's *Jewish Wry*, Wisse's *No Joke*, and Dauber's *Jewish Comedy*.

13 This is covered extensively in J. Hoberman and Jeffrey Shandler's *Entertaining America: Jews, Movies, and Broadcasting*, as well as Laurence Epstein's *The Haunted Smile*.

Selected Bibliography

Caplan, Jennifer. *Funny, You Don't Look Funny: Judaism and Humor from the Silent Generation to Millennials*. Detroit: Wayne State University Press, 2023.

Cohen, Sarah Blacher. *Jewish Wry: Essays on Jewish Humor*. Bloomington: Indiana University Press, 1987.

Dauber, Jeremy. *Jewish Comedy: A Serious History*. New York: W. W. Norton, 2017.

Epstein, Lawrence. *The Haunted Smile: The Story of Jewish Comedians in America*. New York: PublicAffairs, 2001.

Harris, David A., and Izrail Rabinovich. *The Jokes of Oppression: The Humor of Soviet Jews*. Northwale, NJ: Jason Aronson, 1988.

Sholem Aleichem. *Tevye the Dairyman and the Railroad Stories*. Translated by Hillel Halkin. New York: Schocken Books, 1987.

Slucki, David, Gabriel Finder, and Avinoam Patt. *Laughter After: Humor and the Holocaust*. Detroit: Wayne State University Press, 2020.

Tanny, Jarrod. *City of Rogues and Schnorrers: Russia's Jews and the Myth of Old Odessa*. Bloomington: Indiana University Press, 2011.

Telushkin, Joseph. *Jewish Humor: What the Best Jewish Jokes Say About the Jews*. New York: W. Morrow, 1992.

Weiss, Ruth. *No Joke: Making Jewish Humor*. Princeton: Princeton University Press, 2013.

Wex, Michael. *Born to Kvetch: Yiddish Language and Culture in All Its Moods*. New York: St. Martin's Press, 2005.

1

"IS MEL BROOKS ALSO AMONG THE PROPHETS?"

Blazing Saddles, the Biblical Prophets, and "The People of the Land"

Mark Leuchter

In the third season of the juggernaut TV series *The Simpsons*, the producers aired an episode where Krusty the Clown (or "Klown," as the producers often deliberately misspell) comes out as Jewish.[1] Homer is surprised, and Lisa tells him that many entertainers are Jewish, including Lauren Bacall, Dinah Shore, William Shatner, and Mel Brooks. Homer is shocked and responds, "Mel Brooks is Jewish?" The joke, of course, is that with very few exceptions, no American entertainer of the second half of the twentieth century (and the first few decades of the twenty-first) has been more vocal about his Jewishness than Brooks.[2] I often show that particular *Simpsons* episode to undergraduate students when teaching courses on religion in contemporary media. Over time, some of those names have become less familiar to them—many of my students have at least heard of William Shatner, but fewer know Lauren Bacall, and fewer still know who Dinah Shore is. Yet Brooks perseveres. Most of my students still know his name, and those who don't still know his work when I tell them he's the creative force behind it. Recently, Brooks demonstrated his staying power by producing a follow-up to his 1981 film *History of the World, Part I*, a four-part television series entitled *History of the World, Part II*—a gloriously ridiculous bit of sketch writing with a roster of collaborators representing multiple generations of creative talent.[3] It is a testament to Brooks's ongoing influence over the landscape of American comedy.

Brooks's brand of Jewish humor endures because he somehow manages to network it into conceptual kegs that never run dry. One of those kegs, maybe the biggest one, is his satirical concept of the larger Gentile world that surrounds him and his fellow American Jews, and *Blazing Saddles* is a parade example of this.[4] Embedded within *Blazing Saddles* is a moment in Brooks's cinema that is simultaneously horrifying and funny and then horrifying all over again. The film, a spoof of the Western movie genre, possesses a simple setup. A small town called Rock Ridge stands in the way of railroad development, so to drive the population of polite, racist white folk away, a Black man named Bart (played by Cleavon Little) is deliberately installed by local politician Hedy—sorry, that's Hedley—Lamarr (played by Harvey Korman) as the town sheriff. One morning, Sheriff Bart goes out for a stroll and wishes a good morning to an old woman who passes him by. "Isn't it a lovely morning this morning?" he asks her. She replies only with "Up yours," followed by the N-word.

The comedy in the scene is the result of many things that are not really funny, certainly not on their own. One could argue, I suppose, that the comedy derives in part from the image of a prim and proper old white woman in the nineteenth-century American West using such hateful, vulgar language. But it is the next scene that contains the payoff. We fade into a close-up of a depressed Sheriff Bart, with his friend Jim (played by Gene Wilder) seated next to him, who offers some words of context and comfort:

> You've got to remember that these are just simple farmers. These are people of the land. The common clay of the new West. You know—morons.

Dress it up in whatever flowery platitudes or euphemisms you can—simple farmers, the common clay of whatever, proud deplorables—but in the end, these people of the land are morons. This feature is common in Brooks's work: skewer the perpetrator, expose their values, strip away the glamour and the pretense of nobility and reveal the beast for what it is, and then ridicule them mercilessly. In *Blazing Saddles*, the specific moniker identifying the beast is "people of the land," and I would argue that this is not accidental or incidental. Toward the beginning of *Blazing Saddles*, as ideas are floated for getting the people of Rock Ridge—who all have the bland last name of Johnson—to vacate their town, Taggart (played by Slim

Pickens) suggests slaying their first-born children—a clear reference to the Exodus story—which Lamarr rejects as "too Jewish." So, is it possible that the "people of the land" reference is, also, a self-aware reference to a particularly Jewish trope?

I would suggest that this is indeed the case. The phrase "the people of the land" ('*am ha'aretz* in Hebrew) originates in the Hebrew Bible but has a long postbiblical afterlife. The Babylonian Talmud uses the phrase to refer to Jews who are ignorant of Torah learning and who thus have no access to the holiness and prestige it brings. The phrase is a slur, roughly equivalent to calling a rural American resident a "redneck" with all the social and cultural baggage intimated in that label. Indeed, the rabbis tend to see the '*am ha'aretz* as a foil for themselves and even as a threat, presenting a real danger to the sanctity of rabbinic piety and intellectual accomplishment.[5] One passage is especially telling:

> R. Elazar said: It is forbidden to be accompanied by an '*am ha'aretz* on the road. As it is written: For it is your life and the length of your days (Dt 30:20)—he has no concern for his own life—is it not all the more so with regard to the life of his fellow?
>
> R. Samuel b. Naḥmani said in the name of R. Yonatan: It is permitted to tear an '*am ha'aretz* like a fish. (*Pesachim* 49a)

The passage is clearly hyperbolic; few scholars of rabbinic literature think that anything in the Talmud was conceived to be anything but theoretical discourse anyway. It is notable, though, that in dispatching the member of the '*am ha'aretz* in question, the sage should do so as though he were a fish, which invokes echoes of the ancient Near Eastern combat mythology that persisted into biblical literature, where sea monsters constituted cosmic threats to God's dominion.[6] The rabbinic perspective in *Pesachim* 49a is an intriguing example of cultural memory, as it takes up tropes from antiquity that have picked up other mythotypes along the way. Brooks's long career shows more than a passing familiarity with the Jewish intellectual tradition and the place of rabbinic discourse therein; indeed the phrase is still in use in some Orthodox Jewish communities today, and there's no reason to doubt that Brooks was familiar with it when he made the film.[7] But Brooks's "people of the land" critique aligns more closely with what we find in the biblical prophets, especially Jeremiah and Ezekiel, who also use the phrase. This chapter will be less a study of Brooks's film (which warrants a far more extensive treatment) and more an examination of a lemma that the film uses that serves as a sort of hypertext to a much older tradition. It refers to a more expansive network of textual discourse in the prophetic texts of the Hebrew Bible that became foundational for subsequent uses of the lemma in Jewish literature.

Let me briefly summarize my view of who the ʿam haʾaretz actually were in Israelite antiquity. I should note that scholars in my field are divided on the categories and definitions. What I will sketch out is a relatively general picture that has gained a fair degree of consensus among biblical scholars. The term ʿam haʾaretz (henceforth, AH) is found in a variety of biblical texts and narrative contexts; in some, it is a marker of otherness in contradistinction to Israelite identity. The AH appear prominently, for example, in Genesis 23, the story of Abraham's purchase of the Cave of Mahpelah as a family burial site. In the story, Abraham secures the cave from the AH of the Hittite community, who are presented as long-time residents of the territory. The story is by no means historical, and very few biblical scholars would use it to tell us anything about Hittite society. However, the story tells us quite a bit about its Israelite author: he believed that agrarian societies like his possessed a class or caste of rural elites who carried this title (or, at least, parallels to it).[8] From Genesis 23 and other texts, most scholars agree that the AH constitute a sort of "landed gentry," elites of the rural sector in the kingdom of Judah (a political subset of ancient Israelite society) with connections among the powerful in Jerusalem. In envisioning this caste, one should think less of Uncle Jesse from *The Dukes of Hazzard* and more of J. R. Ewing from *Dallas*. They receive a number of mentions in the book of Kings as a powerful political caste that could and did intervene in royal affairs. They were firm fixtures of the Judahite hinterland, though they likely had parallels in the northern kingdom of Israel as well.[9]

It's difficult to determine when this group originated, though the early monarchic period, the tenth century BCE, recommends itself.[10] Yet I would argue that their actual historical origins go all the way back to earliest, emergent Israel, those initial generations of highland settlers who show up in the material record at the outset of the Iron Age, around 1200 BCE, developing among the highland communities of the ensuing century or so.[11] It is likely that they would have become an organized political caste only with the rise of the monarchy roughly two centuries later, at which point new sociological and economic conditions led to new hierarchies of power. By the Persian period (538–332 BCE), well after the fall of the Israelite monarchic states, the term appears to carry a derogatory connotation and is most often presented as a criticism or slight,[12] but the monarchic-era material does not carry this trait. The AH seem to hold an elite position within Judahite society, to the degree that they may have even possessed their own scribal outlets and cultivated literary traditions reifying their own social values (as William Schniedewind has recently argued).[13]

We need to dig a bit deeper, because the AH were not characterized simply by their rural social location but also by a more mythological connection to the landscape on which they resided. Even the name *'am ha'aretz* is suggestive of a mythological status assigned to the members of this group. The word *'am*, after all, means more than just "people" or "nation"; it also means "kin" or "kindred of." So, kin or kindred of the *'aretz*, "the land"? Maybe. The agrarian tradition in ancient Israel is steeped in geomythology, where the identity of the people as a corporate social entity is bound to the landscape in effectively genetic terms. The very oldest text in the Hebrew Bible—the poem known as the "Song of the Sea" (Ex 15:1–18)—explicitly identifies Israel's origins within the landscape in horticultural terms.[14] YHWH, the deity who defeats Egypt (cast as a mythological foe), goes on to claim the landscape as his sacred homestead, wherein he literally "plants" Israel as parts of his cosmic estate (vv. 13–17). The poet declares the deity to be a kinsman-redeemer of Israel because of this; the intimate relationship between Israel and their deity is triangulated through the connection of both to the landscape. In this sense, one might argue that the AH are indeed kinfolk of the land, composed of the soil and its fecundity tended and sustained by YHWH's own devotion and attention. Something of this persists in the later narrative of the Garden of Eden, where the human is made from the very soil of the Earth (*'adamah*) and even named after it (*'adam*, Gn 2:7).

But *'aretz*, in ancient northwest Semitic discourse, also means "underworld." The oracles of the prophet Hosea, who was active around 730 BCE, carry this valence when they mention the term *'aretz*—it is not simply land but the cosmic and chthonic (i.e., ideas related to postmortem existence) dimensions within it, where the dead reside:

And I will give to her her vineyards from thence, and the valley of
Achor for a door of hope; and she shall respond there, as in the days
of her youth, and as in the day when she came up out of the underworld ('aretz)—from Egypt.[15] And it shall be at that day, says YHWH,
that thou shalt call Me "my husband," and shalt call Me no more "my
master" (ba'ali). For I will take away the names of the baals out of her
mouth, and they shall no more be mentioned by their name. (Hos
2:17–19)

The reference to Baal in these verses, the Canaanite deity who rises
from the dead, drives home the double entendre.[16] The 'aretz in AH
may similarly be a metonym for those residing in the underworld—the
dead—in which case, to be part of the AH means that you're not just a
landlubber but a kinsman of the dead, the trustee of their power, the arbi-
ter of their cosmic knowledge emanating from the underworld. The AH,
then, were fixtures of the hinterland who maintained some numinous
dynamic mediating the landscape, the population, the dead, and the sacral
culture shared by all of these. This idea lurks beneath many biblical texts,
most of which derive from the era of the monarchy, but the notion persists even well into the post-monarchic era. The most ancient discourses
about the mythic hero Enoch are deeply connected to a tradition of necromancy; something of this remains in the later treatment of Enoch in the
third century BCE as a source of life-giving wisdom against the forces of
evil connected to death and the underworld (now found primarily in the
"Book of Watchers," 1 Enoch 1–36).[17]

Most of the prophetic literature in the Hebrew Bible is very much
a part of this matrix of ideas, providing revealing critiques of the social
and religious status quo in Israel into which the AH factor. With this in
mind, we will look at four passages that bear witness to the dramatic dis-
ruption of this status quo. We shall consider a text from Jeremiah, a text
from Ezekiel, and two texts from the book of Kings, the latter of which is
widely regarded as redacted by scribes with sympathies to the prophetic
tradition of their day, so this text qualifies, in a way, as prophetic.[18] The
texts from Kings that we will consider are both from the closing chapters
of the work where the AH receive brief but significant attention. But it is
important to bear in mind that the AH are prominent in earlier parts of
the work, reflecting the memory of their privileged position in ancient

Judahite society. It is because of these earlier passages and what they presuppose about this group that the verses below resonate at so potent a narrative frequency:

> [Nebuchadnezzar, the king of Babylon] carried all Jerusalem into exile: all the officers and fighting men, and all the skilled workers and artisans—a total of ten thousand. Only *the enfeebled people of the land* were left. (2 Kgs 24:14)

> And the captain of the guard took Seraiah the chief priest, and Zephaniah the second priest, and the three keepers of the door; and out of the city he took an officer that was set over the men of war; and five men of them that saw the king's face, who were found in the city; and the scribe of the captain of the host, who mustered the people of the land; and *threescore men of the people of the land, that were found in the city*. (2 Kgs 25:18–19)

Both of these passages are part of a larger account of the Babylonian conquest of Judah. The first passage stresses that conditions are so disrupted that the AH have been, as I have translated it here, "enfeebled."[19] Many understand this verse as simply describing the Babylonians not caring about the poorest people of the hinterland and translate the original Hebrew as "the poorest people in the land," but that misses the point. We know from archaeological surveys that most of the Judahite population was not carried into exile but instead internally displaced within the homeland. Approximately 80 percent of the Judahite population remained in the land, including members of elite families with enduring political influence, education, and even some type of priestly status.[20] So it wouldn't just be the "poorest" who remained, and at least some of the AH would have remained as well. But under such conditions—residing within the land but removed from ancestral estates and tombs—how could the AH actually have numinous or social power? How could they be anything *other* than enfeebled?

The second passage comes from a different archival source, and it tells us that sixtyish of the AH were taken captive by the Babylonians.[21] But notice where they are taken *from*: they are huddled like scared mice in the city of Jerusalem, severed from the agrarian source of their power.

The passage cuts them off from this traditional social location and instead deposits them in Jerusalem as mere asylum seekers, vulnerable and desperately huddled in the city. But not for long, because after being taken captive, they're killed, and killed away from the rural tomb spaces where they might normally be interred and become the powerful dead themselves. The significance of this situation is so often overlooked, but it cannot be overstated. Family tombs were not simply spaces where bodies were deposited but also cosmic sites, binding the family to the land and connecting the dead and the living in an ongoing, symbiotic relationship.[22] It was through rites of devotion to the departed ancestors at these tomb sites that Israelite/Judahite religious self-understanding was forged and sustained.

For the AH to die beyond these spaces is a powerful comment about the degree to which society had been conquered and dismantled by the Babylonians. The implication is that there is a complete breakdown in all corners of society, so much so that even the revered AH caste cannot be buried in their family tombs. Indeed, so demolished is the institution of the family tomb and its associated rites over which the AH held sway that the text does not even mention it; in the ears of ancient audiences familiar with the now destroyed social institution in question, the silence of the text would have been deafening. This is both shocking and, yet, unsurprising: the convention among the Mesopotamian powers of that era was not only to assault and destroy the homeland of groups they conquered militarily but also to eradicate their connection to that homeland. One source reports a Mesopotamian ruler disinterring the bones of the ancestors of his captives from their family tombs and then forcing those captives to crush those bones into dust, destroying their own identities in the process.[23] The narratives depicting the fate of the AH in the book of Kings must be understood against this dramatic practice and ideology.

So in these two passages, some of the AH survive, some don't, but as a social category they've been undone, unmade, and barred from any claims to power or even a social or burial location. In dramatic and thematic tone, it is far more Bergman than Brooks, but it gives us important context for looking at the passages in Jeremiah and Ezekiel that make mention of the AH. Biblical scholars generally place the contents of Jeremiah and Ezekiel in the same era as the events depicted in Kings; all are really products of an ancient Judaism dealing with newly imposed conditions of the Babylonian conquest that toppled the continuity of life in the homeland from 587 to 538 BCE.[24] But Jeremiah and Ezekiel provide hot takes on the AH that are different in both tone and substance. Let us view the Jeremiah passage first:

> The princes of Judah, and the princes of Jerusalem, the officers, and the priests, and all *the people of the land* that passed between the parts of the calf; I will even give them into the hand of their enemies, and into the hand of them that seek their life; and their dead bodies shall be for food unto the fowls of the heaven, and to the beasts of the earth. (Jer 34:19–20)

The setting for Jeremiah 34 is a covenant ceremony in Jerusalem in the year 587 BCE where the king and the elites "release" their slaves according to the legislation in Deuteronomy (15:1–6). This ceremony somehow also included a rite involving the chopping up of animals and a ceremonial stroll between the parts, similar to the famous episode in Genesis 15 where Abraham does this with YHWH. But it's only a ritual release, and as soon as the ritual ends, the participants again enslave the poor. This in and of itself is comical, though not in a funny way. It's a parody of what ritual and covenant are supposed to mean and a sign that people like the AH who are entrusted with these sacred rites are completely oblivious to how any of this works. This is a critique that characterizes prophecy even long before Jeremiah's day; Amos (ca. 750 BCE), Hosea (ca. 730 BCE), and both Micah and Isaiah (ca. 720–700 BCE) all lob harsh criticisms at the empty observance of rote ritual. By Jeremiah's time, it was a common prophetic trope. But his application of it here constitutes a dark humor, because the chapter makes clear that this farcical ceremony is taking place while the Babylonian army is literally at the city gates waiting to invade. If ever there was a time to take ritual and ethics *seriously*, it would be in the narrated world of Jeremiah 34, but no such attitude characterizes the AH in this episode.

Jeremiah isn't having any of this, and he brings his A game when it comes to throwing comic shade. Not only will their farcical ceremony not work, but it will have the *opposite* effect. Those who chopped up animals and cast their parts on the ground will suffer the same fate: their own bodies will not be buried. I should note that the threat of nonburial is a huge source of anxiety in Israelite religion for two reasons, the first of which we have already seen with respect to the depiction of the AH in the book of Kings. Burial at a family tomb is a part of the ethno-mythic rhythm of agrarian life, and breaking with that convention introduces chaos into the delicate balance of order. This carried implications for social utility as well, as nonburial was a source of dishonor to the surviving family, suggesting that they are landless and have no space to bury their dead. Nonburial was thus a stigma that marked a family as somehow on the outs not only with their community but also with their deity, since the oldest Israelite theology was one where YHWH planted his people in the land (Ex 15:17). To lack space within this land indicates distance from the patron deity, which could identify people as sources of cosmic danger.

But nonburial also means one cannot enter the underworld and join their departed ancestors through the family tomb. This was the center point of rural family/clan life, and each tomb space served as a cosmic center point, a type of axis mundi, for the clans who resided in the land.[25] Here is where the reference to the AH is important, because the prophet's rebuke here ridicules their claim to power and authority. This is not the first time in the book of Jeremiah that the prophet is presented as ridiculing the status quo of the power system that included the AH and using humor (again, not of the "ha-ha" variety) to do so—humor as social critique is fundamental to Brooks's comedic oeuvre, and it is a cornerstone of this brand of prophetic critique. An early example is found in Jeremiah's famous "Temple Sermon," a speech made in the Jerusalem temple shortly after the shocking death of the powerful King Josiah in 609 BCE. The entire sermon is a master class in philological irony, but one verse stands out:

> Has this house, whereupon My name is called, become a den of thieves (*maʾarat peritzzim*) in your eyes? Behold, I, even I, have seen it, says YHWH. (Jer 7:11)

English translations of this verse typically miss the potent pun on which it turns. The phrase *maʾarat peritzzim* ("den of thieves") plays on the root *peretz*, a term that can mean forceful breaching, brutish behavior, physical roughness or transgression, and so forth. But the name of the clan to which King David belonged was connected to this term as well. There is a long tradition where David himself was known to be a violent mobster, something that even his royal apologists could not fully shake. But significantly,

David's own clan ancestor carried the name Peretz (spelled out in Ruth 4:18–22 but attested in many other texts), perhaps a retrojection of David's own reputation back onto traditions of his own ancestry.[26] Jeremiah's locution is therefore a little joke suggesting that YHWH's temple has become a "den of thieves" (*peritzzim*) because of its association with a corrupt royal line (via Peretz).

We encounter other examples of Jeremiah utilizing dark humor to highlight his social and religious critiques aimed at a variety of groups and practices. He takes issue with the sages of Jerusalem, the priests and prophets on the royal payroll, even some of the kinfolk from his hometown (Jer 11:18–23). Most of these critiques deploy language replete with puns and irony, though the strongest examples are reserved for kings and various elite social sectors. This carries over into the narratives about Jeremiah as well written by later scribes that were added to the book. In one of the most shocking of such tales, Jeremiah 36, King Jehoiakim slices up and burns a scroll containing Jeremiah's oracles in an attempt to nullify their contents, only for the scroll to be completely regenerated despite these efforts (Jer 36:32). It's a potent ridiculing of ancient trends that associated kings with their enculturation in the scribal arts and facility with written revelation and wisdom.[27] In Jeremiah 34, the prophet directs his penchant for ridiculing conventional assumptions against the AH, and I would argue that he does so by making the same joke as Brooks: the people of the land are morons.

Ezekiel was Jeremiah's contemporary but came from a different religious and intellectual corner of Judahite society. Whereas Jeremiah was a Levite of northern descent (and thus a sort of resident alien within Judahite society; see Jer 1:1, 32:6–15), Ezekiel was a member of the Jerusalem priesthood that had ministered at the Jerusalem temple for centuries. His social identity was fully intertwined with the complex strata of Judahite society, and the disruptions that came with the rise of Babylon affected him in a far more traumatic manner. Unlike Jeremiah, who remained in Judah during the course of the Babylonian conquest, Ezekiel was taken captive to Babylon very early on, during the initial phase of Babylonian dominance. Jerusalem was eventually destroyed in 587 BCE, but ten years earlier, in 597, Nebuchadnezzar besieged the city and took its king and several of its leading citizens captive, forcing them into exile and replacing them with puppet leaders. Ezekiel is the only prophet in the biblical tradition,

Moses notwithstanding, whose entire career takes place beyond the land; he receives his first prophetic vision a few years into his own exile, while living in what was a type of refugee camp on the outskirts of Babylon. The uniqueness of his language and the sharpness of his condemnations are rooted in the uniqueness, and the unique trauma, of his experience.[28]

Ezekiel actually talks about the AH far more than Jeremiah. No fewer than seven passages in the book of Ezekiel feature this group, and there is little redeeming, sympathetic, or otherwise optimistic material in any of these texts. One passage is particularly relevant to our discussion here:

> Say to *the people of the land*: "This is what the Lord YHWH says about those living in Jerusalem and on the soil (*'admat*) of Israel: They will eat their food in anxiety and drink their water in despair, for their land/underworld (*'artzah*) will be stripped of everything in it because of the violence of all who reside therein." (Ez 12:19)

Few would view such a statement as funny in any measurable way. But similar to what we saw above with Jeremiah, this too is a joke that satirizes the AH, highlighting that despite their title, they reside only on the soil of Israel (*'admat yisra'el*) and are to be "stripped" away from the cosmic dimensions of the landscape (*'artzah*) with its chthonic, underworld aspects.[29] But when we think about where Ezekiel is when he cooked up these oracles (separated from the ancestral landscape, under foreign imperialism, and in a refugee camp), a dark humor emerges. Unlike those in exile longing to return home, Ezekiel completely repudiated the homeland and rejected those who clung to it in the years leading up to Jerusalem's final destruction, and this is why the AH reference here is relevant. The meal Ezekiel is describing is likely a parody of a *marzeah*, a ritual banquet conducted near ancestral tombs when the numinous power of the dead was shared with the living AH. But in this verse, the AH are stripped from land because of the violence committed by the people residing *in* the underworld. According to Ezekiel, the perpetrators of violence responsible for the exile are the very departed ancestors venerated by the AH.

Of course, insulting an ancestor is a staple of humor, and Ezekiel is engaging in the ancient equivalent of a "your mother" joke. But in this, he's more severe than Jeremiah, because the dead are the actual culprits, deliberately undermining the safety and security of their living descendants.

This goes much further than Jeremiah's own dark humor, which ridicules the perceptions and priorities of the AH but stops short of denying the legitimacy of the mythology upon which their identities were constructed. But then again, and as noted above, Jeremiah and Ezekiel had different experiences and self-understandings when they formed their respective oracles. Levites with northern heritage had long resided in Judah by Jeremiah's day, and their concepts of social identity had adapted to these circumstances in a way that could perhaps more easily navigate culturally seismic shifts.[30] Ezekiel's identity was entirely rooted in the mythos of a fixed temple built atop a cosmic mountain, Zion. Jon D. Levenson famously argued that Zion "absorbed" the Sinai tradition and was thus not bound to the conditions of ordinary time or history;[31] a priesthood that had long served at such a site would invariably see their identity as part of that mythos. For Ezekiel to be forcibly removed from Jerusalem and the temple was a far more severe challenge to his understanding of the underlying ideology of the entire monarchic system that his lineage group had supported for centuries. It is for this reason that Ezekiel turns so strongly against that system, even as it still stood during its final decade of (admittedly compromised) survival.

It is also for this reason that Ezekiel's parody dismantles the entire mythology supporting the social universe of the AH. It is not uncommon among biblical scholars to see a sharp divide between urban and rural cultures in ancient Israel, evidence for which is culled not only from material evidence on the ground but also from relic ideologies preserved in the biblical record. If Ezekiel's roots were set within a long-urbanized priesthood, one might argue that his condemnation of the AH is unrelated to his traumatized repudiation of the Jerusalem mythos. His language in Ezekiel 12:19 might simply reflect his penchant for the Lenny Bruce/George Carlin "burn it all down!" style of locution. But already by the eighth century BCE, we see strong and persistent interaction between urban and rural cultures in the kingdom of Judah, and these persisted in various forms down to the end of the monarchic era in 587 BCE.[32] Ezekiel's harsh parody of the mythology underlying the identity of the AH is part of his overall repudiation of a society that, in his mind, was built on deception and lies, whose civic order was untenable,[33] and that got what it deserved. The couching of this repudiation in what amounts to a joke at the expense of the AH is the icing on the bitter cake.

Some concluding thoughts are in order. It's clear that humor suffuses these prophetic texts, which is to a degree not surprising, since the concept of the mighty and privileged being brought down low is a staple of humor. That, obviously, is not what Brooks is doing in *Blazing Saddles*, because the citizens of Rock Ridge are far from mighty. But in a way, they think they are. They are churchgoing, God-fearing people entitled to claim land and live on it—land, of course, that either they or their immediate ancestors settled and claimed from Indigenous people who (in reality) were systematically dehumanized and brutalized in the name of Manifest Destiny.[34] All of this is unspoken but presumed by the manicured and tepid Christian whiteness of Rock Ridge's population, who see themselves as the sole victims in their community's story. It is they who are the targets of violence and injustice, and it is their alleged God-given dignity that has been sullied as they sing—during a church service—that their town "is turning into shit."

Yet even this turn of events, and the presence of a new lawman who might help improve things, doesn't shake their agrarian entitlement: this is still their town, their land, and their way of life, which shall never be disrupted by corrosive outside forces. For the Johnsons of Rock Ridge, Sheriff Bart's blackness represents the force they believe they must repudiate, oblivious to the fact that it is capitalistic greed (the development of the railroad system) that poses the greatest threat to their existence. So they double down on their identity myths in a way that is really no different than what we find in the prophetic texts surveyed above, where the prophets observe that despite a looming crisis, the "business as usual" behavior of the AH is untenable. And like those prophetic texts, Mel Brooks calls out the townspeople of Rock Ridge on the colossal dumbness of their worldview and mythology. Both Brooks and the prophets use humor to show how ultimately ineffectual such pretenses are and that consequences lurk just around the corner—whether from Nebuchadnezzar or from Hedley Lamarr. Indeed, Brooks's entire goal in making *Blazing Saddles* is to dismantle the myth of the rugged and indomitable archetypes of the Western film genre, a point driven home toward the end of the film when the camera moves back to reveal that the studio where his film is being shot is simply part of a bigger Hollywood mythmaking machine, and the distinctions and taxonomies are easily swept aside as illusory.

In ancient Israel, there were debates about whether Israel's first king, Saul, had prophetic qualities, which led to the slogan "Is Saul also among the prophets?" as reported in the book of Samuel (1 Sm 10:12–13, 19:24). I've riffed on that in the title of this chapter, and I hope that I've made the case that Mel Brooks is, indeed, among the prophets in his own criticism of the people of the land. I'm not suggesting that Brooks is self-consciously making some sort of bid for prophetic qualification; rather, he is drawing from the legacy of the prophets that so strongly affected the trajectory of Jewish self-examination in the context of the larger, hegemonic cultures that Jews encountered throughout history. The canonical shape of the Hebrew Bible, after all, places the prophetic literature at its very heart, and later Jewish theologians would look to the prophets as establishing the precedent for challenging convention and innovating Jewish ethics. Brooks's film and his films en masse affirm this prophetic precedent in their knowing critiques of society at large from the purview of a minority Jewish community navigating its turbulent and threatening features.

Yet there is a difference that we must not forget. In the prophetic texts, the people of the land/AH are part of Israelite society and thus part of Jewish communal tradition, and the biblical narrative eventually offers them opportunities for redemption. In Brooks's film, the people of the land are not Jews, and I'm not sure Brooks is all that interested in letting them off the hook. The final moments in the film break the proverbial fourth wall—the camera pulls back to show that the storyline within the film is actually just part of a film production on the Warner Bros. Studios lot in the timeline of Brooks's mid-1970s audience. This meta-cinematic moment indicates that the people of Rock Ridge are not just characters but archetypes that persist into our own day. As the infamous insurrection of January 6, 2021, demonstrates, the people of the land in *Blazing Saddles* are represented by those who also hold to ideologies involving racism, Christian nationalism, and blood and soil in our real world. The people of the land remain with us, clinging to their myths of ethnic identity, showing themselves to be the very enemy that has already breached the gate.

Notes

1 "Like Father Like Clown," *The Simpsons*, season 3, episode 6, aired October 24, 1991.
2 Matthew R. Meier, "What a Meshugenner! Mel Brooks' Politics of Jewish Humor," in *The Political Mel Brooks*, ed. Beth E. Bonnstetter and Samuel Boerboom (Washington, DC: Lexington Books, 2019), 135–55.
3 *History of the World, Part I* (Brooksfilms, 1981); *History of the World, Part II* (Hulu, 2023).
4 *Blazing Saddles* (Warner Brothers, 1974).
5 For a full consideration of the rabbinic view of this group, see Jonathan Pomeranz, "Did the Babylonian Sages Regard the Ammei-ha'Aretz as Subhuman?," *Hebrew Union College Annual* 87 (2016): 115–43.
6 Genesis 1:2 contains an echo of this, where God creates/controls "the Deep" (*tehom*), cognate to the Babylonian sea demon Tiamat. A more overt nod to this myth is found in Psalm 74, where YHWH defeats the sea monster Leviathan in primordial, mythic time (v. 14).
7 By way of example, I grew up in a modern Orthodox community in the metropolitan Detroit area in the 1980s, and I heard the phrase deployed periodically, mostly in reference to prominent American Jews who were less religious in orientation.
8 Strictly speaking, the author of Genesis 23 was not "Israelite" but "Judahite." Genesis 23 is part of the Priestly source within the Pentateuch, universally regarded as a product of the priesthood in Jerusalem, capital of the kingdom of Judah. Though there is debate as to whether the author of this source was active during or after the monarchic period (which ended in 587 BCE), the group to which he belonged developed their narrative ideologies, and many of their narrative sources, during the monarchic era. However, Judah was part of larger Israelite society in different ways during its political lifespan, sometimes as a subject of the more powerful northern Israelite kingdom or, following the fall of the north in 721 BCE, as the inheritor of its cultural legacies. For the purposes of clarity and simplicity, I will qualify all the biblical texts discussed herein as part of "Israelite" society, with the caveat that this term is applied loosely and that more detailed philological and historical analyses of these materials require greater nuance in determining their cultural patrimonies.

9   The story of Naboth's Vineyard (1 Kgs 21) provides us with an example of one such northern figure, who is presented as the landholder of a desirable territory that Ahab, the king of Israel, wishes to add to his own royal landholdings.

10 It would be at this point that rural elite status would shift from regional and atomistic to something more systematized in the manner of a caste. We encounter similar shifts in recognized titles and group identity labels at this time among other castes; see Mark Leuchter, *The Levites and the Boundaries of Israelite Identity* (Oxford: Oxford University Press, 2017), 94–98.

11 On the premonarchic precursors, see Robert R. Miller, *Chieftains of the Highland Clans: A History of Israel in the 12th and 11th Centuries B.C.* (Grand Rapids: Eerdmans, 2005).

12 See Lena-Sofia Tiemeyer, "The Priests and the Temple Cult in the Book of Jeremiah," in *Prophecy in the Book of Jeremiah*, ed. Hans M. Barstad and Reinhard G. Kratz (Berlin: De Gruyter, 2009), 250.

13 William M. Schniedewind, *Who Really Wrote the Bible? The Story of Scribal Communities* (Princeton: Princeton University Press, 2024).

14 Most biblical scholars regard this poem as among the most ancient, and often *the* most ancient, in the Hebrew Bible. Some have argued that it has gone through a series of subsequent revisions; only a very few scholars have suggested that it is a late work emulating early linguistic styles.

15 Egypt had long been associated with the underworld/the realm of death in Israelite thought by Hosea's day. A parallel may be found in the brief notice in Genesis 37:35, where Jacob exclaims that his own soul has descended into "the underworld," just as Joseph—his favorite son—is taken down into Egypt (Gn 37:36).

16 Leuchter, *The Levites*, 143–44.

17 I discuss this in detail in "The Pre-Pentateuchal Enoch," forthcoming in *Catholic Biblical Quarterly* 86 (2024): 37-62.

18 Jewish tradition regards the book of Kings (i.e., 1–2 Kings) as part of the canonical scriptural category of *nevi'im* ("Prophets"). But the book of Kings is part of what biblical scholars often call the Deuteronomistic History, a work spanning Joshua, Judges, 1–2 Samuel, and 1–2 Kings that stems from the same scribal group that produced the book of Deuteronomy. An excellent overview and analysis of the material and its

connection to the prophetic tradition is that of Jeffrey H. Geoghegan, *The Time, Place, and Purpose of the Deuteronomistic History: The Evidence of "Until This Day"* (Providence: Brown Judaic Studies, 2006).

19 The Hebrew term here is *dalat*, from the root *dll*, which may be translated as "poor," "meek," "weak," etc.

20 For an overview of the archaeological evidence, see Oded Lipschits, *The Fall and Rise of Jerusalem* (Winona Lake, IN: Eisenbrauns, 2005), 158–66. The appointment of Gedaliah by the Babylonians as a regional administrator following 587 BCE (2 Kgs 25:22–24; Jer 40–41) is illuminating, as he belonged to the powerful Shaphan clan that likely held Levite status and that had earlier held influential positions within the royal administration as well. Those who remained in the land were therefore obviously not simply among the most socially and economically marginal.

21 The somewhat piecemeal closing chapters of the book of Kings speak to the different archival sources that were available to its redactors, each of which preserved variant accounts and contrasting details regarding the closing days of the monarchic era. The redactors themselves lived in exile in Babylon and were active probably sometime around 570–560 BCE. They were of the learned scribal caste of Judah, also probably responsible for the redaction of the book of Jeremiah, which draws from (and elaborates on) the same archival material. See Leuchter, *The Levites*, 197–213.

22 An analysis of the ancestral cult and its connection to family-based tomb sites is found in Karel van der Toorn, *Family Religion in Babylonia, Syria, and Israel* (Leiden: Brill, 1996), 206–35.

23 Daniel D. Luckenbill, *Ancient Records of Assyria and Babylonia*, vol. 2 (Chicago: University of Chicago, 1924), 310, sec. 810.

24 Akin to my caveat above regarding the term "Israelite," the term "Judaism" must be used cautiously here as well. Most scholars recognize that the social category of "Jewish" and the ideological construct called "Judaism" are difficult to identify before the Persian period. I use the term "ancient Judaism" to denote that a shift does indeed take place once the continuity of social and religious institutions in Judah was violently disrupted by the Babylonians, which in my view created fundamental social, ritual, linguistic, and ethnographic changes that ultimately led to the categories we can more confidently identify in the Persian period. And it is during the Persian period that the first real self-conscious

interpretation of these exilic-era sources took place among ancient Jews, who saw these texts as part of their cultural heritage. In short, the exilic period creates the preconditions for the emergence of what we can call "Judaism" in later periods, and the earliest proto-stages of Judaism may be traced to this period.

25 Van der Toorn, *Family Religion*, 210–11.

26 Jeffrey C. Geoghegan, "Israelite Sheepshearing and David's Rise to Power," *Biblica* 87 (2006): 55–63.

27 The composition of Jeremiah 36 should be viewed against what James Muilenberg called a "scribal age"; Muilenberg draws attention especially to the claims of the neo-Assyrian king Assurbanipal, who claimed mastery of the scribal arts as a performance of his own royal power; see "Baruch the Scribe," in *Proclamation and Presence: Old Testament Essays in Honour of Gwynne Henton Davies*, ed. John I. Durham and Joshua R. Porter (Macon: Macon University Press, [1970] 1983), 215–38. Jeremiah 36 decidedly denies Jehoiakim any such intellectual distinction.

28 An overview and analysis are provided by Casey Strine, "Was the Book of Ezekiel Written in a Refugee Camp? An Investigation," *Hebrew Bible and Ancient Israel* 11 (2022): 189–203.

29 The motif of stripping the hinterland population from the landscape is earlier found in Micah 3:3, where the two are likened to a single organism ("flesh from the bone").

30 Mark Leuchter, "A Resident Alien in Transit: Exile, Adaptation, and Geomythology in the Jeremiah Narratives," *Hebrew Bible and Ancient Israel* 7 (2018): 316–33.

31 Jon D. Levenson, *Sinai and Zion: An Entry into the Jewish Bible* (San Francisco: Harper Collins, 1985).

32 Richard C. Steiner, *Stockmen from Tekoa, Sycomores from Sheba: A Study of Amos' Occupations*, Catholic Biblical Quarterly Monograph Series 26 (Washington, DC: Catholic Biblical Association of America, 2003).

33 This provides some clarity for Ezekiel's claim that YHWH gave Israel "laws that were not good" by which society could not be sustained (Ez 20:25–26).

34 Jeffrey Ostler, *Surviving Genocide: Native Nations and the United States from the American Revolution to Bleeding Kansas* (New Haven: Yale University Press, 2019).

Selected Bibliography

Geoghegan, Jeffrey H. *The Time, Place, and Purpose of the Deuteronomistic History: The Evidence of "Until This Day."* Providence: Brown Judaic Studies, 2006.

Leuchter, Mark. "A Resident Alien in Transit: Exile, Adaptation, and Geo-mythology in the Jeremiah Narratives." *Hebrew Bible and Ancient Israel* 7 (2018): 316–33.

Meier, Matthew R. "What a Meshugenner! Mel Brooks' Politics of Jewish Humor." In *The Political Mel Brooks*, edited by Beth E. Bonnstetter and Samuel Boerboom, 135–55. Washington, DC: Lexington Books, 2019.

Schniedewind, William M. *Who Really Wrote the Bible? The Story of Scribal Communities.* Princeton: Princeton University Press, 2024.

Tiemeyer, Lena-Sofia. "The Priests and the Temple Cult in the Book of Jeremiah." In *Prophecy in the Book of Jeremiah*, edited by Hans M. Barstad and Reinhard G. Kratz, 233–64. Berlin: De Gruyter, 2009.

van der Toorn, Karel. *Family Religion in Babylonia, Syria, and Israel.* Leiden: Brill, 1996.

2

VISUALIZING THE YIDDISH HUMOR
Sholem Aleichem and Charlie Chaplin

Ber Kotlerman

Yiddish "Cultural Tragedy," or Lost in Adaptation

TEVYE: Chava, I would be much happier if you would remain friends
from a distance. You must not forget who you are and who that
man is.

CHAVA: He has a name, Papa.

TEVYE: Of course. All creatures on earth have a name.

CHAVA: Fyedka is not a creature, Papa. Fyedka is a man.

TEVYE: Who says that he isn't? It's just that he is a different kind of
man. As the Good Book says, "Each shall seek his own kind."
Which, translated, means, "A bird may love a fish, but where
would they build a home together?"
—Joseph Stein, *Fiddler on the Roof*[1]

This scene, taken from the iconic Broadway musical *Fiddler on the Roof*,
showcases the main protagonist, Tevye, catching his daughter Chava in
conversation with her non-Jewish friend (and future husband), Fyedka.
This particular scene aims to capture the familiar essence of Jewish humor,
combining the renowned Yiddish-style wordplay with its characteristic
quasi-biblical expressions. The playwright Joseph Stein always insisted
that his *Fiddler* was merely a homage dedicated "to our fathers," loosely
inspired by Sholem Aleichem's stories but not directly based on Sholem
Aleichem himself. Indeed, in Sholem Aleichem's *Tevye the Dairyman*, we

encounter an alternate rendition of the phrase "Fyedka is a man" as well as a distinct form of humor that warrants a thorough elucidation:

> "No," I said, "I don't know who he is. I've never seen his family tree. But I am sure he must be descended from the sages. His father," I said, "must have been either a shepherd or a janitor, or else just a plain drunkard."
>
> To this Chava answers, "Who his father was I don't know and I don't care to know. All people are the same to me. But Fyedka [Sholem Aleichem uses the Ukrainian version of the name, Khvedke] himself is not an ordinary person, of that I am sure . . . [. . .] Fyedka is a second Gorky."
>
> "But I still don't understand what Fyedka is doing here. I would be much happier if you were friends at a distance. You mustn't forget 'From where you came and where you are going'—who you are and who he is . . ."
>
> "God created all the people equal," she said to me.
>
> "Yes, yes," I say, "God created the first man, Adam, in his own image; but we are not allowed to forget that each man has to look for his equal, as our quotation says, 'Every man shall give as much as he can afford . . .'"
>
> "Marvelous!" she cried to me. "You have a quotation for everything. Maybe you also have a quotation that explains why men have divided themselves up into Jews and Gentiles, into lords and slaves, into noblemen and beggars?"
>
> "Te-te-te," I said, "it seems to me, my daughter, you've driven into the 'sixth millennium'!" And I explained to her that this has been the way of the world since the six days of Creation.
>
> "And why," she wanted to know, "should this be the way of the world?"
>
> "Because," I said, "that's the way God created His world."
>
> "And why," she said, "did God create His world this way?"
>
> "Eh," I said, "if we'll start to ask why this and wherefore that, 'there would be no end to the matter'—a tale without end . . ." [. . .]
>
> "We have an old custom," I told her, "that when a hen begins to crow like a rooster, we take her away to be slaughtered. As we say in the blessing, 'Who gave the rooster the ability . . .'"

As evident from this excerpt, concealed beneath the veneer of more or less politically correct wordplay within the Broadway musical lies an entire realm of a distinct genre of humor. In this vast realm, one discovers a wealth of authentic biblical quotations that are meant to strike a chord with both present-day scholars of Jewish studies and Sholem Aleichem's contemporaries, including those "simpletons" equal in status with Tevye the Dairyman. Drawing upon the concept of hypertextuality, this unique brand of humor evokes a resemblance to the Russian nesting doll, the *matryoshka*. Just as each layer reveals a new dimension, this humor unfolds in a similar manner, offering a multifaceted experience. Here are a couple of samples that exemplify the humor and hypertextuality:

(1) "Chava, I would be much happier if you would remain friends from a distance," said Tevye in the musical, omitting Sholem Aleichem's original quotation from the Talmudic tractate "Ethics of the Fathers" (Avot 3:1): "You mustn't forget '*From where you came and where you are going*.'" Tevye "translates" this Talmudic verse from Hebrew into his Yiddish vernacular as "who you are and who he is" (in Yiddish: *ver bistu un ver iz er*). At first glance, this translation appears noticeably incorrect, thereby generating a comical effect. However, a more literate reader can readily reconstruct the broader context from which the verse was extracted: "Akavia the son of Mahalalel would say: Reflect upon three things and you will not come to the hands of transgression. Know from where you came, where you are going, and before whom you are destined to give a judgement and accounting" (Avot 3:1). In other words, the seemingly straightforward quotation leads the reader toward intricate philosophical and theological notions surrounding judgment and punishment in the afterlife, while also intertwining Chava's actions within the context of the intense Jewish-Christian dialogue. In essence, the utilization of the quotation from "Ethics of the Fathers" serves to underscore the unfeasibility, within Tevye's world, of embracing conversion into Christianity. As highlighted by Ruth Wisse in her seminal work *No Joke*, "Jewish humor is never more anti-Gentile than when it confirms the reality of Jews turning Christian and never more nationalistic than when it admits Jewish infirmity."[2]

Wisse's analysis discerns four distinct categories within Yiddish humor: the anti-religious humor of the Maskilim, exemplified by Joseph Perl's *Megale Tmirin* (*Revealer of Hidden Secrets*); the Hasidic humor embodied by Hershele Ostropoler; the Misnagdic or rabbinic humor prevalent in yeshiva circles; and, last, the women's or folk humor, which includes the works of Sholem Aleichem, particularly the Menakhem Mendl–Sheyne Sheyndl correspondence.[3] However, when it comes to Tevye, it seems that the rabbinic category takes the lead, as a solid understanding of Talmudic culture is crucial to truly appreciate the cleverness and hidden meanings behind the humor in his character. As Aryeh Aharoni, the Hebrew trans-lator of Sholem Aleichem's works, said, "The Jewish 'Homo Ludens' didn't play 'golf' or 'baseball', he played verses. He explained them, commented on them, inflected them—and this for generations."[4] Now, if we take a closer look at Tevye's remarks, we can better ascertain the validity of this claim:

(2) "Fyedka is not a creature, Papa. Fyedka is a man," cried Chava in the musical. The keyword that demands our attention here is "man." The original Yiddish version expands: "God created the first man, Adam, in his own image; but we are not allowed to forget that each man has to look for his equal, as our quotation says, 'Ish kematnas yado—Every man shall give as much as he can afford.'" By referencing from the book of Deuteron-omy (Dvarim 16:17), Tevye potentially alludes to the inherent inequality that exists in the world. However, a more precise translation uncovers an additional layer of meaning within the verse: The literal translation of Ish kematnas yado suggests, "Every man is equal to a gift in his hand," which intriguingly alludes to a book by Maxim Gorky, the present that Fyedka brought for Chava. Considering that just moments prior, Tevye expressed a kind of disrespect toward the Russian proletarian writer Gorky ("Is this your righteous Reb Gorky? I could have sworn I'd seen him somewhere, either by the train carrying sacks or in the woods gathering firewood"), this verse reveals his critical attitude toward Fyedka, his cultural back-ground, and maybe even his political views.

(3) In the musical, Chava naturally protests against such an approach. From the Yiddish original, we gather that Tevye's reaction to Chava's actions is that she has "driven into the 'elef hashishi—sixth millennium'! And I [Tevye] explained to her that this has been the way of the world since the shisha yomey bereyshis—six days of Creation." How exactly does our Jewish "farmer" go about explaining this to his daughter? The phrase "elef hashishi—sixth millennium" within the context of Creation holds significance in Jewish mystical eschatology, elucidated in the renowned Zohar (The Book of Splendor). The humorous effect emerges from the chal-lenge of how a simple man can succinctly explain such intricate theology

during a brief conversation. In essence, Tevye's wit alludes to the concept of the "end of days" and the Messianic Age, encompassing the gathering of the dispersed Jewish diaspora, the arrival of the Messiah, the resurrection of the righteous, and the anticipation of the world to come.

(4) In the Yiddish original, Chava persists with further inquiries, but Tevye is unwilling to delve deeper into the topic: "If we'll start to ask why this and wherefore that," he said, "'*eyn ladovor sof*—there would be no end to it'—a tale without end." At first glance, Tevye's disappointing response of avoiding pertinent questions reveals his inability to confront and address serious issues. However, the Talmudic source of the quotation *eyn ladovor sof*—"there would be no end to the matter"—sends us to tractate "The Day," which reads:

> Seven days before the Day of Atonement (Yom Kippur) the high priest was removed from his house to the cell of counselors and another priest was prepared to take his place in case anything happened to him that would unfit him [for the service]. R. Judah said: Also another wife was prepared for him in case his wife should die. For it is written: And he shall make atonement for himself and for his house. "His house" that means "His wife." They said to him: If so, there would be no end to the matter. (Yoma 1:1)

Tevye's utilization of evasive rabbinic language aligns with what Ted Cohen illuminates in his *Jokes* as hermetic humor, which is "accessible only to those versed in an arcane subject."[5] Even in instances where Tevye indulges in playful antics and fabricates fake quotations like the famous quasi-Aramaic *Askakurda de-farsmakhta de-karnosa de-farsmakhta*, such "yeshivish" humor primarily resonates with insiders, rewarding those who possess insider knowledge and familiarity.

(5) The relatively brief dialogue between Tevye and Chava in the Yiddish original concludes with a description of an old custom, as Tevye puts it: "When a hen begins to crow like a rooster, we take her away to be slaughtered. As we say in the blessing, 'Who gave the rooster the ability.'" It appears that Tevye brings forth this quotation in an associative manner, possibly influenced by his previous mention of a rooster. By introducing the concept of a hen within the context of Chava's situation, Tevye may intend to elicit laughter. However, a reader well versed in Talmudic

culture will promptly decipher the underlying meaning and implications of this quotation from the morning *Shakharit* prayer: "Almighty gave the rooster the ability to discern between day and night." As per R. Asher ben Yekhiel, commonly known as Rosh, one of the influential medieval Talmud commentators, this blessing pertains not to a rooster but rather to a person's ability to discern between good and evil. This holds significance for Chava, who requires such discernment, and it also serves, it seems, as Sholem Aleichem's way of expressing his opposition to the antisemitic atmosphere prevalent in the surrounding society. It is noteworthy that Sholem Aleichem deliberately distanced himself from this society, symbolically "divorcing" it a year prior to writing the Chava story when he permanently departed from Czarist Russia in late 1905.

According to Ruth Wisse, Sholem Aleichem holds a pivotal role in shaping modern Yiddish humor, a humor rooted in a language that "set the Jewish tongue free."[6] This humor thrives on the delicate balance between the sacred and the profane, while also engaging in playful exchanges with Hebrew and other languages. Above all, according to Wisse, Yiddish provided the Jews with a medium for their internal dialogue, encompassing a vast repertoire of "aggressive" hermetic jokes. These jokes, serving as a form of retaliation, became almost the sole means of counteracting the hostile environment. The "cultural tragedy," however, lies in the fact that this humor, which served as a vital cultural expression, gradually became increasingly esoteric even for Jews themselves. This mirrors the decline in the usage of Yiddish and, at best, is now reduced to mere fragments and echoes, as evidenced in works such as *Fiddler on the Roof.*

Sholem Aleichem as "Translator" from Yiddish into Universal Language of Silent Cinema

Undoubtedly, Sholem Aleichem keenly felt the limitations of his writings, which could truly thrive only within the realm of Yiddish. He recognized the inherent richness and nuances that could only be fully expressed through the Yiddish language and its unique cultural context. During my research for my monograph on Sholem Aleichem's cinematic aspirations, titled *Disenchanted Tailor in "Illusion,"*[7] I had the privilege of delving into the writer's inner struggle as he endeavored to "translate" his ironic imagery from the Yiddish language into the universal language of silent cinema.

Archival documents reveal that Sholem Aleichem's professional fascination with the realm of silent cinema drove him to write several film scripts between 1913 and 1915, specifically tailored for international audiences. However, despite his efforts, none of his scenarios made it to the screen, leaving his cinematic aspirations unfulfilled. Living in Switzerland, he established numerous contacts with various cinema figures in Berlin, Moscow, Riga, Odessa, and Warsaw, including the Warsaw branch of the famous French film company Pathé Frères. When he immigrated to America in December 1914, he tried to establish contacts with a whole range of film companies that later became legends of the movie industry, such as Vitagraph, Fox, Universal, Lasky, and Lubin.

Being involved in cinema activities for more than two years, Sholem Aleichem was always searching for the way to visualize the "acoustical-verbal" features (to use the terminology of the Soviet literary critic Meir Wiener),[8] with a pronounced purpose to utilize, even if only partially, Jewish cultural codes—biblical quotes, idiomatic expressions, peculiarities of eastern European Yiddish discourse, and so forth—in other words, all of that speaking complex that characterizes Sholem Aleichem's manner of writing. Some of the humoristic elements he employed look rather well turned. One of his scenarios, *The Enchanted Tailor* (1914), demonstrates that he did gain some mastery over the new genre.

Especially interesting is a scene in which his protagonist the tailor has visions in the middle of the night. This scene, with a title reminiscent of the Passover Haggadah, "In great fear the tailor sees great wonders," is perhaps the most striking and successful specimen of Sholem Aleichem's cinema creations:

> Night has fallen. The tailor, with his goods, finds himself alone in the marketplace, with its locked up shops and folded and covered vendors' stands. He wipes the sweat from his brow. He sits down in the middle of the marketplace. A goat, tied to a strap, takes a seat as well. Frightened, the tailor looks at the animal, and it seems to him that it has human hands rather than the front legs of a goat, and its face also seems to be human-like. Only its beard and horns are like those of a goat (to create this image an actor will put on a goatskin costume

with beard and horns). The goat-man extends his hand to the tailor, sits down next to him, and begins to talk to him like a human being. The tailor looks at him in great fear, trembling all over. Then the goat-man lifts the tailor up from the ground and, having embraced him, suggests that they go for a walk, then, after doing various fantastic tricks with him, starts to dance with him. The tailor does not dare to refuse, and they break into a merry dance to the sound of music (it could be a Russian "Kamarinskaya" folk tune).[9]

Having mastered the visual language of this previously unfamiliar art form, Sholem Aleichem continued to perfect the process of portraying the Jewish world on the screen. The protagonists consistently behave "ethnically" as in the following passages: "He takes hold of his belt, wraps it around himself, snaps his fingers" or "Pale-faced boys in small *yarmolkes* (skullcaps) or peaked caps, small *peyos* (earlocks) and *arba kanfos* (small prayer shawls) with white fringes on the corners . . . sway back and forth pronouncing the words in a sing-song."[10]

However, it is evident that these "pictures" predominantly exhibit a folkloric or caricaturistic style, occasionally even veering into mockery, thereby lacking the distinct Yiddish flavor we previously examined. Perhaps in search of new expressive means, Sholem Aleichem looked closely at Charlie Chaplin's comic acting, trying to make sense of his creative techniques.

The only widespread testimony to this fact comes from the New York Yiddish journalist and translator Naftali Linder (1885–1960), who knew Sholem Aleichem personally. Linder stated several times that the author, almost from the moment he arrived in the United States, was interested in Chaplin. According to Linder's memoirs, the writer was constantly going to the little nickel movie halls, at first in Harlem, then in the Bronx, where he moved with his family, to see the short comedies in which Chaplin was playing.[11] New movies starring Chaplin came out almost every week, and, according to Linder, Sholem Aleichem often went to see them several times. He would tolerate no criticism of Chaplin and once even made fun of a certain young man who had studied theater and cinema in Germany and allowed himself to parody Chaplin disparagingly.[12]

Chaplin as a Visual Perspective to Sholem Aleichem's Heroes

Sholem Aleichem surely noticed that Chaplin's contradictory cinema character was perfectly capable of adding a visual perspective to some of his heroes. The psychologist and philologist Abraham Aaron Robak, who studied the nature of Sholem Aleichem's humor, explained the similarity of Chaplin's and Sholem Aleichem's characters, like Menakhem Mendl, in the progressive irrationality ("surd" in the terminology of Robak's *Psychology of Common Sense*) of their behavior. They both bank "on the immediate future and therefore leave out of account probable, if not absolutely certain, consequences, attributing the results to tough luck, a quirk of fate, or the will of God."[13] To put it differently, it is likely that the outward manifestation of incongruity with the surrounding world, which is a prominent trait of Sholem Aleichem's characters, is what resonated with the writer and drew him to the figure of Charlie Chaplin.

A number of observers noted an inherent similarity between Sholem Aleichem's disfranchised and uprooted heroes and the characters played by Chaplin, in light of Chaplin's "Jewish style" of acting, which has been much discussed over the years. Because of his bowler-hat-wearing, mustachioed Little Tramp character that appears in short films like *The Immigrant*, Chaplin, being non-Jewish, strikes audiences and critics as a Jewish version of the typical comic hero. According to J. Hoberman, to a Jewish audience Chaplin is recognizable as a classic schlemiel and as a David-like figure that is constantly battling Goliath.[14] Because the idea of persecution and resilience is so deeply rooted in Jewish history, it is natural for the Jews to claim Chaplin as their own.

It seems that Sholem Aleichem also discerned a "Jewish style" in Charlie Chaplin's performances. However, there is something more here than the style of acting. Sholem Aleichem may be enchanted seeing a pariah, right like his own luftmensch, triumph over persecution in a way that is as pathetic as it is comic. It was another kind of humoristic "weapon," which was loved by a broader public, Jewish and non-Jewish alike. This kind of acting was worth to be taken as a new model for his own cinema exercises. Linder, writing a quarter of a century after the fact, emphasizes that paradoxically "the Chaplinesque 'playing the fool,' as others called it, never touched Sholem Aleichem." "He was enraptured by the purely childlike naivete of Chaplin's mimicry, how he hitches up his shoulders and twirls his cane." The external expression of incompatibility with the surrounding world characteristic of a lot of Sholem Aleichem heroes, but without any trace of inferiority complex, is what drew the writer to the Chaplin figure. "'His pathetic little moustache, oversized clumsy shoes, trousers too wide, too long, and very worn, jacket too small and soiled, worn top hat, dainty crooked cane, and his whole dance-like stiff-legged gait.' 'You see, this figure,' said Sholem Aleichem with feeling, according to Linder, 'is in itself an artistic production, which no brush and no pen anywhere has ever portrayed before, on canvas or paper.'"[15]

Surprisingly, Chaplin himself described the birth of his famous Tramp in very similar words, which Sholem Aleichem could not have ever seen or heard:

> On the way to the wardrobe I thought I would dress in baggy pants, big shoes, a cane and a derby hat. I wanted everything to be a contradiction: the pants baggy, the coat tight, the hat small and the shoes large.[16]

At first sight, Chaplin's Tramp evokes an association with the "Jewish tramp," Menakhem Mendl, whom Sholem Aleichem created much before his acquaintance with Chaplin's acting. Once Chaplin had been seen, the "foolish" adventures of Menakhem Mendl must have cried out to be put on the screen—in order "to express in pantomime all the wretchedness of a pathetic-comic dandy with his foolish frolicsome (*shlimazldik-kundeysishe*) antics," as Sholem Aleichem expressed it himself, when commenting on Chaplin's "rare abilities."[17] However, in all of his attempts to break into the movies after moving to America, Sholem Aleichem never let slip a word about his desire to put Menakhem Mendl on the screen, although in his previous projects in Europe such a possibility was discussed. However, if he had such a hope, it was perhaps not entirely baseless, as we learn from his private correspondence.

Chaplin's Tramp appeared on the screen at the beginning of 1914, in the period when the actor was working for the Keystone Film Company, which he left a year later for the thriving Chicago firm Essanay Film Manufacturing Company, which turned Chaplin's Tramp into the ultimate symbol of silent film. About the same time, Sholem Aleichem started negotiations with a certain movie businessman, David Keizerstein, who proposed to connect him with some "people higher up" from the world of cinema.[18] Sholem Aleichem asked his brother Berl Rabinowitz, an owner of a kid gloves factory in Newark, to investigate Keizerstein's financial condition. At the end of March, Berl Rabinowitz communicated the information he had received to his author brother. This is his March 1915 letter from which we learn that he checked the financial status of the movie producers George Kirke Spoor and Maxwell Henry Aronson (known as "Broncho Billy" Anderson, thanks to his popular movie hero), owners of the Essanay Film Manufacturing Company.[19] They were perhaps the very "people higher up" whom Keizerstein had mentioned as interested in Sholem Aleichem. Berl's letter clearly shows Sholem Aleichem's attention to this company. He probably never made direct contact with Essanay, but this may simply have increased his interest in Charlie Chaplin.

Keizerstein undertook to promote the stories of Sholem Aleichem's *Motl the Cantor's Son*. The film script based on *Motl* has not come down to us,[20] but an interesting memoir by Ben-Zion Goldberg, then a Columbia University student and the future son-in-law of Sholem Aleichem, tells us how Goldberg joined Sholem Aleichem in Lakewood, New Jersey, to translate the piece into English.

> He performed every role and every scene, while simultaneously playing the role of the audience. When he lifted his finger, showing how the finger would move on the screen, writing the words, "Eli-ink maker," I clearly saw the screen and became totally immersed in the illusion that I was looking at a motion picture. Then we both laughed. Sholem Aleichem laughed with all his might, a frank, heartfelt laughter. I never saw him laugh like that at any other time. . . . If any outsider had seen us then, he would have taken us for a couple of lunatics. There we were, two guys sitting and howling with laughter like frivolous kids at a Charlie Chaplin movie.[21]

All that has been preserved from this project is a short English-language synopsis in Goldberg's translation: *Little Motl Goes to America*, to which Sholem Aleichem gave an additional name in Yiddish, *Shat, mir forn keyn Amerike!* (Shh, We're Going to America!). From its laconic text, it is hard to catch a possible connection with Chaplin's acting, but the second, American, part of the *Motl* stories, written a year later, gives as enough material to speculate about its cinematographic layer.

Motl and his family immigrate to New York. One of the main protagonists of the second part is the family's friend Pini, who is described as a genuinely Chaplinesque type, "putting both hands in his pockets and moving his little cap to the back of his head":

> The rush of people was so powerful that Pini nearly got kicked, just the way he had been in London not long ago when we had only just arrived there. That is, in just a few moments he would already have been lying crushed and trampled on the street. But this time he escaped with only a blow to the side. The blow was so hard, though, that his little cap flew off his head, and, being snatched up by the wind, whirled away somewhere off to the side. . . .
>
> The conductor slammed the door shut. The subway car started off with a jerk. Our Pini, standing by the door pensive and embarrassed, jumped back quickly. In an instant he was lying in the embrace of a Negro woman. She threw him off herself with both hands so strongly that he went flying over to the opposite bench, and his little cap flew off to the door. To top off the whole disaster, loud laughter rang out in the subway car. All the passengers were roaring with laughter.[22]

In April 1916, Sholem Aleichem fell ill and hardly got out of bed, but he continued to write the stories about Motl in America that were being published regularly, every Wednesday, in the socialist Yiddish newspaper *Varhayt*. It was at this time that the name of Charlie Chaplin appeared in a work of his for the first and last time. In the episode called "Hello, Fellow Countryman!" the heroes go to the movies to see a Chaplin film, and on the way they share "information" about the actor:

> My brother asks, For what is Charlie Chaplin so famous?
> Pini answers that they don't pay $1,000 a week to just anyone . . .
> How do you know? You counted his money? asks Eli.
> Pini says that he read about it in the "papers."
> And from where is it known that Charlie Chaplin is a Jew?
> They also write about this, says Pini, in the "papers."

And from where do these "papers" know this? Were they at his *bris* [circumcision ceremony]?

The "papers" know everything!, answers Pini. You see, they know that Charlie Chaplin is mute from birth, that he can't write or read, that his father was a drunk, that he himself was a clown in the circus.[23]

In this short dialogue, in one breath, Sholem Aleichem manages to mention Chaplin's huge fees, the widespread myth about his being Jewish, his lowly social origins, his "circus" past, and even the "silent" character of the early movies. But the main point was that Chaplin was a model worthy of imitation, and little Motl's friend, also named Motl (but called Max in America), does indeed imitate him:

Well, what's he up to, that master craftsman Charlie Chaplin, when he does his various tricks! And Max imitates him in all the little details. When we left the theater, he stuck a couple of little black moustaches like Charlie Chaplin's on himself, pulled a bowler hat over his forehead, like Charlie Chaplin, turned out his feet and began to walk, swaying backward and swinging a slender cane—Charlie Chaplin, as alike as two drops of water![24]

This description reminds us of Sholem Aleichem's enthusiastic response to Chaplin as noted in Linder's memoirs. However, the situation in which it was written gives it a completely different meaning. The episode "Hello, Fellow Countryman!" (no. 16), or to be more precise, its working version, was discovered in the writer's papers after his death, together with two more subsequent episodes. Sholem Aleichem intended to send no. 16 to *Varhayt* the week of his death but did not get around to it. The previous episode in the series (no. 15), his last publication before his death, came out on May 10, 1916.[25] Sholem Aleichem's son-in-law and longtime assistant Itskhok Dov Berkowitz tells of a conversation with his father-in-law on the evening of May 9, just four days before the author's death:

Among other things, he asked me if the editors of "Varhayt" knew . . . that he was sick and told us that during the night . . . he had written, despite his great sufferings, which did not leave him for a minute.

"I lie here and lie here the whole night," he said, breathing with difficulty, "I can't fall asleep, thoughts fly by. . . . What use is there in
lying here this way? I say to Mama: What am I doing, staying here
in bed? It's still a long time until dawn. . . . It would be better to give
me here a pen and folder with paper; at least I will do some writing.
It is much easier for me to write, since in any case thoughts torment
me, they give me no rest. . . . And so, on the sly, I wrote several episodes about Motl."[26]

What were the thoughts tormenting Sholem Aleichem during his last
days? Why, while dealing with Motl's American adventures, did he suddenly remember Chaplin, with his $1,000 a week income, that "they don't
pay . . . to just anyone"? Did he see himself, like Max, as a naive imitator
of the talented movie actor? The conclusion of the story, where Max, who
has learned to speak from his stomach without moving his lips, teases Eli,
would seem to clarify what the dying author felt as he thought about his
cinema projects:

> I-di-ot!—was heard again from behind Eli's back. Eli turned around,
> and Pini, looking at him, also turned around. Max and I followed suit.
> We nearly burst with laughter.
>
> "In America the stones speak . . ." That's the way our friend Pini
> expressed himself. He only wanted to know, whom were they calling
> an "idiot"?
>
> The one who asks, answered Eli.
>
> Then, however, he was amazed, when from underground they
> suddenly heard a muted voice:
>
> You are wrong, Reb Eli! Because, idiot—it is, *takeh*, you yourself![27]

Such an unexpected conclusion to a completely innocent story about Motl
and his friends going to the movies, against the background of Sholem
Aleichem's uniformly unsuccessful efforts to break into the movies, sounds
like an acknowledgment of defeat. Under the words "Because, idiot—it is,
takeh, you yourself," Sholem Aleichem placed two rows of leaders, leaving
the reader to guess what has been left unsaid.

The preserved manuscript of this episode[28] shows that as Sholem Aleichem, on his deathbed, was rereading what he had written and dotting

the last i's, he made several revisions and noted, among other things, that Chaplin "is a great movie star." At the bottom of the last page, he squeezed in one more sentence, as a separate, terse subchapter. That sentence stands out like a caption card epilogue:

> Since that time my brother Eli doesn't go to the "moving pictures" anymore and doesn't want to hear anything about Charlie Chaplin.[29]

Perhaps upon seeing Chaplin's talented acting, Sholem Aleichem felt disappointment at his own clumsy cinematographic exertions (as he said, "You see, this character . . . no brush and no pen anywhere has ever portrayed before!"). It seems that in seeing himself, like Eli, as an immigrant disappointed by his failure to understand reality, Sholem Aleichem is admitting here, with his characteristic melancholy gaiety, his own failure in the field of cinema. Coldheartedly and mercilessly in relation to himself, he sums up his "cinema fantasies," which brought him neither money, nor fame, nor the passionately desired escape of his creative works from the vicious circle of publishers, editors, and theatrical bigwigs into the fast-growing international art of cinema.

Notes

1 Joseph Stein, *Fiddler on the Roof*, based on Sholom Aleichem's stories (New York: Pocket Books, 1964), 991–100.
2 Ruth Wisse, *No Joke: Making Jewish Humor* (Princeton: Princeton University Press, 2013), 92.
3 Wisse, *No Joke*, 92, see also chapter 2, "Yiddish Heartland," 66–103.
4 See Aryeh Aharoni, "Mashehu 'al hahunor shel giborey shalom aleykhem," in Shalom 'Aleykhem, *Khtavim: Tuvya hahalban, Sender Blank, Stempenyu* (Tel Aviv: Sifriyat po'alim, 1997), 7.
5 Ted Cohen, *Jokes: Philosophical Thoughts on Joking Matters* (Chicago: University of Chicago Press, 1999), 17.
6 Wisse, *No Joke*, 17.
7 Ber Kotlerman, *Disenchanted Tailor in "Illusion": Sholem Aleichem Behind the Scenes of Early Jewish Cinema, 1913–16* (Bloomington, IN: Slavica Publishers, 2014).

8 Meir Viner, *Tsu der geshikhte fun der yidisher literatur in 19tn yorhundert (etyudn un materyaln)*, vol. 2: *Mendele Moykher Sforim, Sholem-Aleykhem* (New York: YKUF, 1946), 297; and Meir Viner, "Batrakhtungen vegn Sholem-Aleykhems humor," *Sovetish* 12 (1941): 33.

9 For the original text in the Russian language, see Kotlerman, *Disenchanted Tailor*, 261–62.

10 Kotlerman, *Disenchanted Tailor*, 81.

11 "Ibergegebn fun N. B. Linder," in *Dos Sholem-Aleykhem-bukh*, ed. Itskhok-Dov Berkovitsh (New York: Sholem-Aleykhem bukh komitet, 1926), 360.

12 N. B. Linder, "Sholem-Aleykhem un Tsharli Tshaplin," *Der tog*, April 2, 1939.

13 A. A. Robak, "The Humor of Aleichem," in *Sholom Aleichem Panorama*, ed. Melech Grafstein (London, ON: Jewish Observer, 1948), 22. See also Abraham Aaron Robak, *Psychology of Common Sense: A Diagnosis of Modern Philistinism* (Cambridge, MA: Sci-Art Publishers, 1939).

14 For an overview of Chaplin's "Jewishness," see J. Hoberman, "The First 'Jewish' Superstar: Charlie Chaplin," in J. Hoberman and Jeffrey Shandler, *Entertaining America: Jews, Movies, and Broadcasting* (New York: The Jewish Museum and Princeton University Press, 2003), 34–39.

15 Linder, "Sholem-Aleykhem un Tsharli Tshaplin."

16 Charles Chaplin, *My Autobiography* (New York: Simon and Schuster, 1964), 154.

17 Linder, "Sholem-Aleykhem un Tsharli Tshaplin."

18 Marie Waife-Goldberg, *My Father, Sholom Aleichem* (New York: Simon and Schuster, 1968), 291.

19 Kotlerman, *Disenchanted Tailor*, 169.

20 For the fate of this scenario, see Ber Kotlerman, " 'Going Through the Seven Circles of Hell–Joyfully, à la Motl': Sholem Aleichem's Missing Film Script About *Motl the Cantor's Son*," *Jewish Quarterly Review* 105, no. 2 (2015): 155–73.

21 B. Ts. Goldberg, "Momentn Sholem-Aleykhem," in Berkovitsh, *Dos Sholem-Aleykhem-bukh*, 144.

22 Sholem-Aleykhem, "Motel Peysi dem khazn's. Tsveyter teyl: in Amerike," in *Ale verk fun Sholem-Aleykhem*, vol. 14 (New York: Morgn-frayhayt, 1937), 65, 74. Translated here and thereinafter by Mike Aronson.

23 Sholem-Aleykhem, "Motel Peysi dem khazn's," 185–86.

24 Sholem-Aleykhem, "Motel Peysi dem khazn's," 187.

25 Sholem-Aleykhem, "Motel Peysi dem khazn's in Amerike: mayses fun a ingl a yosem. Mir gehen in di biznes," *Varhayt*, May 10, 1916.

26 See Sholem-Aleykhem, "Motel Peysi dem khazn's," 206–7 (Berkowitz's note).

27 Sholem-Aleykhem, "Motel Peysi dem khazn's," 189.

28 See the original manuscript of *Motl Peysi dem khazns* in Beth Shalom Aleykhem (Sholem Aleichem House) in Tel Aviv.

29 Sholem-Aleykhem, "Motel Peysi dem khazn's," 189.

Selected Bibliography

Chaplin, Charles. *My Autobiography*. New York: Simon and Schuster, 1964.

Cohen, Ted. *Jokes: Philosophical Thoughts on Joking Matters*. Chicago: University of Chicago Press, 1999.

Hoberman, J., and Jeffrey Shandler. *Entertaining America: Jews, Movies, and Broadcasting*. New York: The Jewish Museum and Princeton University Press, 2003.

Kotlerman, Ber. *Disenchanted Tailor in "Illusion": Sholem Aleichem Behind the Scenes of Early Jewish Cinema, 1913–16*. Bloomington, IN: Slavica Publishers, 2014.

Robak, Abraham Aaron. *Psychology of Common Sense: A Diagnosis of Modern Philistinism*. Cambridge, MA: Sci-Art Publishers, 1939.

Stein, Joseph. *Fiddler on the Roof*. Based on Sholom Aleichem's stories. New York: Pocket Books, 1964.

Waife-Goldberg, Marie. *My Father, Sholom Aleichem*. New York: Simon and Schuster, 1968.

Wisse, Ruth. *No Joke: Making Jewish Humor*. Princeton: Princeton University Press, 2013.

3

FRANZ KAFKA AND THE RESISTANCE
Authority and Its Meaninglessness

Lauren Brooks

No Disrespect: Kafka and the Soup Nazis

How can a show use humor with Nazism and "making out during *Schindler's List*"[1] as themes? *Seinfeld* accomplished this feat, invoking reverent images only to expose their unworthiness, much like Kafka's works challenge authority. The Soup Nazi in *Seinfeld* wields power through unreadability, mirroring Kafka's themes of inscrutability and respect for the law. Kafka highlights the authority of authorship, emphasizing that every reading of a text involves claims beyond the text itself. Both Kafka and *Seinfeld* defy reverence for authority figures and objects, fostering compassion for the damage caused by undue respect. Kafka presents the infinite and absolute as effects of our encounter with nonsense and non-meaning, not inherent truths. *Seinfeld*'s Soup Nazi's power lies predominantly in his unreadability; every attempt to follow his rules results in another infraction. Just as the door in Kafka's parable "Before the Law," and its *hiding* of the law, is what produced respect (and not anything we ever see behind the door), and just as the *writing of the law* (and not what the law says) produced power in "The Penal Colony," so does standing in line, waiting, and hoping allow the Soup Nazi to maintain his control. I contend that Kafka plays directly on the authority of authorship: for a text to be read, it must signal some degree of authority and readability, and yet—like the law—there must also be a necessary distance and inscrutability to practice the law. Just as every enforcement of the law requires adding some power to law's authority, every reading of a text requires some claim that is never the text itself.

Kafka and *Seinfeld* share a comic approach to authority, where characters are paralyzed by deference. Kafka's authority figures remain inaccessible, thereby diminishing their importance. In Kafka's novels, humor arises from the fear of an all-knowing, all-powerful authority figure that can never be confronted. This fear of breaking rules, even when the chances of being caught are slim, reflects a deep-rooted concept in human imagination. Kafka's characters mock the power of authority figures due to their unattainable distance. The fear and desire for punishment make authority exist and exert a force larger than life. Kafka's humor stems from an utter lack of respect for authority, both in content and form, with his stories challenging arbitrary authorities and undermining definitive readings. This ambivalent humor leaves interpretations unresolved, making Kafka's counter-authority distinct. Reading Kafka alongside *Seinfeld* allows us to see that the comedy is often generated by our attempts to take things too seriously, even when they lack authority.

The Paradox of Authority

Both *Seinfeld* and Kafka appear to take authority seriously—but this seriousness ultimately undermines authority itself. Their attempts not to laugh in the face of power paradoxically reveal that authority depends on submission to maintain its force. Kafka's characters, like those who appear before the law, never realize that their ongoing deference is what sustains the authority they face. What remains, then, but to laugh—not the cathartic release Freud describes, or with slapstick joy, but with a cryptic, subversive recognition of authority. Laughter here becomes a form of refusal more profound than overt resistance: it exposes the hollowness of power's performance.

In Kafka's "A Report to an Academy," an ape, Red Peter, appears before an "academy" recalling his account of behaving like a human, suggesting how actually simplistic and mundane human life and its rituals are.[2] This scene typically combines Kafka's humor at the level of form and content: the very existence of a talking ape is at once absurd and comical in its deflation of human speech. At the same time, the use of the mode of a "report" is a play on the supposed neutrality of information. Here, and elsewhere, Kafka combined structures of formality—courts, reporting, bureaucracy, judgment—with the contingent bodies of apes, insects, and mice. If we pay attention to the form as a report to an academy, we see how it is nothing but a mockery of the way in which information is consecrated. The "academy" receives its wisdom from an ape, but in that very conveyance of the report, just by being situated in the position of being reported to, the academy becomes authoritative. What does this say about the problem of authority? The ape, in a twisted way, appears to initially represent authority by the means in which he so authoritatively reports. Authority is exposed as an empty form, with the ape freely reporting and the academy duly receiving his statements. What is manifestly a dignified situation of reporting is ultimately as mechanical and forced as Kafka's frequent scenarios of imprisonment. In the end, Red Peter represents our inability to escape authority; therefore, the notion of freedom that Red Peter so fruitlessly searches for in the text does not exist. It is the inaccessibility of freedom that is paralleled with the undesirable way in which it is perceived: those who are hearing the report seem no less compelled or mechanical. These qualities are the weakness of the "Esteemed Academicians," the supposed authority figures in this text. Through the mode of detachment in which the story is narrated, the humor arises. Ultimately, death is the only freedom, and we hear Kafka's voice in Red Peter almost laughing at us and our futile hope for resolution.

In *The Metamorphosis*, Gregor Samsa wakes up one morning to find himself transformed into some kind of monstrous insect. Early in the text, he is horrified to discover he has slept through his alarm; however, instead of rushing to get to work, he lies in bed and fantasizes about quitting his job while also airing his grievances. In this fantasy, Gregor visualizes what would happen after his boss—perched atop a high podium—learns of his true feelings: that he would quite literally fall from his "high" position at his desk.[3] Even in this fantasy, however, Gregor still admires the height of his boss, looking down on his subordinates. This power is then subverted through a weakness—his boss is hard of hearing—since Gregor imagines having to step very close to the podium to be heard. It is as if the boss's perceived authority were produced *because* of his weakness. He must elevate himself and create a literal distance of height. In both situations, there is a Nietzschean quality about Kafka's figures of power: their weakness has forced them to situate themselves above others to establish a constituted authority.

If the *form* of reports, legal hearings, tales, and seemingly objective descriptions provides a way to undermine the authority of the realist and forensic genres, Kafka also disturbs law and order at the level of content. The inability to reach the law and the meaninglessness of authority of any kind—political, judicial, scriptural, or familial—is depicted in almost all his prose, and this is exactly a source from which the humor stems. There is a humor both in the described absurd distance and height of the law and in the formal devices Kafka uses to convey these delays and deferrals. Kafka frequently displays the absence of authority, along with the countless scenes of imposed unreadability: think of the apparatus in "In the Penal Colony" or the maze of bureaucracy as depicted in *The Trial* or *The Castle*, both of which ridicule authority simultaneously at form and content. There is at once the sense that the description of processes will yield an insight that never arises, while the very machines and processes that are described act to reduce and deflate the law to nothing more than mechanics. Kafka's humor emerges from a disrespect for authority that has a way of generating a new relationship with form and content of his work. He not only describes a law that is an inhuman machine; his texts operate in the same way—a promised sense that never arrives. It is in this respect that we might ask a question of Kafka that we should ask of *any* author but that must have particular force in a writer whose work seems at once enigmatically simple (in the form of the parable or the tale) and impossibly enigmatic (in the interpretation of the actual text, or content): How can "the law" appear at one and the same time as inescapable and empty? The distance and contingency these authoritative figures create coincide with a particular type of humor that easily connects us to *Seinfeld*.

Several instances from *Seinfeld* are reminiscent of scenes from Kafka's *The Trial* and *The Castle* or the parables "Before the Law" and "Give It Up." Each one of these moments from the Seinfeldian universe builds on traditions of the absurd and presents situations that are unsettling. Such Kafkaesque elements permeate postmodern American popular culture, with the humor in *Seinfeld* providing an implicit critique of modern urban futility. For example, in one episode, "the law" prohibits a bounced check on display from being taken down—much to Jerry's dismay—where the store clerk claims that even he, as the owner, is not above the policy.[4] In another episode, with Mr. Bookman, the library cop ("Bookman? The library investigator's name is actually Bookman?"),[5] Jerry is accused of not returning a twenty-five-year overdue library book and thus, according to Bookman, considers himself above the law.[6] We also see that intense interrogation of postal employee Newman will never reveal the greater conspiracy of the US Postal Service when Kramer insists on canceling his mail.[7] In "The Chinese Restaurant," Kafka's parable "Before the Law" comes to life. In Kafka's parable, you encounter a man standing outside of a door waiting to be told when to enter, a door to which he never gains access even though it is only meant for him. In *Seinfeld*, Jerry, Elaine, and George fruitlessly wait for a table and leave the restaurant out of frustration when only the audience hears "Seinfeld, four!"[8] These scenes function as an allegory for the act of reading: when we stand before authority, anticipating its summons, we are disappointed when the law offers us only silence. Approaching a text to seek meaning reveals that any meaning has come from our own construction. Thus, if we choose to not interpret and simply submit to the law, all that remains is laughter. These Seinfeldian issues remain unresolved, and though not redemptive for the characters on the show, they provide us as viewers with some kind of redemption since these situations are relatable. There is no "happy ending" in *Seinfeld*, and throughout the show's nine-year run, there is no redemption for Jerry, Elaine, George, or Kramer.

In the show's final episode, the crazy antics and tomfoolery of the *Seinfeld* four come to a halt in a courthouse in the small town of Latham, Massachusetts, where they are tried for breaking the newly created "Good Samaritan" law, which requires citizens to *do* something if they see something, the opposite of the show's supposed premise. They are sentenced to confinement for one year in order to "contemplate the manner in which they have conducted themselves."[9] It is their passivity and lack of ethics that is the cause of their demise. The show ends up with the four of them sitting, unperturbed, in a jail cell discussing George's button, a conversation that resembles one in the very beginning of the series. They have come full circle and learned nothing. The Kafkaesque outcome of the series finale leaves audiences disappointed and dissatisfied, contemplating the unanswered and unresolved, and this is exactly the point. After nine seasons, nothing has changed; the characters keep surrendering to the very stasis that encapsulates them. There was never anywhere for them to go.

Although a lot happens in the show, nothing is learned or gained, and this creates the same kind of moral ambiguity and humor that one finds at the end of Kafka's *The Metamorphosis* and *The Trial*, for example. We question "whether justice has actually been served or if justice even exists as a concept."[10] There is more to the *Seinfeld* show than just comedy. This comic tradition is evident in Kafka's writing as well. Philip Roth described Kafka as "the poet of the ungraspable and unresolved, someone whose fiction refutes every easy, touching, humanish daydream of salvation and justice and fulfillment with densely imagined counter dreams that mock all solutions and escapes."[11] Through the gravity of Kafka's stories dealing with themes of profound anguish, depression, and suffering, we can read the humor portrayed in Kafka's works through a Seinfeldian lens.

Humor and Authority

Both in works of Kafka and in episodes of *Seinfeld*, we witness the characters' heightened anxiety and their relentless preoccupation with proper conduct, situating them within excruciatingly uncomfortable scenarios, all the while employing moments of humor to alleviate the stress inherent in the psychological narratives.[12] *Seinfeld* finds comedy in the tragedy of life, whether by adding levity in the death of Susan (George's finance, who dies from licking cheap wedding invitations that George insisted on buying) or by bringing a fundamental issue such as abortion to the same level as picking toppings on a pizza; all of these events are tragic and yet framed by humor. What is the correct behavior when someone has been hospitalized? Can one stop to get a box of candy on the way to the hospital? Is it wrong to eat Junior Mints while watching "the fat bastard" being sliced up? Or how about dropping a Junior Mint that happens to land directly in the wound during surgery? Dying and being hospitalized are fears and situations we avoid thinking about but are plausible events in life nonetheless. Who makes these rules? And why do we so blindly follow them? This brings us to the question that is practically at the core of every episode of *Seinfeld*: Why do we want to conform to the norms of society when there is no purpose? Why obey laws only written to give some semblance of control and order in life? *Seinfeld* was known for being the television show that changed the way Americans looked at sitcoms, and it was the first of its kind not to center the plot around family, familial values, and typical norms that society values and expects. In this vein, this rejection of what we know, we witness a pure disregard of the authority of the norm.

In the way that *Seinfeld* refuses the authority of what a sitcom is, the series represents not only the death of the so-called American Dream but also the dissolution of the family unit. There is no mention of children, unless you consider the main characters as childlike adults, with no responsibilities. In the episode "The Engagement," Jerry and George think the thing that is missing in their life must be marriage. Why is that? By presenting a constant series of frustrations, *Seinfeld* at once hints at what might be fulfillment but also exposes that our ideas of fulfillment are given only through the obstacles and frustrations that make up damaged life. No matter what, there will never be *the one* or *the date*, we will never be redeemed, and what we desire or think we desire will constantly be deferred and postponed. Through this we are given some kind of delayed hope of an unattainable goal or achievement.

In this state of deferral, we also find that societal norms can also shape what we believe to be *moral* and *right*, and as such *morality* takes on new definitions in the show. There is a "medley of rules with no clear relationship to one another."[13] In "The Parking Garage," we see the true face of humankind as represented by the people in the parking garage who refuse to help Elaine—or the other three, for that matter—find their car. When Elaine questions the compassion of a passerby, he claims that nothing can be gained by helping them. She pushes him further, suggesting that he would feel good about himself knowing that he helped people, and, she adds, he would also save the dying fish in her plastic bag. The passerby shamelessly admits that he would not feel any better by helping them and is perfectly okay with going about his day. Our four characters search endlessly in a parking lot that eerily resembles life in the sense that we are constantly wandering and following signs that lead to nowhere. One interpretation of this show is that it demonstrates the banal repetition of life with no end goal or purpose in sight. But is life really this banal and pointless? Yes.

Authority serves little purpose, only to confuse our tragic heroes, and there is little respect for authority figures and their supposed necessity. Every chance the *Seinfeld* characters have to subvert putative authority, they do so. This disregard for authority is perhaps better thought of as an affirmative nihilism—the tragic yet laughable realization of the absence of the law. In a Kafka text and an episode of *Seinfeld*, we have childlike heroes who never attain adulthood, nor strive to attain it, because of an ultimate meaninglessness. "What is the point of it all?" is a question posed in many episodes. In "The Engagement," Jerry and George, in a very Nietzschean discussion, contemplate, once again, the purpose of life and come to the absurd conclusion that getting married will fix it all. This two-minute scene demonstrates the pointlessness of their existence. On the one hand, they know that they are pathetic and that it is ridiculous to break up with a woman because she "shushed" him, which completely goes against the idea of "normal," yet, for some reason, albeit only for a short instance, they believe they are capable of marriage. On the other hand, we know that nothing is going to change and that their circular reasoning will leave them right back to where they started, as in the series finale. "No learning" at its finest. And as if marriage were really the solution to it all! Neither man is capable of caring for others, let alone himself. Jerry and George make a pact to marry, but Jerry breaks the pact almost immediately, and by the time George finds out, he has already proposed to Susan. Even Kramer later tries to explain to Jerry that marriage is a "man-made prison." Kramer points out that there is nothing more to life than what they currently have or know. "Is there more to life? Let me clue you in on something. There isn't."[14] George becomes more and more miserable as the episode progresses, and we see that what the two men initially thought was the ticket out, or the thing that would define them as men, is nothing what it seems or anything like they had imagined. One of the reasons is because they are just too selfish and self-absorbed, and since these are qualities that resonate with audiences today, we drift further and further away from those values and norms once considered traditional. All characters in *Seinfeld* are better off being alone. Relationships are portrayed as arbitrary—as arbitrary as someone eating their peas one at a time.

Let's consider the repetitive nature of the Seinfeldian settings, the fixed natures of characters, and how time plays no essential role in the show. It's a given that Kramer will persistently concoct unconventional plans; George will perpetually struggle with managing self-assurance and maintaining steady employment; Elaine will persist in her on-and-off relationship with David Puddy, all the while aspiring to find a partner who is both more intellectually stimulating and accomplished; and Jerry will inevitably discover minor reasons to end his romantic relationships.[15] If we return to the conversation George and Jerry have about marriage, it invokes the feeling that the struggle is fruitless because there is no end goal in life other than death due to humankind's finitude. And yet somehow we are always trying to find meaning from our actions. But not these four characters! They appear to want change, but nothing ever changes for them; although the world around them changes, they do not. They endlessly imagine that there will be *the date* or *the job* but simply meander through life waiting for its arrival, doing nothing that would count as action.

The Ultimate Dismantling of the Patriarchal System

Autobiographical elements played a critical role in Kafka's work, and the focus here is "The Judgment," written in 1912. There are at least two ways that one might think of biography in relation to a body of work: It can serve as a supposed foundation, an ultimate law or authority—just out of reach—that we continually appeal to in search of the "right" interpretation. Alternatively, an author's life can have a deflationary effect, reframing the grand questions posed in the work as expressions of the minor enigmas of "a" life. In this view, the author's character is not a final authority but another fragment to consider in the broader interpretive process. In his diary entries, Kafka wrote extensively about the similarities between himself and Georg Bendemann, the son character in "The Judgment." He even breaks down the character's name: "Georg" has the same number of letters as "Franz," and "Bende" matches "Kafka" in length, with the vowel e placed similarly to the vowel a in Kafka. Furthermore, Georg's love interest is named Frieda, while Kafka's longtime love interest was named Felice. And, finally, Kafka also wrote extensively about—and is widely known for—his tense relationship with his father. The father-son conflict, therefore, lends itself as a logical connection between many of Kafka's texts and episodes of *Seinfeld*. This theme is central to Kafka's work, and although the conflict is not necessarily an autobiographical one, this same theme plays a central role in *Seinfeld*, particularly in the relationship between George Costanza and his father. In "The Judgment," readers witness Georg Bendemann's futile struggle with his authoritative father and Georg's ceaseless desire for his father's approval and respect, which is ultimately never earned. This same struggle defines the dynamic between George and Franz Costanza throughout *Seinfeld*, manifesting in everything from physical confrontations to groundings and failed job pursuits.

Both Bendemann and Costanza are presumably in their midthirties and live in uncomfortably close proximity to their fathers—evident in the short distance Bendemann must carry his father to bed and in the cramped Costanza apartment in Queens. Both sons are also entangled in their father's professional lives: Bendemann owes his success entirely to his father's business, while Costanza either gets job interviews through his father, such as the infamous bra salesman interview, or works directly with him, as in the basement computer-selling venture with Lloyd Braun. Furthermore, the two characters harbor a deep fear of conjugal commitment. Consider Costanza's eating cheese half-naked after his fiancée died from licking cheap wedding invitation envelopes during his self-proclaimed "Summer of George." Similarly, Bendemann is scolded by his father for his engagement to Frieda only after his mother's death—implying that he could not face the judgment of both parents at once. These eternal bachelors share an awkward, complicated, and deeply dependent relationship with their fathers. Yet, this relationship is a necessary evil. Their father's interference is essential to the sons' perceived success. Bendemann's father reminds him that the company's achievements were his doing and that his son merely rode the coattails of this success. Both sons allow their fathers to maintain control over their lives, revealing a deeper reluctance to take decisive risks. Instead, they choose to suffer within their own self-constructed circumstances. They prefer to live in fictitious worlds sustained by their own lies rather than confront reality—a trait shared by many of Kafka's antiheroes.

Just as Bendemann lives in a self-delusional state, we witness a similar dynamic in Costanza. In many episodes of *Seinfeld*, Costanza's futile attempts to impress others—particularly women—rely on elaborate fabrications about jobs and experiences he has never had. His relentless fondness for lying is demonstrated throughout the show by his unstable personal and professional life: He cannot maintain a romantic relationship, repeatedly loses jobs, and frequently gets himself fired. Costanza claims to own a house in the Hamptons after his fiancée dies from licking the cheap wedding invitations he insisted on purchasing; he pretends to be disabled to access comfortable, spacious bathrooms; he even fakes a mysterious elbow twitch—and, at one point, his own death. As he tells Jerry one day at Monk's: "Jerry, it's not a lie, if you believe it."[16] But Costanza never gets away with his lies. Like Bendemann, his deceit is inevitably exposed in the most humiliating ways: lying face down on the floor with his pants around his ankles or caught having sex in his parents' bedroom. He often finds himself in absurd situations and becomes the object of ridicule, especially when he remains oblivious to the comedy of his predicament. Not only does he contribute to his own downfall—the same hand that doomed him as a failed hand model—but he also unintentionally challenges the prescriptive norms of the status quo. This includes how topics like marriage, homosexuality, and promiscuity are represented and discussed. By clinging to his own naivete, Costanza remains to keep going, never striving for conventional measures of success—such as a stable job, a family, or a house. In a similar way, Bendemann remains unmarried and continues to live and work with his father. This complacency of both characters amounts to a life without responsibility. And, yet, it is precisely through this refusal to conform that these figures subtly challenge the authority of socially constructed norms, disrupting the very system that society demands they uphold.

Turning toward the father figures—Bendemann's father in "The Judgment" and Frank Costanza in *Seinfeld*—we see that both initially appear weak, only to later reveal a strength that contradicts that appearance. This strength is primarily demonstrated through the fear they invoke in their sons and the way they maintain their roles as patriarchal figures—an archetype neither son is ever able to attain. In "The Judgment," the father is introduced as a frail old man, sitting in soiled dressing gowns and barely able to finish his breakfast. Bendemann wrestles with guilt over his father's neglect and resolves to take better care of him. He undresses his father and carries him to the bedroom, where he attempts to tuck him in. But the absurdity of the scene escalates when the father, in a sudden fit of rage, leaps up, dances on the bed, and ultimately sentences his son to death by drowning. Bendemann, obedient and bewildered, follows through—flinging himself from a bridge. The reader is left shocked by the father's transformation and Georg's submission, struggling to make sense of the surreal yet terrifying turn of events. A similar dynamic plays out in *Seinfeld*, where Frank Costanza celebrates Festivus, a holiday created in protest against the commercialization of Christmas. Festivus includes two key rituals: the "Airing of Grievances" and the "Feats of Strength." After Frank decides to revive the holiday, George is once again humiliated by childhood memories. In a restaurant scene, Frank plays an old cassette tape in front of Jerry and Kramer, in which a young George is heard being called weak. Just like Georg, George storms out of the building, screaming and crying. Later, in the "Airing of Grievances," Frank momentarily loses his train of thought while berating George's boss and promptly receives pity from his guests. But, as with Bendemann, Frank quickly regains his footing—demanding the "Feats of Strength," where George is forced to compete against him. George is completely terrified, and he whimpers at the idea of fighting him.[17] His father bellows, "Stop crying and fight your father!" and in the background, we can hear George's mother saying encouragingly, "I think you can take him, Georgie!"[18] In both mediums, even as the father figure reaches an elderly age, neither son is capable of overcoming him. Theoretically, both George and Georg possess the physical strength to do so—but they never succeed, nor do they seriously try. Their fear renders them inert. While these scenes are masked in humor, the terror George feels toward his father cuts through the sitcom's comedic surface and reveals something darker. Neither George nor Georg can escape the raging patriarch. Their fathers remain, to the end, inescapable forces of domination.

In the end, we might say that Kafka's figures escape the patriarchal system that once dominated them. In "The Judgment," Georg finds relief from his father's wrath through death. His plunge can be read as his first step toward freedom. The ambiguous ending invites the question: Was there ever the possibility of a "life after the father" for Georg?[19] What if *not understanding* and *being baffled, defeated,* or *self-undermining* were not only literary themes but existential attitudes one might embrace as a form of learning? Kafka will continue to uphold his reputation for being depressing, misanthropic, and existential; but through a Seinfeldian lens, we can begin to see how distance from the law, from authority, or from full disclosure creates space for humor as well as angst. Kafka brilliantly depicts a sense of constant motion that leads nowhere—a stasis embedded in everyday life—while simultaneously challenging routine social structures. Similarly, *Seinfeld* uncovers life's paradoxes and invites viewers to recognize the absurdity hidden within life's trivialities. Costanza will always remain a comedic character, but through Kafka, his situation takes on a deeper resonance. For a "show about nothing," *Seinfeld* boldly challenged the unspoken rules of society, confronting conflicts, catastrophes, and social discomforts all too familiar in Western culture. Although *Seinfeld* aired its finale in 1998, the show remains widely available through syndication and streaming—and reading Kafka through Seinfeldian eyes offers a more accessible and surprising approach to Kafka's work.

Conclusion

In this chapter, I have demonstrated how humor is intrinsic to Kafka's writings, evoking both amusement and emotional discomfort in readers. Kafka's portrayals of authority figures resonate with lived experiences, where those in power often exploit their authority for personal amusement, either through ambiguity, inaccessibility or performative seriousness. By drawing parallels between Kafka's literary world and *Seinfeld*'s sitcom universe, we uncover the shared absurdity of authority—and the futility of seeking definitive interpretations in either law or literature. It is perhaps ironic, then, that Kafka himself has become an authoritative figure in literary scholarship. As a canonical author, his work is often treated with an almost religious reverence, requiring detailed exegesis, fidelity to historical context, and deference to critical lineage. But is this the only—or even the most meaningful—way to read Kafka?

Both Kafka and *Seinfeld* expose the paradox of power: The more seriously we take authority, the more we reveal its hollowness. Whether it is a man waiting forever outside a door "only meant for him" or Jerry, Elaine, and George waiting for a table that will never become available, the comedy lies in our persistent submission to systems that do not serve us. And, yet, that very submission sustains them. In both Kafka's works and *Seinfeld*, characters meet these systems with resignation, confusion, and, often, laughter—a laughter that is not cathartic or liberatory but dry, ironic, and unresolved. Kafka's literary works and *Seinfeld* might appear to occupy different cultural spheres—early twentieth-century existential literature and late twentieth-century American sitcoms—but they converge in their commentary on modern life. Themes of alienation, absurdity, bureaucracy, and failed communication that saturate Kafka's stories still echo in *Seinfeld* and in contemporary society. Their shared refusal to offer closure, moral lessons, or redemptive arcs makes them kindred critics of modernity's rituals and contradictions. Reading Kafka through a Seinfeldian lens—seeing the comedy in deferral, the absurdity in reverence, and the power of refusal—offers not only a more approachable interpretation of Kafka's work but also a renewed understanding of humor itself. Whether through literature or popular culture, both Kafka and *Seinfeld* remind us that meaning is often a performance, authority a fiction, and laughter a strangely honest response to both.

Notes

1 In "The Raincoats," Jerry's nemesis, Newman, spots him and his girl-friend Rachel "making out" while at the movies watching *Schindler's List*. Jerry and Rachel behave inappropriately and thus show no respect according to societal norms. When Jerry's parents eventually hear of the disrespect shown toward *Schindler's List* they are horrified. Jerry's parents and Newman grant *Schindler's List* all the weight and reverence that perhaps ought to be bestowed on art after Auschwitz. Jerry does not *really* feel guilty but is more shocked at the gravity of how his action has become interpreted, by his parents, nonetheless.

2 "Gentleman, esteemed academicians! You do me the honour of inviting me to submit a report to the Academy on my previous life as an ape." In Michael Hofmann's translation of "A Report to an Academy," in Franz Kafka, *The Metamorphosis and Other Stories* (London: Penguin Books, 2007), 225.

3 Hofmann, translation of "A Report to an Academy," 88–89: "If I didn't have to exercise restraint for the sake of my parents, then I would have quit a long time ago; I would have gone up to the director and told him exactly what I thought of him. He would have fallen off his desk in surprise! That's a peculiar way he has of sitting anyway, up on his desk, and talking down to his staff from on high, making them step up to him very close because he is so hard of hearing."

4 *Seinfeld*, season 8, episode 11, "The Little Jerry," written by Jennifer Crittenden, directed by Andy Ackerman.

5 *Seinfeld*, season 3, episode 5, "The Library," written by Larry Charles, directed by Joshua White.

6 *Seinfeld*, "The Library."

7 *Seinfeld*, season 9, episode 5, "The Junk Mail," written by Spike Feresten, directed by Andy Ackerman.

8 *Seinfeld*, season 2, episode 11, "The Chinese Restaurant," written by Larry David and Jerry Seinfeld, directed by Tom Cherones.

9 *Seinfeld*, series finale, season 9, episodes 23, 24, "The Finale," written by Larry David, directed by Andy Ackerman.

10 Rosa Rosenberg, "Larry David's 'Dark Talmud'; or Kafka in Prime Time," *Studies in American Jewish Literature*, no. 32 (2013): 167.

11 Philip Roth, *A Philip Roth Reader* (New York: Farrar, Straus, Giroux, 1980), 157.

12 Jeffrey Meyers, "Kafka's Dark Laughter," *Antioch Review* 70, no. 2 (2012): 761.

13 Thomas S. Hibbs, *Shows About Nothing: Nihilism in Popular Culture* (Waco: Baylor University Press, 2012), 118.

14 *Seinfeld*, season 7, episode 1, "The Engagement," written by Larry David, directed by Andy Ackerman.

15 William Irwin, *"Seinfeld" and Philosophy: A Book About Everything and Nothing* (Chicago: Open Court, 2003), 89.

16 *Seinfeld*, season 6, episode 16, "The Beard," aired February 9, 1995, written by Carol Leifer, directed by Andy Ackerman.

17 *Seinfeld*, season 9, episode 10, "The Strike," aired December 18, 1997, written by Larry David and Jerry Seinfeld, directed by Andy Ackerman.

18 *Seinfeld*, "The Strike."

19 I say "ambiguous" because while we know he "lets himself fall," drowning is never confirmed.

Selected Bibliography

Hibbs, Thomas S. *Shows About Nothing: Nihilism in Popular Culture*. Waco: Baylor University Press, 2012.

Irwin, William. *"Seinfeld" and Philosophy: A Book About Everything and Nothing*. Chicago: Open Court, 2003.

Kafka, Franz. *The Metamorphosis and Other Stories*. Translated by Michael Hofmann. London: Penguin Books, 2007.

———. *Vor dem Gesetz. Romane und Erzählungen*. Edited by Michael Müller. Stuttgart: Reclam, 2019.

Meyers, Jeffrey. "Kafka's Dark Laughter." *Antioch Review* 70 (2012): 760–68.

Rosenberg, Roberta. "Larry David's 'Dark Talmud'; or Kafka in Prime Time." *Studies in American Jewish Literature* 32 (2013): 167–85.

Roth, Phillip. *A Philip Roth Reader*. New York: Farrar, Straus, Giroux, 1980.

Seinfeld, Jerry, Larry David, Jason Alexander, Julia Louis-Dreyfus, and Michael Richards. *Seinfeld: The Complete Series*. Sony Pictures Home Entertainment, 2007.

4

FOR WHOSE BENEFIT?

Jean Carroll Performing "Jewish Humor" Through Fundraising

Grace Kessler Overbeke

"Tonight, I'm so proud to be Jewish, I'd give anything to have my old nose back!" quipped Jean Carroll, America's first Jewish female stand-up comedian, at Madison Square Garden in 1948. According to Carroll, the joke was met with a few moments of silence, before the "ground swell" of twenty thousand people's laughter.[1] The event at Madison Square Garden was a celebration of the state of Israel being recognized by the United Nations and was attended by high-profile speakers and performers ranging from clergy and Holocaust survivors to comedians. American Jewish entertainers like Carroll often devoted their celebrity platform to raising money and support for the new nation-state.

Although Jewishness was not expressed in the *content* of her comedy (in dialect or religious and cultural references), it was often expressed in what Susan Bennett would call the performance's "outer frame," or "all the cultural elements which create and inform the cultural event."[2] For instance, elements of a performance's outer frame would include its venue, marketing, and social occasion. For Jean Carroll, a frequent outer frame of her performances was that of charitable benefit for the state of Israel. While it is problematic to equate Jewishness with Israel in any kind of essential way, it is revealing to examine the phenomenon that Carroll exemplifies, of midcentury American Jews expressing their Jewish identity through support of the new Jewish state. This fervent Zionism was Carroll's way of expressing a Jewish identity that had been stunted by assimilatory pressure in the midcentury United States. This chapter argues that what made Jean Carroll's comedy "Jewish" was not simply the content of her jokes but the cause for which she told them.

This idea of "cause over content" is a significant departure from other paradigms for understanding what makes Jewish humor "Jewish." Israeli scholar Avner Ziv located the Jewishness of Jewish humor in psychological characteristics like a desire to distort reality, a strong sense of social cohesion, and a tendency toward self-disparagement.[3] Henry Eilbert, author of *What Is a Jewish Joke?*, classifies Jewish humor as humor that stems from conditions of Jewish life or experiences, involves Jewish language, or shows supposed Jewish characteristics or stereotypes.[4] Traits such as an attention to language,[5] a dialectical mode of thinking, an impulse toward subversive attacks on people in power, and a perpetual "outsider" mindset[6] are commonly invoked as characteristics of Jewish American humor.[7] Jeremy Dauber counters the multifaceted nature of Jewish humor by setting two simple conditions: Jewish humor must be "produced by Jews" and must "have something to do with either contemporary Jewish living or historical Jewish existence."[8] What these classifications have in common is their location of "Jewishness" in the content of the comedy. Examining the benefit performances of a Jewish American comedian such as Carroll shifts the focus away from the content of the comedy and toward the cause that it benefits. The phrase "follow the money" is commonly used to suggest that a politician's values and priorities are more clearly revealed by their financial dealings than by their rhetoric. So, too, this chapter suggests that a comedian's "Jewishness" ought to be assessed by the financial beneficiaries of their performance as much as by their one-liners. Classifying Jean Carroll's stand-up benefits as Jewish humor insists that Jewishness can be present in the outer frames of performance rather than simply within jokes.

Jean Carroll's Coded Jewish Comedy

A joke can be a revealing cultural artifact, and Carroll's joke about wanting her "old nose back" is a neat encapsulation of the ambivalence that American Jews faced regarding their assimilation into mainstream culture in the United States. According to historian Sander Gilman, the practice of cosmetic surgery was a "seemingly universal" mode of acculturation for Diaspora Jews following the Shoah.[9] Rhinoplasty had been a way of "passing"—disavowing one's Jewishness as a way to claim whiteness in America. So, to yearn for one's "old nose" was to express what Matthew F. Jacobson called "the assimilation blues": the ambivalence of wanting both the privileges of whiteness and a sense of connection with one's biological and cultural roots.[10]

For Jean Carroll (born Sadie Zeigman), her career as the first Jewish woman (and arguably the first woman)[11] to perform the still nascent form "stand-up comedy" in the United States had demanded a marked omission of Jewish content. After moving from Paris (where her father was imprisoned for defecting from the Russian army) to America as an infant, Carroll experienced a childhood that was largely defined by being a Jewish immigrant. At home, she and her mother spoke in what one journalist called "an acid patois that is half-American, half-Yiddish."[12] She grew up in the Bronx in the 1920s, when Jews made up over half the neighborhood's population.[13] And her earliest performances as a solo comic involved nods to Yiddishkeit with parodies like "Yiddish River Shannon" (a send-up of "Where the River Shannon Flows")[14] and "When I Began with Levine" ("Begin the Beguine").[15] These performances took place, however, before she had become established as a mainstream stand-up comic.

By the height of her career in the mid-1950s, when she was touring comedy clubs nationwide and making frequent appearances on *The Ed Sullivan Show*, her act had lost its ethnic flavor. Instead, her Jewish content became subtle and coded, with the more overt elements of her stand-up focused on more generic, stereotypically "feminine" themes like dress shopping, her husband, and her "rotten kid." Some of her beloved quips included digs at her husband, like "Our romance was one of those triangles. He and I were both in love with him."[16] Other popular bits jabbed at her daughter, with lines like "I'm the happiest woman in the world! What do you think happened to me today? My mother went back to her own house and I hit my kid! Did you ever try to hit your kid with a grandmother running interference?"[17] A reviewer of Carroll's 1953 appearance at Chicago's Palmer House gives a clear overview of the kind of material that Carroll addressed in her stand-up:

> Miss Carroll's comedy is found in events close to everyday living. She
> tells about buying a dress—or, rather, merely shopping—and she has a
> few verbal notations about love, PTA meetings, a day at the race track,
> the movies and dogs. Everything she relates is true-to-life, in conver-
> sational tone, and extremely hilarious. When the ladies in the audi-
> ence laugh "out-loud," you may be sure that Miss Carroll has given
> familiar occurrences a real sugar-coating of commentary.[18]

In order to be "true-to-life" and "familiar," Carroll leaned away from
speaking directly to experiences that were more specifically Jewish. In
other words, not only did she get a new nose, but she also got a new act.

In spite of her omission of overtly Jewish content, Carroll's Jewish
identity continued to be paramount. However polarizing, the new state
of Israel played a major role in Carroll's Jewish identity. In this respect,
Carroll was part of a larger trend of American Jews in the midcentury
connecting Jewishness to Zionism. For most American Jews, this trend
was more firmly cemented in the 1960s, evident in the success of films like
Exodus and Broadway musicals like *Milk and Honey*.[19] But for Jean Carroll and a number of her Jewish comedy contemporaries, this attachment
began well before that. For instance, Georgie Jessel boasted that he raised
$25 million in bonds for the new nation of Israel by leaving "no Cohen
unturned."[20] Likewise, Eddie Cantor played an active role in fundraising
for Jews in Palestine starting in 1929.[21]

Tucked into Carroll's personal scrapbook is an interview from *The
Jewish Chronicle*, in which she discloses her plans to learn Hebrew and visit
Israel. Both the content of the article and its privileged place in her scrapbook reveal the importance that this trip held for Carroll. With a headline
trumpeting "America's First Comic Takes Hebrew Seriously," the article
takes an incredulous tone regarding her "burning desire" to visit Israel:

> Fancy going to meet America's top TV and cabaret star and find-
> ing her in the middle of a Hebrew lesson! This was Jean Carroll,
> the glamorous single-act star who for the past month performed
> at the Savoy restaurant. She was sitting there in her suite with her
> teacher, Iakov Gilboa wrestling with verbs. . . . Her teacher told me
> she was one of his most apt pupils. She needs to learn the language,

she told me, because of a burning desire to be in Israel for the Bar Mitzvah year of the state.[22]

Another article from the scrapbook, released around the same period, included the subhead "Keen to Learn Israeli Lingo," indicating Carroll's strong desire to study Hebrew. In this piece, the interviewer confesses that they "interrupted Jean at just the wrong moment," describing how their arrival forced Carroll to put away her book, which taught her how to "speak Israeli." The same piece quotes Carroll "fervently" professing, "I'm crazy about the language. . . . I feel I just must speak it."[23] These multiple published references to Carroll's Hebrew study suggest that at that point in her life, she was making a point of publicly proclaiming her commitment to visiting Israel. This heavily publicized expression of enthusiasm for Israel enjoyed a prominence that her American Jewish identity never did.

Jean Carroll: A Fixture in the "Night of Stars"

Another way that Carroll publicly allied herself with Israel as an expression of Jewishness was her commitment to fundraising for Israel through benefit performances such as those of the United Jewish Appeal for Refugees and Overseas Needs. Throughout her career, Carroll said it was her responsibility as a Jewish person to "lend my talent"[24] to Jewish causes, and she often made little distinction between American Jewish causes and American causes to benefit Israel. In the late 1940s, one of the most high-profile Zionist events was the "Night of Stars" show for the United Jewish Appeal an organization that helped Jewish refugees from central and eastern Europe to relocate to Palestine.[25]

The "Night of Stars" was a variety show mainstream enough to be covered by both the Jewish press and trade publications, who charted its headliners with great detail. In 1948—the first year of Israel's statehood—*Variety* boasted a celebrity-packed bill that included Jean Carroll, Red Buttons, Milton Berle, Myron Cohen, Danny Kaye, Mickey Rooney, Henny Youngman, and even the Rockettes.[26] The Radio City Rockettes, best known for their annual Christmas Spectacular, are a particularly noticeable attestation to the event's mainstream status. The next year, however, *Variety*

noticed the event was "marked by extreme difficulty in getting many performers to respond." Offering reasons ranging from lack of new material
to show, union restrictions, or weariness of working without pay, many of
the big stars opted out.[27] Those who remained, such as Jean Carroll, Henny
Youngman, Harry Hershfield, and Joey Adams, were predominately Jewish
and expressed personal commitment to Israel. In 1950, *Variety* did not
even cover the "Night of Stars" event, though *Jewish Advocate* recorded the
continued participation of devotees like Carroll, Youngman, and Adams.[28]
But in 1951, the event was apparently back to mainstream prominence.
Variety wrote that the Rockettes were back on the bill, which featured
not only comedy sets by Jean Carroll, Ed Sullivan, and others but also
an address in which Mayor Impelliterri declared, "What Israel stands for
in the Near East is what the United States stands for here."[29] By sticking
with the "Night of Stars" benefit even when other celebrities' enthusiasm
waned, Carroll showed a deep commitment to the United Jewish Appeal
and its efforts to raise money for "European relief and Israel resettlement."[30]

Even after Jean Carroll began moving away from professional comedy, she made her retirement home in an American seat of Jewish life, the
Catskill Mountains. This location allowed her to continue to do stand-up
benefits for the United Jewish Appeal and other Zionist organizations as a
way of performing her Jewish identity. By 1960, she was publicly outspo-
ken about no longer working in show business. Headlines announcing her
retirement blared, "With Jean, It's the Family First, Show Biz Second."[31]
However, shortly after the 1967 Arab-Israeli War—a point when American
Jewish support of Israel experienced an upswell—Carroll's visit to Israel
prompted her to emerge from retirement for at least a few occasions. She
did a set of performances benefiting the United Jewish Appeal's Ellenville
chapter.[32] Moreover, she intensified her involvement with the Sullivan and
Ulster County Israel Bond Committee, winning their State of Israel Bonds
Woman of the Year award in 1971 (see fig. 4.1).

The award recognized her efforts to raise over $175,000 for the eco-
nomic development of Israel.[33] The description of the award commended
her for leveraging her "rewarding career in the entertainment field" into
leadership, "providing Israel with this vitally needed investment capital,"
as well as offering "her many contributions to Jewish Philanthropies and
civic causes."[34] The equivalency in this wording is apt; Carroll's fundraising
efforts for Israel are held up alongside (and implicitly equated with) her

State of Israel Bonds Woman of the Year, Jean Carroll is pictured at last week's Israel Bond dinner which raised over $175,000 for the economic development of Israel with David Levinson, chairman of the Sullivan-Ulster Division, and Leon Greenberg of Monticello at the Homowack Lodge in Spring Glen. Over 150 honored Miss Carroll for her leadership in the drive.

Israel Bond Dinner Raises $175,000

Over $175,000 for the economic development of Israel was raised at an Israel Bond dinner in honor of Jean Carroll last week at the Homowack Lodge in Spring Glen.

Dave Levinson, chairman of the dinner, announced the total of Israel Bond sales during the event to the more than 150 persons who turned out to honor Miss Carroll for her leadership in the Israel Bond drive.

Miss Carroll, a prominent personality in the entertainment field, resides in Wurtsboro and is active in Hadassah. She also is chairman of Tay-Sachs and Allied Diseases.

Levinson pointed up the urgency of this year's campaign by noting "an unprecedented goal of $400 million in Israel Bond investment capital has been set for 1971. This is because Israel never has faced greater problems in building a firm foundation of economic security and peace."

Proceeds from the sale of Israel Bonds constitute the principal source of investment capital for the expansion and development of Israel's industry, agriculture, commerce, and housing, it was pointed out.

1971
NOV

FIGURE 4.1. Photograph of Jean Carroll as State of Israel Bonds Woman of the Year, saved in Carroll's personal scrapbook, 1971. (Personal collection of Susan Chatzky)

fundraising efforts for American Jewish "civic causes." And, indeed, Carroll herself made little distinction between fundraising for Jews in Israel and fundraising for Jews in the United States. Her performances benefiting the United Jewish Appeal and the Israel Bond Committee are matched by a long history of performances benefiting American Jewish organizations.

Joking Jewishly in the United States: Carroll's Comedy in Domestic Jewish Fundraising

Throughout her career, Jean Carroll expressed her Jewish identity by performing stand-up to benefit American Jewish organizations like the Hillel Academy in Pittsburgh and the Jewish Memorial Hospital in Boston. The Hillel Academy, a prestigious Jewish school in Pittsburgh, managed to turn their school's anniversary fundraiser in 1951 into a premier event featuring headlining comedians like Jean Carroll and Georgie Jessel. Promotional articles in the Pittsburgh Jewish newspapers touted "Top Flight Stars"[35] and the "Greatest Array of Talent,"[36] boasting of Carroll's appearance as "her first here since she was skyrocketed to theatrical fame via her amazingly successful television shows."[37] The latter paper, *American Jewish Outlook*, also recognized her anomalous status as a female stand-up: "When hardened theatrical men take time out to hail a new star, that's news. And when that star happens to be a young comedienne, that's headlines."[38]

Carroll made more headlines with her decision to volunteer her talents on behalf of the Jewish Memorial Hospital at the "Celebrities Night" benefits in 1951 and 1957. Billed as "New England's Greatest Show," this annual event received tremendous coverage in the *Jewish Advocate*. In 1951, the annual event's second year running, Jean Carroll's name was trumpeted alongside "Myron Cohen, Jon Pearce, Red Buttons, Billy Williams . . . and many other guest stars."[39] *The Advocate* promoted Jean Carroll's participation in another "Celebrities Night" benefit six years later, where she appeared alongside Jackie Miles, Barry Gray, and the Winged Victory Chorus,[40] before a crowd of thirteen thousand people.[41] That article was illustrated by a photograph that depicted Carroll surrounded by an overwhelmingly male crowd of performers and hospital executives. This image draws attention to how conspicuous Carroll's female body was among the male performers. Even when she was in a Jewish space expressing the Jewish identity that she shared with costars like Cohen and Buttons, Carroll was still othered by her gender.

In addition to the events benefiting the United Jewish Appeal, Hillel Academy, and Jewish Memorial Hospital, Carroll "lent her talent" and her celebrity status to many other charitable events for Jewish causes. Those that she memorialized in her personal scrapbook range drastically in the scale and profile of the event. A program from the Shield of David Institute for Retarded Children's Eleventh Annual Cavalcade of Stars at the famed Madison Square Garden[42] was tucked away next to a newspaper profile of a small performance she hosted at her home to benefit Hadassah Hospital.[43] Others range from an Actors' Temple benefit headed by Rabbi Bernard Burstein[44] to multiple events for the National Tay Sachs and Allied Diseases Association—a matter of particularly Jewish concern since, as Carroll and *Variety* both pointed out, the disease is "associated with Ashkenazi Jews."[45] Carroll was so involved with the National Tay-Sachs and Allied Diseases Association that she was named "Tay-Sachs Woman of the Year" in 1964, during which she headed "a new Speakers Bureau which will bring the Tay Sachs story to many organizations in the metropolitan area."[46] In sum, Jean Carroll used her stand-up skill—and the celebrity status it earned her—to act as an advocate for Jewish causes in a distinctly public way. Her humor may not have had "Jewish" content, but it was for a Jewish cause.

"I Do Think That's a Jewish Thing": Civic Engagement as Jewish Identity

Jean Carroll's granddaughter, Susan Chatzky, provides valuable insight about the connection between Carroll's Jewish identity and her fundraising efforts, benefit appearances, and public awareness work. Chatzky confirms that Jean Carroll's Jewish identity was rooted not in theological or ideological commitments but in social engagement and philanthropy. When asked about her grandmother's Jewish practices, Susan Chatzky responded, "She was socially active, which I think she would probably connect to her Judaism. . . . It was important to her to support charities. I think to her (and to me) it is part of the social tradition of Jews to care about their community. I do think that's a Jewish thing."[47]

Of course, being invested in one's community is not specifically or exclusively a "Jewish thing"; but it is significant that Chatzky asserts that her grandmother drew a connection between community engagement and Jewishness. Chatzky also revealed that her grandmother was invested in an uncomplicated and idealistic vision of Israel that did not account for the nation's complicated relationship with other Palestinian populations. For Carroll, and perhaps many other Jewish Americans, Israel was a symbol. Perhaps for a Jewish immigrant like Carroll, whose sense of belonging in the United States may have been unstable, it was a symbol of home. It was a symbol of safety from persecution, of democracy and scientific advancement. To borrow Mayor Impelliterri's vague but hopeful words, Israel symbolized the same values as the United States. Carroll's version of Israel as an idealistic seat of democracy was a privilege that allowed her to view it as interchangeable with American Jewish institutions like hospitals.

The clearest testimony to Jean Carroll's connection between her American Jewish identity and her connection to Israel is her emotional account of her appearance at Madison Square Garden on the night Israel became a nation, when she gave her famous joke about being such a proud Jew that she wanted her old nose back. In an interview with Stephen Silverman, Carroll recounted:

> The night Israel became a nation . . . I was appearing at the Capital Theatre, and they asked me to please come over and do something for Israel that night. It was a wonderful night. . . . Strauss, who had just come back from Israel, is on stage talking about the battle for survival. . . . This handful of heroic people . . . children fighting . . . and women fighting, grandmothers fighting. And then when *America* gave the deciding vote, the United States, that Israel was a nation . . . I was trying hard not to cry, like I am right now. . . . Madison Square Garden is packed to the rafters. . . . They had a priest, who sang some religious song. And the rabbi . . . and a choir did Hatikvah. And how you could keep from weeping, I don't know! And that's how I felt. Well, I've always felt that way about Israel anyway. And then he introduces me. . . . I defy anybody to go out and be funny following that! So I went out, and I said to the audience, "I'm finding it very difficult not to cry. I've always been proud of the Jewish people. Proud of their

contribution to mankind. And because of their persecution, they are the kindest to everybody. . . . So long before it became chic to say that you were Jewish, I was a proud Jew." But I said, "Tonight I'm so proud to be Jewish, I'd give anything to have my old nose back again!" And there was . . . at first there was silence. Then there was a ground swell of laughter that started. And 20,000 people got up off their feet and . . . right now, I'm finding it tough not to cry. In my life, I will never know that kind of sensation. To be able to make people laugh in the face of such horror . . . that they were able to wrest victory out of the horrors?[48]

Carroll's celebration of Israel's statehood is as uncomplicated as the logistical particulars of her anecdote are dubious. The official night that Israel became a state was May 14, 1948. There were a number of events memorializing its statehood, including one at Madison Square Garden, chaired by a man named Nathan Strauss. However, this Madison Square Garden event documented in *Variety* took place on Monday, November 15, 1948, six months after Israel was recognized by the United Nations.[49] What is less dubious is the reception to Carroll's quip about wanting her old nose back. This uncharacteristic "Jewish joke" enjoys a totally disproportionate presence in Carroll's scant biographic record. In fact, it is one of her most well-remembered jokes, appearing in joke books,[50] in comedy anthologies,[51] and even in her obituary in the *New York Times*.[52]

To Carroll, the audience's laughter also signified a greater truth— laughter as a mode of empowerment, of "wresting victory out of the horrors." This act of laughter as resistance to "horror" is precisely the way she positioned it in her autobiographical narrative. In the grand tradition of Sholom Aleichem and Yiddish comedy, Carroll used laughter as a way to avoid tears and overcome obstacles. Laughter was the way by which she wrested financial autonomy and acceptance from a patriarchal society that had little interest in welcoming Jewish women. It was how she had dealt with an abusive father, faced down the prejudices of her colleagues, and, now, flown in the face of the "horrors" of World War II. A month after the event at Madison Square Garden, Carroll appeared in another celebration of Israel outside of Boston. There, she appeared alongside Dr. Jorge Garcia Granados, chief delegate of Guatemala to the United Nations, as he praised how the Jewish people "took the situation into their own hands . . . with all the courage and spirit which I have so much admired."[53] While it is impossible to speculate on the root of Carroll's attachment to Israel, part of it may have been that she identified with the implausible achievements of a nation whose recognition came, as Dr. Granados put it, "against all odds."[54]

Cause, Not Character

Carroll's seeming disavowal of Jewishness in her comedy is complicated by her pronounced public performances of engagement with Zionist and Jewish causes like the United Jewish Appeal. But one reading of this apparent tension can be illuminated by an editorial written by one of Carroll's colleagues that was published in *Commentary*, the prestigious journal of Jewish intellectual discourse. In 1952, comedian Sam Levenson wrote a scathing indictment against comedians who leaned heavily on Jewish dialects and other forms of explicitly Jewish comedic material, proclaiming, "It is my belief that any Jew who, in humor or otherwise, strengthens the misconceptions and the prejudices against his own people is neither a good Jew nor a responsible human being." He went on to recommend his own technique of assimilation, in which he "consciously omitted the word Jew from the entire discourse. I was afraid that if I said they were Jews the audience's prejudices might come into play and destroy the beautiful picture I had built up."[55] Levenson's reasoning—that a comedian identifying as Jewish risks hailing the audience's prejudices—presupposes a degree of antisemitism in the audience. But his move to omit the word "Jew" from his act also refuses to use Jewishness as a punchline, persona, or other comic device. In a cultural moment when comedians like Myron Cohen and Gertrude Berg made successful careers from exaggerated Jewish comedy, Levenson's deliberate move away from explicitly Jewish content was a way to resist the comedy industry's caricaturing of Jews.

Levenson's article offers another reading of Carroll's similar turn away from Yiddishkeit toward "universal" feminine subject matter. Rather than simply finding that her overtly Jewish comedy limited her audience, she may have found that it risked disseminating images of Jews as caricatures, flattening the complexity of Jewishness into superficial behaviors like a voice or a gesture. So, like Levenson, she expressed her Jewish humor not through caricatures to play but as a cause to support. This cause also aligned with her own oft-expressed commitment to using her talent in service of Zionism and the American Jewish community. In other words, by performing Jewishness through involvement with Jewish and Israeli organizations rather than jokes, Carroll made a strong statement: Jewishness was a cause to champion, not a character to perform. Her humor would not mock Jewish people—it may not even directly reference them—but it would contribute to them.

Notes

1 Jean Carroll, Jean Carroll Interview Transcripts, interview by Stephen Silverman, November 6, 2006, Stephen Silverman Personal Collection, New York City, New York.

2 Susan Bennett, *Theatre Audiences: A Theory of Production and Reception* (London: Routledge, 1990).

3 Arthur Asa Berger, *Jewish Jesters: A Study in American Popular Culture* (Cresskill, NJ: Hampton Press, 2001), 105.

4 Henry Eilbert, *What Is a Jewish Joke?* (Northvale, NJ: Aronson, 1995).

5 In Anthony Lewis's essay "The Jew in Stand-up Comedy," he quotes Leo Rosten's claim that Jews have a heightened linguistic ability as a result of growing up with multiple languages—Hebrew for prayer, Yiddish for secular domestic life, and the national language for professional life.

6 Epstein cites Sam Janus's interview-based study (1975) finding that Jewish humor emerges from "intense alienation" from American culture.

7 Lawrence J. Epstein, *The Haunted Smile: The Story of Jewish Comedians in America* (New York: PublicAffairs, 2002).

8 Jeremy Dauber, *Jewish Comedy: A Serious History* (New York: W. W. Norton, 2017).

9 Sander L. Gilman, "Proust's Nose," *Social Research* 67, no. 1 (2000): 61–79.

10 Matthew Frye Jacobson, *Roots Too: White Ethnic Revival in Post–Civil Rights America* (Cambridge, MA: Harvard University Press, 2009).

11 Depending on the definition of "stand-up," that distinction may go to Jackie "Moms" Mabley.

12 Joan Michel, "Women at Work: Contradictory Comedienne," For and About The Family, n.d., p. 81, Jean Carroll Scrapbook. Personal Collection of Susan Chatzky.

13 "New York City," Jewish Virtual Library, 2007, accessed October 23, 2018, https://www.jewishvirtuallibrary.org/new-york-city.

14 "Night Club Reviews: Thunderbird, Law Vegas," Variety (Archive: 1905–2000), April 29, 1953, 963286984, Entertainment Industry Magazine Archive.

15 Jerry Gaghan, "Cross Town," n.d., p. 29, Jean Carroll Scrapbook. Personal Collection of Susan Chatzky.

16 Qtd. in Kliph Nesteroff, The Comedians: Drunks, Thieves, Scoundrels, and the History of American Comedy (New York: Grove Press, 2016), 255.

17 The Ed Sullivan Show, CBS, April 29, 1956, SOFA Entertainment.

18 Charlie Dawn, "Comedienne Stars in Empire Room Revue," Chicago American, October 22, 1953, 59, Jean Carroll Scrapbook. Personal Collection of Susan Chatzky.

19 Ben Sales, "Israel at 70: How 1948 Changed American Jews," Jewish Federation of San Diego, April 28, 2018, https://www.jewishinsandiego.org/jewish-community-news/israel-at-70-how-1948-changed-american-jews.

20 Qtd. in Burns, All My Best Friends, 178.

21 David Weinstein, The Eddie Cantor Story: A Jewish Life in Performance and Politics (Waltham, MA: Brandeis University Press, 2017).

22 Sadie Levine, "America's First Comic Takes Hebrew Seriously," November 4, 1960, p. 77, Jean Carroll Scrapbook. Personal Collection of Susan Chatzky.

23 "With Jean It's the Family First, Show Biz Second," n.d., p. 78, Jean Carroll Scrapbook. Personal Collection of Susan Chatzky.

24 Carroll, Jean Carroll Interview Transcripts, 4–16-4–17.

25 The United Jewish Appeal actually supported refugee relocation to a number of places other than Palestine. The United Jewish Appeal united three organizations that funded three different immigration paths for refugees. The United Palestine Appeal funded "immigration and settlement in Palestine," whereas the National Coordinating Committee Fund dealt with German refugees coming to the United States, and the Joint Distribution Committee dealt with German and Austrian refugees in other parts of Europe. "3 Jewish Groups Unite for Refugees: Combined Appeal to Be Offered to Nation for Fund of Three or Four Times That Given Year

Heightened Crisis Citied Agencies to Retain Separate Duties in Pressing Common Cause for Victims. 'Tragic Setbacks' of 1938 Noted Function of Palestine Appeal," *New York Times* (1923–Current File), January 13, 1939, 102797829, ProQuest Historical Newspapers: The New York Times.

26 "Vaudeville: 'Night of Stars' Benefit Nets 110G for UJA," *Variety* (Archive: 1905–2000), November 17, 1948, 1285917848, Entertainment Industry Magazine Archive.

27 "Vaudeville: Talent Problem Vexes 'Night of Stars' Show but 125G Gross at Par," *Variety* (Archive: 1905–2000), November 16, 1949, 1285944272, Entertainment Industry Magazine Archive.

28 Nathan Norman Weiss, "Bostonian on Broadway," *Jewish Advocate* (1909–90), August 17, 1950, 887016774, ProQuest Historical Newspapers: U.S. Jewish Newspaper Collection.

29 "Vaudeville: PJA 'Night of Stars' Pulls 110,000 at N.Y. Garden," *Variety* (Archive: 1905–2000), November 21, 1951, 1401266273, Entertainment Industry Magazine Archive.

30 "Vaudeville: PJA 'Night of Stars' Pulls 110,000 at N.Y. Garden."

31 "With Jean It's the Family First, Show Biz Second."

32 Julius Slutsky and Louis Zipperman, "United Jewish Appeal Letter," June 13, 1967, p. 22, Jean Carroll Scrapbook. Personal Collection of Susan Chatzky.

33 "Israel Bond Dinner Raises $175,000," November 1971, p. 73, Jean Carroll Scrapbook, Personal Collection of Susan Chatzky.

34 "Program from the Sullivan and Ulster County Division of State and Israel Bonds," November 16, 1971, pp. 87–88, Jean Carroll Scrapbook, Personal Collection of Susan Chatzky.

35 "Top Flight Stars to Shine at Hillel Academy Anniversary Celebration," *Jewish Criterion*, February 9, 1951, vol. 117, no. 16, Pittsburgh Jewish Newspaper Project.

36 "Hillel Anniversary Show Dated March 2," *American Jewish Outlook*, January 25, 1952, vol. 35, no. 14, Pittsburgh Jewish Newspaper Project, http://doi.library.cmu.edu/10.1184/pmc/OUT/OUT_1952_035_014 _01251952/OUT_1952_035_014_0125195.

37 "Hillel Academy Celebration to Feature Popular Comedienne," *American Jewish Outlook*, January 26, 1951, vol. 33, no. 14, Pittsburgh Jewish Newspaper Project.

38 "Hillel Academy Celebration Has Spectacular Entertainment," *American Jewish Outlook*, February 9, 1951, vol. 33, no. 16, Pittsburgh Jewish Newspaper Project.

39 "Display Ad 3—No Title," *Jewish Advocate* (1909–90), April 19, 1951, 886751178, ProQuest Historical Newspapers: U.S. Jewish Newspaper Collection.

40 "Extravaganza Aids Memorial Hospital," *Jewish Advocate* (1909–90), September 12, 1957, 889068219, ProQuest Historical Newspapers: U.S. Jewish Newspaper Collection.

41 "Photo Standalone 14—No Title," *Jewish Advocate* (1909–90), October 3, 1957, 889054010, ProQuest Historical Newspapers: U.S. Jewish Newspaper Collection.

42 "Program: Madison Square Garden," May 26, 1952, p. 51, Jean Carroll Scrapbook. Personal Collection of Susan Chatzky.

43 "Miss Jean Hostess for Hadassah," *Ellenville New York Press*, December 14, 1967, p. 82, Jean Carroll Scrapbook, Personal Collection of Susan Chatzky.

44 "Actors' Temple Benefit," *New York Times* (1923–Current File), December 9, 1949, 105885987, ProQuest Historical Newspapers: The New York Times.

45 "Chatter: Broadway," *Variety* (Archive: 1905–2000), September 18, 1968, 962938491, Entertainment Industry Magazine Archive.

46 "Foundation to Honor Wurtsboro Comedienne," *Times Herald*, March 21, 1968, 73, Jean Carroll Scrapbook. Personal Collection of Susan Chatzky.

47 Susan Chatzky, Personal interview with Susan Chatzky, by Grace Overbeke, October 7, 2016.

48 Carroll, Jean Carroll Interview Transcripts, 4–14.

49 "Legitimate: Night of Stars," *Variety* (Archive: 1905–2000), November 17, 1948, 1285945792, Entertainment Industry Magazine Archive.

50 Rosemarie Jarski, *The Funniest Thing You Never Said 2: The Ultimate Collection of Humorous Quotations* (London: Ebury Press, 2010), 100.

51 Mary Unterbrink, *Funny Women: American Comediennes, 1860–1985* (Jefferson, NC: London: McFarland, 1987).

52 Margalit Fox, "Jean Carroll, Stand-Up Comedian, Dies at 98," *New York Times*, January 2, 2010, accessed July 12, 2023, http://www.nytimes.com/2010/01/03/arts/03carroll.html.

53 "1,000 B-B-N Zionists Attend Meeting Featuring Dr. Granados as Speaker," *Jewish Advocate* (1909–90), December 23, 1948, 908944313, ProQuest Historical Newspapers: U.S. Jewish Newspaper Collection.

54 "1,000 B-B-N Zionists Attend Meeting Featuring Dr. Granados as Speaker."

55 Sam Levenson, "On the Horizon: The Dialect Comedian Should Vanish," *Commentary Magazine* (blog), August 1, 1952, https://www .commentarymagazine.com/articles/on-the-horizon-the-dialect -comedian-should-vanish/.

Selected Bibliography

Bennett, Susan. *Theatre Audiences: A Theory of Production and Reception.* London: Routledge, 1990.

Berger, Arthur Asa. *Jewish Jesters: A Study in American Popular Culture.* Cresskill, NJ: Hampton Press, 2001.

Carroll, Jean. Jean Carroll Interview Transcripts. Interview by Stephen Silverman, November 6, 2006. Stephen Silverman Personal Collection, New York City, New York.

Chatzky, Susan. Personal interview with Susan Chatzky. By Grace Overbeke, October 7, 2016.

Dauber, Jeremy. *Jewish Comedy: A Serious History.* New York: W. W. Norton, 2017.

The Ed Sullivan Show. CBS, April 29, 1956. SOFA Entertainment.

Eilbert, Henry. *What Is a Jewish Joke?* Northvale, NJ: Aronson, 1995.

Epstein, Lawrence J. *The Haunted Smile: The Story of Jewish Comedians in America.* New York: PublicAffairs, 2002.

Fox, Margalit. "Jean Carroll, Stand-Up Comedian, Dies at 98." *New York Times,* January 2, 2010. http://www.nytimes.com/2010/01/03/arts/03carroll .html.

Gilman, Sander L. "Proust's Nose." *Social Research* 67, no. 1 (2000): 61–79.

"Israel Bond Dinner Raises $175,000." November 1971, p. 73. Jean Carroll Scrapbook. Personal Collection of Susan Chatzky.

Jacobson, Matthew Frye. *Roots Too: White Ethnic Revival in Post–Civil Rights America.* Cambridge, MA: Harvard University Press, 2009.

Jarski, Rosemarie. *The Funniest Thing You Never Said 2: The Ultimate Collection of Humorous Quotations*. London: Ebury Press, 2010.

Jewish Advocate (1909–90). "1,000 B-B-N Zionists Attend Meeting Featuring Dr. Granados as Speaker." December 23, 1948. 908944313. ProQuest Historical Newspapers: U.S. Jewish Newspaper Collection.

Levenson, Sam. "On the Horizon: The Dialect Comedian Should Vanish." *Commentary Magazine* (blog), August 1, 1952. https://www.commentarymagazine.com/articles/on-the-horizon-the-dialect-comedian-should-vanish/.

Michel, Joan. "Women at Work: Contradictory Comedienne." For and About the Family, n.d., p. 81. Jean Carroll Scrapbook. Personal Collection of Susan Chatzky.

"Miss Jean Hostess for Hadassah." *Ellenville New York Press*, December 14, 1967, 82. Jean Carroll Scrapbook. Personal Collection of Susan Chatzky.

Nesteroff, Kliph. *The Comedians: Drunks, Thieves, Scoundrels, and the History of American Comedy*. New York: Grove Press, 2016.

"New York City." Jewish Virtual Library, 2007. Accessed October 23, 2018. https://www.jewishvirtuallibrary.org/new-york-city.

New York Times (1923–Current file). "3 Jewish Groups Unite for Refugees: Combined Appeal to Be Offered to Nation for Fund of Three or Four Times That Given Year Heightened Crisis Citied Agencies to Retain Separate Duties in Pressing Common Cause for Victims. 'Tragic Setbacks' of 1938 Noted Function of Palestine Appeal." January 13, 1939. 102797829. ProQuest Historical Newspapers: The New York Times.

Sales, Ben. "Israel at 70: How 1948 Changed American Jews." Jewish Federation of San Diego, April 28, 2018. https://www.jewishinsandiego.org/jewish-community-news/israel-at-70-how-1948-changed-american-jews.

Slutsky, Julius, and Louis Zipperman. "United Jewish Appeal Letter." June 13, 1967, p. 22. Jean Carroll Scrapbook. Personal Collection of Susan Chatzky.

Unterbrink, Mary. *Funny Women: American Comediennes, 1860–1985*. Jefferson, NC: McFarland, 1987.

Weinstein, David. *The Eddie Cantor Story: A Jewish Life in Performance and Politics*. Waltham, MA: Brandeis University Press, 2017.

"With Jean It's the Family First, Show Biz Second." N.d., p. 78. Jean Carroll Scrapbook. Personal Collection of Susan Chatzky.

5

THE OUTRAGEOUS OUTRAGE OF ROMAIN GARY

A French-Yiddish Take on Holocaust Humor

Ariane Santerre

The year 1967 saw the start of the Wilhelm Harster trial in Munich for his involvement in the murderous deportations of tens of thousands of Dutch Jews, mainly to Auschwitz and Sobibor, during which the ex-SS general admitted having been hired as a civil servant in the 1950s by the state of Bavaria with full knowledge of his previous conviction of "abuse of duty" by a Dutch court.[1] The very same year, Jewish French writer Romain Gary published his novel *La Danse de Gengis Cohn*, featuring the eponymous Yiddish cabaret comedian who, after having been executed during the Holocaust, spends his time in modern Germany as a dybbuk, haunting the consciousness of Police Commissioner Schatz, the ex-SS officer responsible for his death, now in charge of solving a case of serial murders in the German town of Licht. Steeped in outrageous humor from the start, the novel in fact reflects the outrage felt by Gary himself toward the European reaction to the memory of the Holocaust as it was being rekindled in the wake of the Adolf Eichmann trial in 1961. As a result of the heated social debates, the Holocaust found its way into the fictional literature of a variety of nations, which would turn into what Ellen S. Fine called an "explosion of works"[2] in the 1970s and 1980s.

Hence, in France, André Schwarz-Bart published *Le Dernier des Justes* in 1959, a fictional family chronicle that ends in the gas chambers of Auschwitz. The novel was an immediate success and won the Goncourt Prize. In the United States, Philip Roth described the attempts of suburban assimilated American Jews to rid themselves of their new religious neighbors who are survivors of concentration camps in his short story "Eli, the Fanatic," published in *Goodbye, Columbus and Five Short Stories* (1959). Edward Lewis Wallant published *The Pawnbroker* (1961), "one of the first Jewish American novels to focus on a Holocaust victim,"[3] followed by Norma Rosen's *Touching Evil* (1969) and Saul Bellow's *Mr. Sammler's Planet* (1970). In Germany, the *Schuldfrage* emerged around the same time following the 1963–65 Auschwitz Trials in Frankfurt, seeing the publication of Wolfgang Hildesheimer's *Tynset* (1965), which multiplies evocations to the Holocaust without explicitly mentioning it, allowing for an interpretation of the narrator as a "Holocaust survivor representing, in stream-of-conscousness [sic] fashion, his struggle not only with the past, but also with the present in postwar Germany."[4]

The evocation and representation of the Holocaust in quick succession in the cultural sphere led to the emergence of a Holocaust literary trope that in turn became problematic, as Efraim Sicher puts it:

> The memory of the Holocaust . . . has become public property for the postwar generation, a ready trope for political protest, bracketed with Hiroshima, Vietnam, Cambodian killing fields, and Serbian ethnic cleansing, in a denunciation of state tyranny or simply authority, or, as in Sylvia Plath's poetry, a convenient trope for private pain inflicted by the "Nazi" father on his daughter Electra.[5]

Romain Gary's *Danse de Gengis Cohn* falls right into the first wave of exploitation of that literary trope, but its originality lies in shifting it from the dramatic mode into the comedic repertoire, hence breaking the clichés that were already starting to crystallize around the subject of the Holocaust. To better appreciate where that peculiar form of humor is coming from, a biographical summary is surely in order.

Born Roman Kacew in Vilnius's Jewish Quarter in 1914, at the time part of the Russian Empire, Gary was quickly deported with his mother, Mina, in 1915, to central Russia as Baltic Jews suspected of German espionage. He returned to Vilnius only in 1921 at the age of seven. He then spent two years in Warsaw before immigrating to Nice, France, with his mother in 1928. France became his *mère-patrie*: his attachment to the nation was always profound and sincere, as his wartime allegiances later proved. In June 1940, as a young pilot and sergeant, Romain Gary heard Général de Gaulle's famous "Appel" on the radio and immediately decided to join him. After effectively stealing a plane of the French army, now in a state of armistice, he flew over the Mediterranean into North Africa, before finally joining the Free French Air Forces in Great Britain, where he was assigned until the end of the war. His missions took him to Africa (Ghana, Libya, and Al-Habash in today's Ethiopia), the Middle East, and Great Britain. He was decorated with the Croix de Guerre and was named Compagnon de la Libération and commander of the Légion d'Honneur.[6] He published *Éducation européenne* in 1945—the first of a whopping thirty-one novels—and with the end of the war started his writing vocation, along with a diplomatic career that took him to Bulgaria, Switzerland, Bolivia, and the United States, where he was consul general of France in Los Angeles from 1956 to 1960. But in his native Lithuania, his father, Arieh-Leyb, who had remarried, was murdered in the Holocaust along with Gary's stepsister Walentyna and stepbrother Pawel.[7]

In this chapter, I will investigate Gary's provocative humor according to three specific dimensions that emerge from a panorama of humor commentators. The underlying question at work concerns how his humor ties in with both his French and his Yiddish backgrounds—among the many cultures that he managed to acutely comprehend throughout his wandering life as a Jewish child in exodus, a war hero, and a diplomat and that transpire in *La Danse*. An important cultural point to keep in mind while exploring this novel is the fact that Gary wrote it in French and then translated it himself into English the following year; both versions will be given here, with the original French in notes. As we will see, the English translation presents quite a different version that sheds light on Gary's mastery of both French and American cultures,[8] while erasing some of the typically French humor found in the original that deserves to be underlined. Nevertheless, what remains in both the French and the English versions is the all-important language of Yiddish. Throughout the analysis, I argue that Gary's outrageous form of humor, far from aiming to offend the memory of the Nazis' Jewish victims, serves in fact as a powerful vehicle of denunciation, of reflection, and of reconnection to the Yiddish culture that was annihilated by the Holocaust.

Humor in Three Dimensions

Before delving into Gary's *Danse de Gengis Cohn*, I would like to offer my own take on what emerges from a panorama of humor commentators concerning what I see as the three main dimensions of humor: analytical, artistic, and historical. I would like to underline nonexhaustive aspects of each of these dimensions that will be relevant for this chapter, as all three are represented in Romain Gary's *Danse*.

The analytical dimension focuses on the functions of humor and appears frequently in scholarly works as they aim to peel back its layers. The analytical dimension comes in handy in cases of controversy, as a more weighted viewpoint can go beyond the immediacy of emotions, as is often the case when a joke touches on a sensitive issue such as the Holocaust. The validity and effectiveness of that kind of humor is then measured in terms of its functions and the context of its enunciation (who says it, to whom, who is the real butt of the joke, etc.).[9] Functions such as coping, better remembering the past, arming against various forms of fascism, denouncing hypocrisy, challenging authority, and unifying a marginalized community are often put forward in order to understand and explain the raison d'être behind a type of humor that can seem baffling or even offensive.[10] One of Gary's strengths in writing his novel is that, envisioning accusations by critics, he starts it off by addressing them head-on through his protagonist:

> Allow me to introduce myself: the name is Cohn, Genghis Cohn: my real name was Moishe, but Genghis went better with my rather wild stage personality. I'm a comedian, and in the old days I used to be very well known on the Yiddish burlesque circuit: first at the Shwarze Shikse, in Berlin, then at the Mottke Ganeff in Warsaw, and finally in Auschwitz. . . . It's true that many people objected to my brand of humor. They often felt shocked and shaken and some critics expressed strong reservations about my act: they thought that it lacked dignity. My wit, or *khokhme*, as we call it, they found either too arrogant or too self-deprecating, either too biting and cruel or, on the contrary, self-pitying and close to black despair. One of the critics wrote in the *Nasz Przeglad* of Warsaw: "Mr. Genghis Cohn's humor occasionally sounds like some kind of helpless and hopeless self-defense. This

comedian seems unable to find a middle ground between a sort of Jewish Uncle-Tomism and hostility, often sinking to downright provocation and abuse."

. . . Maybe they were right. In Auschwitz, one day, I told a fellow inmate such a funny joke that he literally died laughing. He was undoubtedly the only Jew who ever died laughing in Auschwitz. The German guards were furious.[11]

Let us note that the English translation goes even further than the French original in describing at length the critics' condemnation of humor, emphasizing an antithetical tendency that ends up in pure contradiction that underlines how humor can be perceived, by those who practice it, as a balancing act that will never go unchallenged. Nevertheless, having acknowledged his critics' reservations right from the start, Genghis Cohn proceeds immediately (with his story about the Auschwitz fatal joke), and then throughout the novel, with his "wild stage personality." The functions of such "cruel," "provocative," and "abusive" humor will be addressed in the next section of this chapter.

The artistic[12] dimension focuses on the techniques of humor—or the art of delivering a joke—and mostly comes up in the discourse of comedians themselves. It is often linked to orality (and the gestures it implies[13]), in the context of a performance. Intonation, timing, rhythm, and rhyming are discussed by comedy professionals with the same acuteness that poets talk about writing. When reflecting on Yiddish as a funny and "expressive language," *YidLife Crisis*'s Eli Batalion mentioned that it is linked to "the intonation, how it raises and falls that has something that is really rhythmic. And comedy is largely about rhythm."[14] In Alan Zweig's documentary *When Jews Were Funny*, comedian Modi Rosenfeld gave this anecdote as an example of the art of timing:

I'll tell you the funniest thing in the world, and its timing. . . . And Jews have this type of timing. . . . I'm at a Shabbat dinner in Brooklyn, and they sit me next to this guy who is a survivor of the Holocaust. Old man. Wearing a short-sleeved shirt, you see the numbers and everything. And a conversation began at the table about the synagogue, and somebody in the synagogue who moved a chair and didn't put it back, or borrowed a book . . . it was nonsense. Nonsense! This old man out of nowhere picks his head out of the soup, and in Yiddish, says: "*Ikh gedenk im fun dem Lager,*" which means "I remember him from the Lager, from the death camps." You have to understand: the whole room is like . . . he's got our attention . . . the floor is yours, right? And he says this in Yiddish. . . . They're talking about a guy in the synagogue, who must be a hundred years old also, who took a book and didn't bring it back. Nonsense, right? . . . He begins to tell this story: "'*S'iz geven a nakht*" (there was a night) "*az ikh hob gehat a kartofl*" (I had a potato), "*un er hot nisht gehat [keyn] kartofl*" (and he didn't have a potato), "*un ikh hob im gegebn mayn kartofl*" (and I gave him my potato). . . . And he takes the perfect pause, and says: "If I had known back then he'd be doing the things he's doing today, I wouldn't have given him the potato."[15]

This metadiscourse by comedians themselves surrounding humor shows the level of careful craftsmanship and serious self-reflection that is at the core of comedy. In Gary's *Danse*, the timing described by Modi, mixed with cabaret-style humor, is portrayed when the dybbuk intervenes (through Schatz's mouth) in a discussion involving the commissioner and two German aristocrats. One of them, the ridiculously named Baron von Pritwitz, is concerned after his wife's disappearance, which appears clearly to everyone but him to be the result of a love affair with the gamekeeper Florian (a humoristic reference to D. H. Lawrence's *Lady Chatterley's Lover*):

> "What about the gamekeeper?" [asks Commissioner Schatz.]
> "He was . . . inoffensive. He had been the victim of a shooting accident in France. . . . You see what I mean?" . . .
> "Why should the Baroness have gone off with a eunuch?"
> "Because he is harmless."
> "*Then one might just as well stay with one's husband.*"
> I rub my hands. That's a good one, in the best Shwarze Shikse tradition.[16]

As a comedian, Genghis Cohn is depicted by Gary with many of the artistic attributes necessary to deliver a powerful punchline: The strength of his jokes relies on the gravity of its subject matter, while the dramatic topic is more easily addressed through laughter. The finesse, or the exaggeration of the delivery in this case, better carries the intention behind the humor. Among the dybbuk's comedic arsenal are well-placed Yiddish words, and the use of Yiddish itself as a form of psychological torture against Schatz (the language embodying the collective culture destroyed by the Nazis), which act as one of the comedy/tragedy leitmotifs of the novel.

The historical dimension focuses on the trajectory of humor and its triggers, and it is often found in scholars' and comedians' discourses alike. Addressing Jewish humor in particular almost never comes without mentioning the long tradition of catastrophes that has driven Jews to address it through either lamentation or laughter. Francis Veber, one of the most iconic French comedy screenwriters—renowned for *Le Dîner de Cons* (1998), an immensely acclaimed film that turns superciliousness on its head—starts his autobiography accordingly: "I was born in Neuilly of a Jewish father and an Armenian mother. Two genocides, two bloody Wailing Walls, everything to create a comedian."[17] Wars and political persecutions are often cited as triggers of a people's humor,[18] and the traumatic postmemory persists through laughter when stories are carried over through the generations. Romain Gary's understanding of Jewish humor stems from its historical dimension. Hence, in *La Danse*, Cohn reflects on the reason why he showed Schatz his *tokhes* right before being shot:

> I suppose it was . . . a kind of prophecy, a premonition, almost as if I had foreseen that the Jews would one day be accused of having gone to their death like sheep, without fighting back? [So I used the only weapon—purely symbolic, in truth—that we had managed to keep just about intact through the ages].[19]

The Jewish weapon of humor is portrayed here as an internalized cultural legacy that manifests itself in moments of terrible adversity.

Gary's Aggressive Humor

As mentioned earlier, *La Danse de Gengis Cohn* is steeped in outrageous humor right from the start. This profusion of provocative humor is even portrayed within the speech pattern of the comedian protagonist according to what I call the "stand-up principle," as this example shows:

I now recognize the two distinguished gentlemen who are waiting for Schatz. I have seen their pictures in the Society column of the *Zeitung*. They have amassed considerable fortunes since what is known as the "German miracle," and they spend this money generously: they build museums, patronize the arts, finance symphony orchestras, and offer their Dürers and their Rembrandts to the City's Hall of Culture. I must admit that right now beauty is greatly encouraged all over the world. In the U.S.A. there is such an overflow of art treasures, music, and books that you could rape your grandmother there, no one would notice.

   I have no reservations about our culture vultures. If Christ—peace to His ashes—were to rise again and look at all the splendors and beauty of the Renaissance crucifixions, He would be indignant, insulted in every drop of His blood. It has always appeared to me that to make beauty out of His agony, to use His martyrdom to procure delight, is not very Christian. I think the popes ought to have looked into it. In my humble opinion, the Church should have forbidden the Renaissance masters to capitalize on the Crucifixion and should have left the artistic exploitation and profiteering of the Fra Filippo Lippi and Giotto type to us unworthy Jews, like the practice of usury.[20]

Let us follow the steps of this excerpt. There is first a general contextual setting (Genghis recognizes the two men who walked in the room and explains their background). He then says something exceedingly shocking (the grandmother rape) to draw the attention of his target audience. From this uncomfortable setting point, he then proceeds with a social commentary (the proximity of high culture to suffering in Western civilization) that aims to make that audience think. Finally, he concludes the commentary with a last provocative joke (by getting into the antisemitic register and its stereotype of Jewish usury, which he in fact reverses by arguing that Jews should be given the monopoly to capitalize off the Crucifixion). Through the medium of writing, we just attended a stand-up routine.

   Formally, Gary renews with the specific brand of comedy that is usually performed orally in front of spectators. Content-wise, he provides a context that is typically Jewish, while also making explicit and implicit references to the cabaret-style "sarcasm and verbal aggression that had characterized Yiddish comedy of the interwar era."[21] Using an irreverent form of humor fulfills many functions, in this example that of underlining the contradictions of a given society (in this case Western civilization) and encouraging the audience to reflect further upon its hypocrisy (in this case, the obsession of high culture with barbarity and its relationship to money). This passage applying the stand-up principle thus features both the artistic and the analytical dimensions of humor in a way that subtly places standard comedian jokes within the bigger framework of the genre of stand-up comedy, therefore evoking the multiple elements of that architext.[22]

The "verbal aggression" of Gary's French version of Yiddish humor does not hold anything sacred, not even the Holocaust. When describing the moment of his death, when he is shot with other Jews in a grave that they were forced to dig themselves, Genghis Cohn mentions one of the most horrible facts of the genocide, the murder of children. In a particularly dark form of humor, Genghis keeps linking it to the archetypical Jewish mother, insisting on the fact that his death was so terrible to experience because of their shrieks: "At a moment like that, a Jewish mother can make a lot of sound, at least a thousand decibels,"[23] and yet again:

> It wasn't so much fear that made my hair stand up this way [like some sort of ghostly Harpo Marx]: it was the noise. I've always been easily unnerved by noise, and all those mothers with their kids in their arms waiting to be shot made a helluva noise. I don't want to sound anti-Semitic, but nothing screams like a Jewish mother when her kids are being murdered. After all these centuries, they're still unable to adjust. I didn't even have any earplugs on me. I was completely helpless.[24]

It is important to note that Gary's dark humor goes so far as to mention the anguish of the mothers a split second before the execution, but not as they are being shot, and that their description remains within the boundaries of a caricature rather than opting for a realistic form of representation.[25] More importantly, the children themselves are only alluded to as "accessories" to the Jewish mothers and are never described in the face of death. Nevertheless outrageous, this type of humor serves to emphasize, in turn, the outrageous criminal behaviors that took place during the Holocaust. It is through comedy that it becomes possible to talk about traumatic facts excruciatingly difficult to address still twenty years after the genocide.[26]

Humor, in that sense, allows the preservation and perpetuation of a collective memory that, as harrowing as it is, should not be repressed and eventually risk being forgotten. Going beyond the *refrain* of "remembering the Holocaust," the memorialization process that humor sets in motion addresses the most horrific aspects of the genocide, slightly askew, allowing a way to enter the mass grave.

This rekindling of memory through humor is the main reason behind Gary's desacralization approach, as is shown in Genghis Cohn's subversive understanding of high art as a sophisticated method to profit from other people's tragedy:

> I fear that by becoming intoxicated with culture, our biggest crimes will fade entirely. Everything will shine with such beauty that the massacres and famines will only be literary or pictural effects under the pen of a Tolstoy or the brush of a Picasso. And as soon as some mass grave finds its admirable artistic expression, it will be classified as a historic monument and will only be considered as a source of inspiration, a material for *Guernica*, war and peace becoming, for our immense joy, *War and Peace*. In truth, it is another sign of our proverbial avarice: I fear that someone else, a writer, a painter, will make a killing on my back and profit from my misfortune.[27]

The desacralization approach aims to avoid a definite, crystallized opinion of a particular subject, as is true for anything complex that is hastily and easily grasped as having only one facet. Desacralizing the masterpieces of literature encourages discussions and debates; desacralizing the Holocaust can help keep its memory alive. The power of humor lies in its reversal of clichés and the official culture of memory[28] that can only get frozen in time.[29]

Throughout the course of writing this novel in the 1960s, Gary uses aggressive humor that also turns against contemporary Germany's complicated relationship with its own memory of the Holocaust:

> I dance off whistling the *Horst Wessel Lied*. Tunes from the last war are quite popular in Germany now. New recordings are made of them, old ones are dusted off. Chancellor Erhard went to the United States to ask for nuclear weapons; he came back empty-handed and was

removed from office. We're having a quiet little Renaissance here. The
new Chancellor Kiesinger had even belonged to the Nazi Party in a
burst of youthful enthusiasm and idealism that lasted briefly from
1932 to 1945. Which reminds me that when Professor Herbert Lewin
was named head of the Offenbach General Hospital near Frankfurt
some years ago, the majority of municipal councilors opposed the
appointment on interesting ethical grounds. They gave as their reason that—and I quote—"it is impossible to trust a Jewish doctor and
expect him to treat German women impartially, after what happened
to the Jews." I clipped this precious little item from the magazine section of the London *Sunday Times*, October 16, 1966, and tacked it
on the wall over the john in Schatzchen's bathroom, so that he
wouldn't feel safe from me, even in there.[30]

Far from being the product of fiction, the facts mentioned above about
Erhard, Kiesinger, and Lewin are historically accurate. Gary's outrage
toward modern Germany turns in *La Danse* into bitter irony about the
country's real ability to change. Within the storyline of his novel, he adds up
several instances underlining its conveniently chronic selective memory.
For example, when discussing the serial murders, Schatz surmises:

> "They were in a state of ecstasy. . . . There's got to be something mys-
> tical about it. Ritual murders?"
>
> "Come now, sir, we're not dealing with Aztecs. Human sacrifices
> do not take place in Germany."
>
> It's then that Schatz makes a statement that I simply cannot
> accept, particularly when you consider that it comes from a friend.
>
> "It's the first time in all my experience," he declares solemnly,
> "that somebody's carrying out mass murders without a motive, with-
> out a shadow of a reason . . ."
>
> That's too much. I can't let him get away with such *hutzpeh*, such
> gall.[31]

The function of the humor here is to denounce modern Germany's opposition to truly accept *Kollektivschuld* and live with the memory of its crimes.

Gary's aggressive humor, therefore, is twofold: It is both a shield and
a weapon. A shield because, through laughter, he protects himself against

the horrors of human cruelty: "Provocation is my preferred form of legitimate self-defense,"[32] he would write three years later in *Chien blanc* (*White Dog*). A weapon because, through irony, he fights against those who minimize or even ignore the past, in the best tradition of what Yiddish comic writer Moyshe Nudelman called "*vits-gever*" (weapon of jokes), which he considered as a form of revenge and resistance.[33]

Laughing with Rabelais: The French Intertext

The French side of Gary's Jewish humor has not yet come into play, which is what this section proposes to do by looking into its intertextual references, which are not as clear for someone reading the English translation of *La Danse* since it is rewritten for a different target audience. It is first important to underline a recurring joke present in both versions that, however, comes directly from Gary's French humor. Throughout the novel, the narrator and characters repeatedly misattribute quotes and works of art, a very French type of humor that pokes fun at the tendency of some to pretend to be more cultured than they are. Taken individually, most of these misattributions are without consequence to the general argument of the novel, but others bear much more significance. An example of this can be found when Cohn refers to a poem supposedly written by an unnamed Yiddish poet in the fall of 1943 that contains the words "the sobbing of the violins of autumn."[34] The words of this poem erroneously—and purposefully—attributed to a Yiddish poet in fact come from the first stanza of Paul Verlaine's poem "Chanson d'automne," published in 1866. The false date affixed to the poem in *La Danse* is a clue to the meaning of the intertextuality in the context of the Holocaust: Verlaine's nineteenth-century stanza was used by Radio Londres in June 1944 (and not in the fall of 1943) to signal to French railway saboteurs to get ready to do their work. Mixing funny jokes with high culture, Gary points to a network of intertextuality that, in this case, is reminiscent of the history of the Resistance and the Holocaust (as Nazism's victims were deported by train).

In both the French and English versions, a particular phrase is repeated throughout the novel, as is shown in this example:

You probably all remember a certain snapshot of a Hasidic Jew, one of those Jews who look so funny with their beards and long locks of hair, *peyes*, falling on their cheeks, their hats and their long, black caftans? A soldier is posing in this famous photograph: he is laughing for posterity, while pulling the Hasidic Jew by the beard. And what do you think the Hasidic Jew is doing while being pulled by the beard, standing there all alone among the laughing, humorous German soldiers? *He is laughing too.* As Montaigne so rightly said, laughter is a deeply human characteristic.[35]

While the formula of the last sentence is wrongly—and, again, purposefully—attributed every time to Montaigne in the English version, the French version never alludes to the author of the redundant "*le rire est le propre de l'homme.*" However, to anyone with a French education, it is a famous sentence: It is part of Rabelais's opening of *Gargantua* (1534): "*Mieux est de ris que de larmes écrire / Pource que rire est le propre de l'homme*"[36] (It is better to write with laughter than tears / Because laughter is natural to man). In the English translation, Gary likely decided to continue his comedic trend of misattributions by associating Rabelais's quote to his contemporary Montaigne, humorously confusing Rabelais's novels with the more serious, religious, and philosophical writings of Montaigne. In his novel, Gary always uses Rabelais's laughter formula to conclude a passage about the laughter of the offended and the oppressed,[37] which serves as a sort of intertextual metadescription explaining his authorial choice to resort to humor to talk about the humiliation and murder of his people: "*Mieux est de ris que de larmes écrire,*" a French pendant of the Yiddish "*gelekhter durkh trern*" (laughter through tears).[38] Romain Gary makes many other references to French writers, including funny ones like Molière, but Rabelais's formula comes back as a *refrain* to remind his readers of his importance. A pillar of French literature, the sixteenth-century Humanist writer François Rabelais created an oeuvre that offered a comical, vernacular, scatological counterpart to the rigid writings endorsed by the Church at the time, and his novels were the precursors of the philosophical novels of the Enlightenment. Through Rabelais's words, Gary harkens back to the great French traditions and hints at a key fact: French literature was, in fact, born in humor.

Medieval narratives written in the Old French that derived from the *"parlers romans"* (the roman dialects of the Vulgar Latin) gave its name to what we know today as one of the most important literary genres, the *roman* (novel). Breaking away from the Classical Latin mastered by the elites, many of the medieval writings in Old French were targeting a popular public. The *Fabliaux érotiques*,[39] for instance, were comic tales often staging a fair lady caught in a compromising situation with her priest, hence humorously bringing together the sacred and the profane. Widely considered as the first *romancier* of French literature, Chrétien de Troyes presents his readers with a universe of *merveilleux*, love and adventure, but also of comical circumstances, as the scene of *Yvain ou le Chevalier au Lion* (between 1178 and 1181) in which the lion attempts to commit suicide can attest.[40] Interestingly, it is thought that Chrétien de Troyes, as his many insistences on his name could indicate, might have in fact been a Jew converted to Christianity.[41] If that were revealed to be the case rather than a mere hypothesis, one could even *dare* submit that the origins of the French *roman* are rooted in Jewish humor.

Throughout its history, French literature continued to be involved with humor. If Voltaire was one of France's greatest thinkers, he was also one of its funniest writers: One has only to read his ironically witty *Dictionnaire philosophique* (1764) to be convinced of it. That very oeuvre might have inspired Flaubert's *Dictionnaire des idées reçues* (written in the 1850s and published posthumously in 1913), which dissects the mentality of its time in a hilariously satirical way.[42] In the twentieth century, Marcel Proust continued in the same vein with *La Recherche du temps perdu*, in which he casts an ironic gaze upon the salon-going upper class that he himself had had the luxury of observing at length as a younger man.[43] As with Sholem Aleichem's crucial impact on the development of Yiddish literature, it becomes evident that forging literature by incorporating vernacular language in a way that can make it transcend itself into a new stratum of significance requires a form of creativity able to play on words and their double meanings—a mastery of language that is found among writers and comedians. At the very root of literature and humor alike, one can appreciate the penchant of humankind for creative language and storytelling. Who knows, maybe the first story ever told was a *vits*.

This short review of French literature's ties to humor underlines the relevance of reading Gary's Jewish humor in the original French. Similar to reading Sholem Aleichem in English, the intertextual jokes are, in effect, more than mere jokes: They open up a cultural universe that, in English or any other language, gets lost in translation. The memorialization process of the Holocaust at the heart of the novel finds its foundation in history and culture. Through its references to literary history, Gary's *Danse* has the particularity of upholding both Jewish and French cultural traditions in its quest to better remember the tragedy and to keep its memory alive through their typical forms of humor.

Conclusion

A common thread among commentators of *La Danse de Gengis Cohn* is the observation of Gary's denunciation of Western European culture as a factor that led to the Holocaust.[44] Though this observation is accurate, I argue that he does not blame it altogether, seeing as humor is, undeniably, part of culture. Indeed, the humor within European culture was mobilized throughout history to criticize society (let's think of Rabelais, Molière, Flaubert, etc.) and could have been a conduit to rethink and reshape Western society itself. And it is in this very type of humor that reflects upon itself through irony and self-deprecation that Western European culture connects with Jewish civilization—Gary's attempt, perhaps, at reconciling in laughter the two sides of his identity in his outrageous staging of Genghis Cohn.

The novelist's complex duality is summed up perfectly by Jean-Marie Catonné, Gary's first biographer, when he describes his entire oeuvre as an "idealistic farce": According to Catonné, Gary's narrative voice throughout his work can be seen as having two paradoxical sides, an idealist versant believing in human fraternity and a disillusioned versant denigrating the Humanistic principles.[45] It would appear that oscillating between these two sides was his sense of humor, which, in a self-deprecating way, allowed him to poke fun at his own idealism without giving it up entirely. Upon closer examination, the clash between the ideal of fraternity and the disillusionment in the face of human nature is linked to Gary's complex identity as a Frenchman and as a Jew born in eastern Europe. One of France's greatest ideological achievements coming out of the Revolution was the invention of its universalist national motto: *Liberté, Égalité, Fraternité*.[46]

For anyone schooled in France with the values of the Republic, as was Gary from the age of fourteen, it was commonplace to believe strongly in the Humanistic concept of universality—a word that suggests secularity but that in fact finds its origins in Catholicism.[47] Gary's constant negotiation between idealism and reality, universality and distinct cultural tradition, follows his life path of growing up with French Republican values and then growing out of them with the ruthless experiences of the twentieth century. Through its analytical, artistic, and historical dimensions of humor, *La Danse de Gengis Cohn* is but one example of the memorial functions of global Jewish humor in the context of the Holocaust: for a German reader forced to acknowledge the horrific nature of his countrymen's crimes, for a French audience introduced to the killing fields of the East in this way, and for a general (even Jewish) audience who would rather not confront the horror but is perhaps able to do so through the less threatening use of humor. Laughter, in that sense, is the first utterance that can be mobilized to start the dialogue.

Notes

1 "Nazi General on Trial for Deporting Dutch Jews Testifies in Court," *Jewish Telegraphic Agency Daily News Bulletin* 34, no. 17 (January 25, 1967): 3, accessed August 15, 2023, http://pdfs.jta.org/1967/1967-01-25_017.pdf?_ga=2.15521328.709787542.1684158006-397933926.1684158006.

2 Ellen S. Fine, "Transmission of Memory: The Post-Holocaust Generation in the Diaspora," in *Breaking Crystal: Writing and Memory After Auschwitz*, ed. Efraim Sicher (Urbana: University of Illinois Press, 1998), 186.

3 Efraim Sicher, *The Holocaust Novel* (New York: Routledge, 2005), 89.

4 Corey Lee Twitchell, "The German Jewish Post-Holocaust Novel: Narrative and a Literary Language for Loss," PhD diss., Washington University in St. Louis, 2015, 8.

5 Efraim Sicher, "The Holocaust in the Postmodernist Era," in Sicher, *Breaking Crystal*, 315–16. Let us underline that Sylvia Plath (1932–63) wrote her Holocaust-themed poem "Daddy" in 1962, which was published posthumously in 1965 in her collection of poems *Ariel*.

6 "Romain Gary," *Musée de l'Ordre de la Libération*, accessed August 15, 2023, https://www.ordredelaliberation.fr/fr/compagnons/romain-gary.

7 His father was probably killed by the Einsatzgruppen in Lithuania
   (Myriam Anissimov, *Romain Gary, le caméléon* [Paris: Gallimard,
   2006], 70), while the children and their mother were killed in the
   Klooga camp in Estonia after having been incarcerated in the Vilnius
   ghetto (63).
8 See also Nancy Huston, "Gary se traduit," *TransLittérature*, no. 58 (2020):
   51–62.
9 See, for example, Slucki, Finder, and Patt's take on Larry David's *Saturday Night Live* host appearance and his joke about a pickup line in a
   concentration camp and on Jeff Ross's *Historical Roast* of Anne Frank
   (David Slucki, Gabriel N. Finder, and Avinoam Patt, "Introduction: To
   Tell Jokes After Auschwitz Is Barbaric, Isn't It?," in *Laughter After: Humor
   and the Holocaust*, ed. David Slucki, Gabriel N. Finder, and Avinoam Patt
   [Detroit: Wayne State University Press, 2020], 2–4).
10 See Slucki, Finder, and Patt, "Introduction," 1–11; Eli Lederhendler and
   Gabriel N. Finder, "Preface," in *A Club of Their Own: Jewish Humorists
   and the Contemporary World*, ed. Eli Lederhendler and Gabriel N. Finder
   (Oxford: Oxford University Press, 2016), vii–xii.
11 Romain Gary, *The Dance of Genghis Cohn* (New York: World Publishing,
   1968), translated from the French by Romain Gary with the assistance of
   Camilla Sykes, 3–4. Original passage:

Mon nom est Cohn, Gengis Cohn. Naturellement, Gengis est un pseu-
donyme : mon vrai prénom était Moïché, mais Gengis allait mieux avec
mon genre de drôlerie. Je suis un comique juif et j'étais très connu jadis,
dans les cabarets yiddish : d'abord au *Schwarze Schickse* de Berlin, ensuite
au *Motke Ganeff* de Varsovie, et enfin à Auschwitz. Les critiques faisaient
quelques réserves sur mon humour : ils le trouvaient un peu excessif,
un peu agressif, cruel. Ils me conseillaient un peu de retenue. Peut-être
avaient-ils raison. Un jour, à Auschwitz, j'ai raconté une histoire tellement drôle à un autre détenu qu'il est mort de rire. C'était sans doute le
seul Juif mort de rire à Auschwitz. (Romain Gary, *La Danse de Gengis
Cohn* [Paris: Gallimard, coll. "Folio," 1967], 11–12)

12 In her analysis of Gary's humor in *La Danse*, Esther Grimalt describes
   Genghis's dance rather than humor as a form of art, whereas I see humor
   as being itself a form of artistic expression (Esther Grimalt, "La mise

en fiction de la Shoah dans *La Danse de Gengis Cohn* de Romain Gary, *Inglorious Basterds* de Quentin Tarantino et *The Passenger* de Mieczyslaw Weinberg," PhD diss., Université d'Avignon, 2019, 104).

13   Paul Zumthor, "Oralité," *Intermédialités*, no. 12 (Fall 2008): 196.

14   "Yiddish Makes Everything Funnier: Reflections from the Co-Creators of *YidLife Crisis*," *Yiddish Book Center*, accessed on August 15, 2023, https://www.yiddishbookcenter.org/collections/oral-histories/excerpts/woh-ex-0004747/yiddish-makes-everything-funnier-reflections-co-creators-yidlife-crisis.

15   Alan Zweig, *When Jews Were Funny* (Canada: Sudden Storm Entertainment, 2013). I wish to thank Mario "Moishele" Alfonso for the Yiddish corrections on the written form of this excerpt.

16   Gary, *The Dance*, 60. Original passage: " 'Pourquoi la Baronne serait-elle partie avec un eunuque?' 'Justement . . . J'imagine que c'est parce qu'il est . . . inoffensif.' 'Dans ce cas, on est aussi bien en restant avec son mari.' Je pouffe. Je suis content d'avoir placé cette *khokhmé*, dans la meilleure tradition du *Schwarze Schickse*" (Gary, *La Danse*, 85).

17   Francis Veber, *Que ça reste entre nous* (Paris: Robert Laffont, 2010), 7; translation mine.

18   See, for example, Olesia Yehorova, Antonina Prokopenko, and Anna Zinchenko, "Towards a Typology of Humorous Wartime Tweets: The Case of Ukraine 2022," *European Journal of Humour Research* 11, no. 1 (2023): 1–26, accessed August 15, 2023, https://europeanjournalofhumour.org/ejhr/article/view/746/705; and Anastasiya Astapova, "Soviet Meta-Jokes: Tradition and Continuity," *European Journal of Humour Research* 8, no. 3 (2020): 60–82, accessed August 15, 2023, https://europeanjournalofhumour.org/ejhr/article/view/463/pdf.

19   Gary, *The Dance*, 23. Original passage: "Peut-être pressentais-je qu'on allait un jour reprocher aux Juifs de s'être laissé massacrer sans résister : j'ai donc utilisé la seule arme, purement symbolique, certes, que nous avions réussi à conserver à peu près intacte à travers les âges" (Gary, *La Danse*, 32). Note that I modified the translation of the last sentence to better convey the meaning of the original, as the translated official version of the same sentence reads "The only weapon we had was our bare ass, so I used mine."

20   Gary, *The Dance*, 35–36. Original passage:

Ils ont fait, depuis le miracle allemand, des fortunes considérables et ils dépensent leur argent généreusement : ils bâtissent des musées, protègent les arts, financent les orchestres symphoniques et font don à la ville de tableaux admirables. Dans le monde entier, d'ailleurs, les signes extérieurs de la beauté sont en ce moment très encouragés. Aux États-Unis, c'est un tel débordement de trésors artistiques et de grands ensembles culturels, que vous pourriez violer votre grand-mère, là-dedans, personne ne le remarquerait. Ça éblouit. J'avoue que je me sens assez mal à l'aise devant ces efforts. Imaginez—une simple supposition—que le Christ renaisse soudain de Ses cendres et se trouve nez à nez avec nos splendeurs d'art sacré et avec la beauté enivrante de toutes les crucifixions de la Renaissance. Il serait indigné, insulté, jusqu'à la dernière goutte de son sang. Tirer de sa souffrance atroce de telles beautés, utiliser son agonie pour donner du plaisir, ce n'est pas très chrétien. Il y a du Sade, là-dedans, sans parler d'une façon de faire fructifier un capital de souffrance où le pape devrait mettre son nez. Il devrait interdire aux chrétiens la pratique de l'art sacré et le laisser aux Juifs, comme l'usure. (Gary, *La Danse*, 48–49)

Note the difference of cultural references in both versions: the French Marquis de Sade is replaced with Filippo Lippi and Giotto in English.

21 Marc Caplan, "Too Soon? Yiddish Humor and the Holocaust in Postwar Poland," in Slucki, Finder, and Patt, *Laughter After*, 50.

22 See Gérard Genette, *The Architext: An Introduction* (Berkeley: University of California Press, [1979] 1992), translated from the French by Jane E. Lewin.

23 Gary, *The Dance*, 9. Original passage: "Ça fait au moins mille décibels, une mère juive, à ces moments-là" (Gary, *La Danse*, 18).

24 Gary, *The Dance*, 14–15. Original passage: "Ce n'était pas tellement la peur qui m'avait ainsi fait dresser les cheveux sur la tête : c'était le bruit. Je n'ai jamais pu supporter le bruit et toutes ces mères avec leurs gosses dans les bras, ça faisait un tam-tam terrible. Je ne veux pas paraître antisémite, mais rien ne hurle comme une mère juive lorsqu'on tue ses enfants. Je n'avais même pas de boules de cire, sur moi, j'étais complètement désarmé" (Gary, *La Danse*, 23).

25 When looking at the novel more generally, Charlotte Wardi notes that the murdered protagonist Genghis Cohn is, paradoxically, the only true

lively character of the novel with whom the reader can identify (Charlotte Wardi, *Le Génocide dans la fiction romanesque : Histoire et représen-
tation* [Paris: Presses universitaires de France, coll. "Écriture," 1986], 56).

26 See also Marc Caplan's analysis of *Undzere kinder*'s funny moments in the
immediate postwar (Caplan, "Too Soon?," 49).

27 Gary, *La Danse*, 61; translation mine. Original passage:

Je crains qu'à force de nous griser de culture, nos plus grands crimes
s'estompent complètement. Tout sera enveloppé d'une telle beauté que
les massacres et les famines ne seront plus que des effets littéraires ou
picturaux heureux sous la plume d'un Tolstoï ou le pinceau d'un Picasso.
Et dans la mesure où quelque charnier, soudain entrevu, trouvera aussitôt
son expression artistique admirable, il sera classé monument historique
et ne sera plus considéré que comme une source d'inspiration, du maté-
riau pour *Guernica*, la guerre et la paix devenant, pour notre bonheur,
Guerre et Paix. Au fond, il s'agit là encore de notre avarice proverbiale,
de notre esprit de lucre : j'ai peur que quelqu'un d'autre, un écrivain, un
peintre, fasse une affaire sur mon dos, tire des bénéfices de mon malheur.

The English official translation omits this passage.

28 See, for example, Catherine Coquio's reservations about the "duty of
memory" and its derivatives that she calls the "culture of memory"
(Catherine Coquio, *Le Mal de vérité ou l'utopie de la mémoire* [Paris:
Armand Colin, coll. "Le temps des idées," 2015]).

29 This is what Slucki, Finder, and Patt suggest from psychoanalyst Sla-
voj Žižek's take on humorous films about the Holocaust in the wake of
movies such as *Schindler's List*: "For Žižek, the emergence of Holocaust
comedies on film is directly related to the 'elevation of the holocaust itself
into the metaphysical, diabolical Evil'" (Slucki, Finder, and Patt, "Introduction," 6).

30 Gary, *The Dance*, 17–18. Original passage:

Je m'éloigne en sifflotant le *Horst Wessel Lied*. Il y a en ce moment en
Allemagne une véritable renaissance des marches militaires. On enre-
gistre des disques. On chantonne. On se prépare. Le chancelier Erhard est
allé aux États-Unis pour réclamer des armes nucléaires. Il est revenu bre-
douille et a été limogé. Dix-neuf ans de démocratie, c'est lourd à porter,

lorsqu'on a un passé. Le nouveau chancelier Kiesinger avait appartenu un instant au parti nazi de 1932 à 1945, dans un moment d'idéalisme et de fougue juvéniles. Bref, c'est peut-être ça, cette chaleur, qui vient par bouffées, et qui me trouble un peu : le renouveau. Je me souviens d'ailleurs que lorsque le professeur Herbert Lewin avait été nommé, il y a quelques années, à la tête de l'Hôpital Général d'Offenbach, à côté de Francfort, la majorité des conseillers municipaux s'y était opposée sous prétexte, et je cite, qu'*il n'est pas possible de faire confiance à un médecin juif et de lui permettre de traiter des femmes allemandes impartialement après ce qui est arrivé aux Juifs.* J'ai même découpé cette citation récemment dans le supplément illustré du *Sunday Times,* du 16 octobre 1966, et je l'ai épinglé au-dessus du siège dans les waters de mon ami Schatz, pour qu'il se sente moins seul. (Gary, *La Danse,* 25–26; emphasis by the author)

31 Gary, *The Dance,* 13. Original passage: " 'En tout cas, ils ont tous été tués en pleine extase, dit Schatz, sombrement. Il y a sûrement un aspect mystique. Crimes rituels ?' 'Allons donc. Nous ne sommes pas chez les Aztèques. Des sacrifices humains, en Allemagne . . . Vous voulez rire.' Schatz a alors une phrase que je trouve assez inouïe, lorsqu'on considère qu'il s'agit d'un ami. 'C'est la première fois, dans mon expérience, dit-il solennellement, que quelqu'un se livre à un massacre collectif sans trace de motif, sans l'ombre d'une raison . . .' En voilà assez. Il n'est pas question de laisser passer une telle *hutzpé,* sans réagir" (Gary, *La Danse,* 22).

32 Romain Gary, *Chien blanc* (Paris: Gallimard, 1970), 59; translation mine.

33 Moyshe Nudelman, *Gelekhter durkh trern: Zamlung fun humoristish-satirish shafungen funem nokhmilkhomedikn lebn fun poylishe yidn* (Laughter Through Tears: A Collection of Humoristic-Satirical Creations on the Postwar Life of Polish Jewry) (Buenos Aires: Tsentral-Farband fun Poylishe Yidn in Argentina, 1947), 15–16, translated by Marc Caplan; qtd. in Caplan, "Too Soon?," 43; see also 52.

34 Gary, *The Dance,* 108. Original passage: "comme l'a écrit un poète yiddish, *les sanglots longs des violons de l'automne*—automne 1943, pour être précis" (Gary, *La Danse,* 165; emphasis by the author).

35 Gary, *The Dance,* 37; emphasis by the author. Original passage:

Vous avez sans doute tous vu, dans vos illustrés, une certaine photo d'amateur, prise par un soldat bon enfant, au moment de l'entrée des troupes allemandes en Pologne. On y voit un Juif *khassid*, vous savez, ceux qui étaient si ridicules, avec leurs cheveux en papillotes sur leurs joues, et leurs longs caftans noirs. Sur la photo, un autre soldat posait pour son camarade : il tirait en riant la barbe du *khassid*. Et qu'est-ce qu'il faisait, le Juif *khassid*, que l'on tirait par la barbe, tout seul parmi les soldats allemands bons enfants qui riaient ? *Il riait, lui aussi.* Je vous l'ai dit : le rire est le propre de l'homme. (Gary, *La Danse*, 50–51; emphasis by the author)

36 François Rabelais, "Aux Lecteurs," in *Gargantua* (Paris: Imprimerie natio-nale, coll. "Salamandre," [1534] 1997), 55.
37 See also Gary, *The Dance*, 27–28 and 69–70; for the French version, see Gary, *La Danse*, 37–38 and 97–98.
38 See Avinoam Patt, " 'Laughter Through Tears': Jewish Humor in the Aftermath of the Holocaust," in Lederhendler and Finder, *A Club of Their Own*, 113–31.
39 *Fabliaux érotiques : Textes de jongleurs des XIIᵉ et XIIIᵉ siècles* (Paris: Librairie Générale Française, 1992).
40 Angelica Rieger, "La bande dessinée virtuelle du lion d'Yvain : Sur le sens de l'humour de Chrétien de Troyes," in *Arthurian Literature XIX: Comedy in Arthurian Literature*, ed. Keith Busby and Roger Dalrymple (Cambridge: D. S. Brewer, 2003), 49–64.
41 Françoise Pont-Bournez, *Chrétien de Troyes : Père de la littérature européenne* (Paris: L'Harmattan, 2010), 8. Let us add that the town of Troyes in the northeast of France was the birth town of the famous medieval Rabbi Rashi (1040–1105), also known in French as Salomon de Troyes. His rabbinical school made Troyes the center of Western Jewish thought in the eleventh and twelfth centuries, at the time of Chrétien de Troyes.
42 For example, under "Académie française," one can read: "Denigrate it, but attempt to become a member if possible," "Anglais" (Englishmen): "All rich," and under "Roman" (novel): "Deprave the masses" and "Only historical novels can be tolerated because they teach history" (Gustave Flaubert, *Dictionnaire des idées reçues* [Paris: Louis Conard, 1913], with an introduction and commentary by E.-L. Ferrère, 43, 46, and 89–90, translation mine, accessed August 15, 2023, https://www.sas.upenn.edu/~cavitch/pdf-library/Flaubert_Dictionnaire.pdf).

43 On a topic related to the one at present in this chapter, the recent exhibit *Marcel Proust du côté de la mère* presented at the Musée d'art et d'histoire du Judaïsme in Paris, focusing on the novelist's maternal family and his ties with Judaism, showed how Proust's particular writing method of using the margins of his working sheets and what he called "*paperoles*" that he would add on to extend certain passages—and which had amazed literary geneticists for decades—seems to have in fact been inspired by the Talmud (see *Marcel Proust du côté de la mère* [Paris: Musée d'art et d'histoire du Judaïsme, 2022], exhibit catalogue, 23–33).

44 Judith Kauffmann, "La Danse de Romain Gary ou Gengis Cohn et la valse-horà des mythes de l'Occident," *Études littéraires* 17, no. 1 (1984): 72; Wardi, *Génocide*, 62.

45 Jean-Marie Catonné, "La farce idéaliste," *Europe*, no. 1022–23 (June–July 2014): 36–37.

46 Though the last word of that triad was the last one to be affixed to it later, since other terms such as "Justice" and "Patrie" were considered, it was without a doubt Gary's most cherished one, the one that he had managed to find on a smaller scale within his army unit but that was never to be known again (on the French motto, see Mona Ozouf, "Liberté, Égalité, Fraternité," in *Les Lieux de mémoire*, ed. Pierre Nora [Paris: Gallimard, 1992], vol. 3, no. 3, 587); on Gary's idealism of fraternity, see Romain Gary, *La Promesse de l'aube* (Paris: Gallimard, coll. "Folio," [1960] 1980), 326; Romain Gary, *La Nuit sera calme* (Paris: Gallimard, coll. "Folio," 1974), 203.

47 Maurice Samuels, *Le Droit à la différence : L'universalisme français et les juifs* (Paris: La Découverte, 2022), 7–8.

Selected Bibliography

Anissimov, Myriam. *Romain Gary, le caméléon*. Paris: Gallimard, 2006.

Gary, Romain. *The Dance of Genghis Cohn*. New York: World Publishing, 1968. Translated from the French by Romain Gary with the assistance of Camilla Sykes.

Gary, Romain. *La Danse de Gengis Cohn*. Paris: Gallimard, coll. "Folio," 1967.

Lederhendler, Eli, and Gabriel N. Finder, ed. *A Club of Their Own: Jewish Humorists and the Contemporary World*. Oxford: Oxford University Press, 2016.

Slucki, David, Gabriel N. Finder, and Avinoam Patt, eds. *Laughter After: Humor and the Holocaust*. Detroit: Wayne State University Press, 2020.

6

HOW IT EMERGED FROM ODESSA

Mordecai Richler and Montreal Jewish Humor

Jarrod Tanny

"Your father, he once said to me, was one of your real wild Jews. A bonditt. A mazik. A devil. I could have sworn he was out of Odessa."[1] These were the words of Irv Nussbaum, a character in Mordecai Richler's final novel, *Barney's Version*, describing, with more than a touch of admiration, Barney Panovsky, the book's picaresque protagonist. This is my starting point for this chapter, in which I explore whether one can speak of a distinct Montreal Jewish humor, as seen through the writings of Mordecai Richler. Richler is considered part of the twentieth-century canon of Jewish literature, rightfully placed on the same virtual shelf as Philip Roth, Saul Bellow, and Joseph Heller, who gave the American public unforgettable portraits of Jewish anxiety and alienation through irreverence and satire in an age of upward mobility. Richler's writings, however, have a distinctive edge to them, a grittiness embodied by his characters who in certain respects share as much with the comical thugs, gangsters, and tricksters in Odessan Jewish lore, made famous by Isaac Babel and many others, as they do with their American counterparts, be it Roth's Alexander Portnoy, *Catch-22*'s Captain John Yossarian (who is usually read as Jewish), or, for that matter, *Annie Hall*'s Alvy Singer and other Jews in Woody Allen's 1970s films, who have equally played a defining role in post–World War II Jewish humor. An analysis of Mordecai Richler's novels as well as his nonfictional writings suggests that his work is well within the orbit of the Silent Generation's American Jewish humor, but it packs a dissolute punch, largely absent from what his counterparts south of the Canadian border produced. This chapter argues that Richler's sardonic pluck is the product of the unique social, cultural, and political landscape of Montreal, a historically cosmopolitan city and a site where competing nationalisms have clashed, much like Odessa of the late nineteenth and early twentieth centuries.[2] In this sense, Montreal Jewish humor constitutes an important link between Odessa's legendary Jewish wit and the Jewish humor that gestated and bore fruit in New York, Los Angeles, and other American cities.[3]

There is a vast literature on Jewish humor, and most recent scholarship on the subject either avoids defining it or instead focuses on unpacking certain facets of Jewish comedy.[4] Even if one focuses exclusively on the hegemonic Ashkenazi humor that emerged in eastern Europe and then took root in the United States, the obvious patterns, common themes, and recurring comedic tropes often belie the great variety and richness in the copious material produced by the "people of the joke."[5] Mel Brooks, Woody Allen, Joan Rivers, and Larry David have much in common, but their contributions to the canon are nevertheless distinct. The diverse array of chapters in this volume attests to the heterogeneity of Jewish humor, or rather "Jewish humors," once we widen our gaze to include non-Ashkenazi communities from around the world. That said, if one examines the Jewish humor that exploded in the United States during the late 1950s and 1960s beginning with Lenny Bruce and Philip Roth and that continues to flourish in the twenty-first century with Sarah Silverman, Larry David's *Curb Your Enthusiasm*, and the nostalgic *Marvelous Mrs. Maisel*, it is possible to construct a working definition of American Jewish humor, one that is hardly all-encompassing, but one whose rhetorical style and tropes are easily recognizable and, most significantly, set it apart from the humor produced by other ethno-cultural communities.[6]

So, what are the defining attributes of *this* Jewish humor, which undisputedly played a pivotal role in shaping American entertainment in the latter half of the twentieth century?[7] Modern Ashkenazi Jewish humor emerged during the eighteenth and nineteenth centuries in eastern Europe, during a time of ferment and upheaval, when movements such as the Haskalah transformed the Jewish perspective on the Jewish place within the surrounding world, inducing many to question their seemingly precarious existence amid a sea of hostile Christians. "Jewish humor," writes Sarah Blacher Cohen, was "born out of the vast discrepancy between what was to be the 'chosen people's' glorious destiny" of eternal election and their desperate reality of juridical segregation, destitution, and impeded upward mobility in Russia's Pale of Settlement.[8] Divine chosenness seemed to imply abandonment on earth, or, more precisely, special selection for punishment and suffering. As modernization engendered religious reform and secularization, many Jews came to see the absurdity of traditional Judaism's conception of exile. This absurdity became the cornerstone of Ashkenazi diasporic humor.

What makes this diasporic Jewish humor distinctive is the use of sardonic self-deprecation to underscore this incongruity between Jewish misery in an antisemitic world and a lingering hope for a glorious future as God's chosen people. This tension between the ideal of chosenness and the expected sufferings of exile is at the root of kvetching—the need to express oneself through complaint in almost every situation. "Judaism is defined by exile," as Michael Wex puts it, and "if we stop kvetching, how will we know that life isn't supposed to be like this? If we don't keep kvetching we'll forget who we really are."[9] The Diaspora Jew cannot express fulfillment, for to do so is to forget he is in exile. His kvetch is his declaration of an unattainable entitlement, rooted in Jewish theology but denied by history with an ironic vengeance.

This is not merely self-deprecation, let alone self-hatred—as other scholars have incorrectly argued[10]—because the Jewish kvetch harbors a subversive undercurrent, manifested though a sophisticated linguistic practice that also derives from traditional Judaism. This is a legacy of the Talmud, which is structured around argument and debate, infamous for what appear to be endless discussions and meandering digressions. The comical Jew exploits so-called Talmudic logic to achieve subversive ends, and this is why Jewish tricksters are adept at linguistic manipulation. Accordingly, the linguistic foundations of Judaic tradition can be a means of empowerment, a technique to escape the expected anguish of exile. This legacy of premodern normative Judaism found its way into modern Jewish humor. The impact of Talmudic discourse on Jewish comedy can best be seen on the hit television series *Seinfeld*, a show seemingly about nothing, but one in which "the excruciating minutia of every single daily event" is dissected through painstaking deliberation.[11]

The two million east European Jews who came to America between 1880 and 1920 brought their humor with them. However, their comedy evolved on a slightly different trajectory on this side of the Atlantic, because of America's distinct social, political, and racial context. In Europe the Jews were marked as inveterate outsiders, Christ killers, and commercial exploiters, stereotypes that medieval Christendom had bequeathed to the modern world. But in America the status of the Jews was ambiguous. On the one hand, they carried their Old World legacy of religious heresy in an overwhelmingly white Christian country. On the other hand, America has historically been defined as a nation of immigrants, a land of promise for outsiders to prosper in freedom. The American Jew did not have to surmount ghetto walls and centuries of legal exclusion—the common lot of his European ancestors and his new African American neighbors. Jewish identity in America, particularly in the post–World War II era, has reflected this duality: an unprecedented sense of inclusion and confidence but one that is tinged by a historical consciousness of persecution and exile. American Jews were now securely positioned to express their Jewishness in public, but the enduring memory of alienation and suffering has tempted Jewish comics to use humor to subvert the dominant values of white Christian America.[12] As a fictional Jewish satirist in one of Michael Wex's novels puts it, "Every time a Jew is born, the rest of the world gets a headache. Most of us do it inadvertently; the difference between me and the rest of the Jews is that I want to cause headaches on purpose."[13] A ticket of admission to the Anglo-American public sphere proved to be a license for ironic rebellion and a demand for restitution. The Jews were cashing in on centuries of victimhood through the vehicle of comedy.

Mordecai Richler falls squarely into this tradition; his characters deliberately cause headaches. Much like Roth's and Allen's Jews, they exude a sense of alienation rooted in a collective memory of inherited Jewish persecution, and they take great pleasure in expressing it in public. "Are you, ah, Jewish?" asked the prosecutor to a witness on the stand in *St. Urbain's Horseman*, when he was brought a New Testament to take the oath. "For purposes of census, taxation, and pogroms . . . I am a Jew," he replied in a swelling voice.[14] Similarly, when Barney Panovsky was tried for a murder he did not commit in rural Catholic Quebec and took one look at the jury, made up of "local yokels, pig farmers . . . a mortician . . . [and] a snow-plough operator," he knew he was "going to be hanged," especially once his friend Irv Nussbaum, wearing a yarmulke, testified that Barney was "a pillar of the community . . . who had done more than his share for the Israel Bond drive."[15] "Sliding into a sweat," Barney grieves,

I felt I was now destined to join a long line of Jewish martyrs. Captain Dreyfus, languishing on Devil's Island for years before he was not adjudged innocent, yet accepted a pardon. Menahem Mendel Beilis, victim of a blood libel in Kiev in 1911. Accused by the Black Hundreds of the ritual murder of a twelve-year-old Christian boy, he endured two years in prison before he was acquitted. Leo Max Frank, son of a wealthy Jewish merchant, charged with the murder of a fourteen-year-old girl, tried and convicted, and lynched by a mob in Georgia in 1915. I passed the time making mental notes for my address to the court before I was to be sentenced.

"I did not poison your wells," it began, "and neither did I murder your babes in quest of blood for my Passover matzohs. If you prick Panofsky, does he not bleed?"[16]

Richler's characters' intrinsic sense of persecution, seeing antisemitism everywhere as the imagined source of their misery, is a generational phenomenon; most of Richler's characters—like Roth's and Allen's—were born in the 1930s and, despite coming of age in the New World, inherited their grandparents' memories of Cossacks, pogroms, and blood libel. For the Jews of Newark in Philip Roth's alternative historical novel *The Plot Against America*, the United States' drift into xenophobic politics on the eve of World War II "had activated an atavistic sense of being undefended that had more to do with Kishinev and the pogroms of 1903 than with New Jersey thirty-seven years later."[17] Similarly, albeit with a touch of irony, the principal character in *St. Urbain's Horseman* is disaffected by the Christmas tree his Gentile wife places in their living room, fulminating that "his forebears hadn't fled the shtetl, surviving the Czar, so that the windows of the second generation should glitter on Christmas Eve like those of the Black Hundreds of accursed memory."[18] Much like the American Jews of their generation, Richler's Canadian Jews continued to be haunted by this past, even after attaining socioeconomic mobility, unprecedented financial success, and, to a certain extent, entry into Gentile society.[19]

But Richler's characters are not doctors, lawyers, and accountants; they are hardly purveyors of respectable commerce. Consider Duddy Kravitz, a wheeler-dealer who achieves his first breakthrough at the age of nineteen after producing a rather questionable bar mitzvah video for wealthy Montreal Jews, featuring a montage of the boy's haftorah reading, with a close-up of a bris and some rather graphic African tribal rituals. Or consider the Gurskys, who made their fortunes as bootleggers and hardly became upstanding businessmen in later years. Or consider Barney Panovsky, who, after working as a middleman exporting goods of dubious origins, became a self-proclaimed "sinner," a producer of Canadian cultural schlock: third-rate films and a junk Royal Canadian Mounted Police (RCMP) TV show, "which," as he puts it, "is big on bonking scenes in canoes and igloos."[20] They are all unabashedly proud of their socioeconomic mobility despite a lack of education and their anti-intellectualism, as evidenced by Barney's high school diploma, ostentatiously framed and hanging on the wall of his office, headquarters of his company, aptly named Totally Unnecessary Productions.

To be sure, Richler's Jews of the so-called Silent Generation[21] are hardly Isaac Babel's Benya Krik, and they did not join a regiment of Cossacks during a bloody civil war to pillage and plunder. They are not murderers or violent thugs; their wheeling, dealing, and chiseling certainly skirt close to the edge of criminality and intermittently cross into it. But criminality and thuggery are their inheritance; it is in their *yichus*, and it profoundly shapes their outlook.[22] Duddy Kravitz's father is a cab driver, but he pimps on the side; Jacob Hirsch is obsessed with his older cousin Joseph, known as "St. Urbain's Horseman," an alleged Montreal mobster who fought in the Spanish Civil War, made *aliyah* in 1948 to fight Arabs, and then went to the jungles of South America to hunt down Josef Mengele. Jake prizes the possession of his cousin's journal, which, quoting Babel's play *Sunset*, states that a Jew who gets up on a horse stops being a Jew.[23]

Joshua Shapiro's father, a former minor league boxer named Reuben, always put down "bill collector" as his occupation on official forms and would never answer the door when a stranger rang, instead sending his wife or child, "hanging back himself, a length of lead pipe in his curled fist."[24] Indeed, to the anguish of Joshua's mother's wealthy Jewish family, who lived in Montreal's opulent Outremont neighborhood, Reuben came from "a family of thugs out of Odessa,"[25] and his own grandfather worked as a "crippler back in Russia."[26] "If you didn't want to serve in the Czar's army," Reuben explained to his son, "he would put one of your balls on an anvil and smash it. Or shoot a toe off for you. Or maybe just puncture an ear drum. It was good work, but seasonal."[27] Joshua's mother took to her husband's cultural milieu. Instead of throwing a traditional bar mitzvah for Joshua, she had a slumber party, where Joshua's classmates were treated to Mrs. Shapiro performing an elaborate striptease down to her panties, belt, and stockings. Attentive to the guests, she concluded by asking: "Now I want everybody who got a hard-on watching my act to be a good boy and put up his hand."[28]

Conversely, we have Barney's father, Izzy Panovsky, who was not a gangster; rather, he was a police officer, hardly a typical Jewish profession in the first half of the twentieth century. But he was a thug who took pleasure in horrifying respectable Jews with tales of how he used to extract confessions from suspects in the good old days. "We'd arrest a guy, we'd take him downstairs to open him up, if you know what I mean?" Izzy explains matter-of-factly to his son's future in-laws, "They don't want to talk, you take them down below."[29] And much like the sagas of old Odessa, Izzy's tales of violence contain an unabashed undercurrent of Jewish vengeance. "Let me give you another for instance," Izzy continues:

> In 1951 this was, I found those bearded rabbinical students were being beaten up outside their school on Park Avenue by all those punks. Just because they were Jews. . . . Anyways their leader, this Hungarian roughneck, just off the boat, was caught, and I drove him to Station 17 to have a look at him. He's got those boots on, you know those big boots, rough as hell, I shut the door. What's your name, I says? I don't care about anybody, he says in that accent they have. His English is terrible. So I slammed him good, mister. Down he goes. He passes out. Jesus Christ. I thought he would die. I tried to give him first aid. You know what passed through my mind? Just imagine . . . JEW POLICE OFFICER KILLS . . . if the guy died. So I rushed up an ambulance and we get him to come to.[30]

Izzy proudly defied Jewish stereotype until the end of his life, dying of a heart attack in a brothel right after ejaculating.

Finally, we have the patriarch of the Gursky clan, Ephraim, a forger of documents proficient in Latin, Russian, Hebrew, and Yiddish and an escaped convict from London's Newgate prison who was later exiled to Van Diemen's Land and somehow eventually made his way to Canada, surviving aboard the lost Franklin expedition of 1845, of which there were allegedly no survivors. Where Reuben Shapiro and Izzy Panovsky echo Babel's gangsters, Ephraim Gursky exudes more than a trace of Ostap Bender, the celebrated rogue from Soviet literature—created by the Odessan satirists Il'ia Il'f and Evgenii Petrov—who swindles his way across the USSR through elaborate scams, subterfuge, and impersonation.[31]

Richler's brazen knaves seem to be at odds with the dominant stereotypes of Canadians, who are imagined as an amicable, civilized, well-mannered, anti-militaristic people, especially when juxtaposed to Americans.[32] Richler and his characters repeatedly satirize Canada and its populace in such a manner. "The truth is Canada is a cloud-cuckoo-land," declares Barney Panovsky, "an insufferably rich country governed by idiots, its self-made problems offering comic relief to the ills of the real world out there, where famine and racial strife and vandals in office are the unhappy rule."[33] "The bulk of our undeniably vast domain remains uninhabitable," writes Richler in one of his many musings on Canadian identity, "and to this day most of us are snuggled within a hundred miles of the 49th parallel, intimidated by the punishingly cold tundra on one side and American pizzazz on the other."[34] "History, for us, was a spectator sport." No Spanish Armada, no revolution, "we even lacked an Alamo."[35] When Confederation was authorized in 1867 by the British House of Commons, the chamber was three-quarters empty; but as soon as it was passed, the House "filled up immediately for a debate on the dog tax bill."[36] Lack of historical memory and cultural capital compared to Canada's southern neighbor led to bouts of Canadian nationalism, which themselves often proved comical. In one of his memoirs, Richler describes once tangling with "one of the new nationalist zealots, a novelist-cum-publisher," who would not read any American novels on principle, "because they were all contaminating."[37]

But Barney Panovsky greeted the void of Canadian identity as an opportunity, which he used to sell his junk television production *McIver of the RCMP* to politicians at home and voyeuristic audiences abroad who delighted in Canadian stereotype:

> I did a quick change in the hypocrite's phone booth, slipping into my Captain Canada mode, and appeared before the committee. "We are defining Canada to Canadians," I told them. "We are this country's

memory, its soul, its hypostasis, the last defence against our being over-
whelmed by the egregious cultural imperialists to the south of us."[38]

Ephraim Gursky also understood Canada to be a landscape of opportunity
and, after surviving his disastrous Arctic shipwreck, founded a community
of seminomadic Inuit, whom he convinced to worship him, concocting
a rather inventive theology that ostensibly combined Judaism with Inuit
practices:

> Ephraim disappeared into his igloo and emerged again wearing his
> silk top hat and his talith. He sang: "Who knows One? I know One:
> One is God in Heaven and Earth. Who knows Two? I know Two: Two
> is the Tablets, One is God in Heaven and Earth." He rolled over in
> the snow, simulating convulsions, froth bubbling from his lips. Then
> he stood up, and at the rising of the moon he lifted his arms and
> the eclipse began. The astonished Eskimos cried out, falling to their
> knees, pleading with Ephraim not to become a raven and pluck out
> their eyes.[39]

Gursky even "bestowed on his followers a version of Yom Kippur," with
all the requisite Judaic prohibitions coupled with his personal deification,
"telling them that . . . from the time the sun went down, until it rose and
went down again, any of his flock who was thirteen years old or older was
not to fuck or eat any food, but instead must pray to him for forgiveness
of his sins."[40] Disaster occasionally struck, however, such as the time a
group of his followers who "wandered too far north in search of seal in
October . . . [discovered once] the sun went down they were obliged to
remain celibate and fast until it rose once more several months later,
not sinking below the horizon again for many more months."[41] But this
would-be tribe of Arctic Israelites persisted, and Efraim remained their
deity even after he had vanished, as evidenced by fragmentary reports
from missionaries about natives chanting in Hebrew or by the fact that
when the federal government forced the Inuit to take surnames in the
1960s, not all of them opted for "Anglalik or Pekoyak," choosing instead
"Gor-ski, Girskee" and some other unexpected monikers of Polish origin.[42]

The emptiness of the tundra made Canada a land of opportunity for
Jews on the make, much as the frontier town ethos of old Odessa enabled

the dissolute behavior of the city's Jewish rogues. But there is far more than the improbable Jew on the frontier, an inverted fish out of water, to understanding Richler's Odessa connection. The missing ingredient is the city of Montreal, especially from the perspective of Richler's generation.

Richler grew up on St. Urbain Street, which "used to be the heart of Montreal's swirling Jewish quarter."[43] It was an era when Montreal was a wide-open city, replete with casinos and bordellos that were technically illegal but flourished, even following the raids by a corrupt police force, who after being paid off would padlock the bathroom rather than the front door to show they'd done their job.[44] Much like New York, the archetypal immigrant metropolis of the time, Montreal radiated a freewheeling yet deceptive cosmopolitanism. "It was," writes Richler, "a sequence of alienated self-contained tribal bastions—French, WASP, Jewish, enriched in recent years by settlements of Italians, Greeks, Portuguese, and Haitians. Growing up, I was nourished and to some extent misled in a warm world that was just about entirely Jewish, and enjoined to be suspicious of those who weren't."[45]

The insularity of Montreal Jewry was not merely shaped by rival ethnic groups in an immigrant sea each claiming its turf, defined against the nation's WASP heartland, as one might describe New York of that era. It was an island of diversity, but one engulfed in a sea of French Quebecois homogeneity, a cultural community of resentment that itself was a minority island in a much larger sea of Canadian Anglophone hegemony. Montreal Jews were long denied entry into the WASP establishment, which was replete with antisemitism, yet Quebec's French nationalists—who were no less antisemitic—saw the Jews as agents of Anglophone Canada, upstarts and colonialists, intent on decimating Quebecois culture from within.[46] "In the Quebec of that era," writes Ira Robinson, "overtly anti-Jewish manifestations seemed to proliferate, and there was a widespread perception that antisemitism in Quebec was worse than the rest of Canada."[47] According to Morton Weinfeld, "anti-Semitism was and is no stranger to anglophone Quebec, yet it differed from the French variety."[48] "The former," Weinfeld maintains, "represented the snobbish elitism of the economically powerful—it was for the most part 'polite' anti-Semitism; the latter was more populist in nature, reflecting the resentment of the economically disadvantaged, with more physicality and potential for violence—the anti-Semitism of the mob."[49]

Richler's Joshua Shapiro may have married into a Montreal WASP family, but they viewed him as an interloper: "A tall, loping, bushy-haired stranger, obviously street-wise; a lean, middle-aged hawk with a hooked nose, a pockmarked face, who, practicing God knows what necromancy in depraved Europe years ago, had seduced their [daughter nicknamed] Trout and might yet poison the wells or abscond with one of their babes, its blood required for his Passover rituals. Beware."[50] And the French were worse. "I was brought up in a Quebec," writes Richler in one of his memoirs, "that was reactionary, church-ridden, and notoriously—corrupt—a stagnant backwater—its *chef* for most of that time, Premier Maurice Duplessis, a political thug—and even its intellectuals sickeningly anti-Semitic for the most part."[51] Signs worded with "A bas les Juifs [Down with the Jews]" littered the highway to St. Agathe, a popular destination outside Montreal, where the English and French each had their resorts from which Jews were excluded.[52]

The rise of Quebec separatism in the 1960s and the explosion of linguistic nationalism only made matters worse. "Jews who have been Quebecers for generations," writes Richler, "understand only too well that when thousands of flag-waving nationalists march through the streets roaring 'Le Quebec aux Quebecois!' they do not have in mind anybody named Ginsburg."[53] For Richler, the meaning was abundantly clear, which is why, when giving a speech in Trier, Germany, he audaciously stated that in their envisioned independent Quebec, "there would obviously be only *ein Volk, eine Kultur.*"[54]

Much like his American counterparts, Richler saturates his writings with humor about antisemitism and the Holocaust. Hence Barney Panovsky imagining himself during his trial to be the next Jew who will have suffered martyrdom in the tradition of Alfred Dreyfus, Mendel Beilis, and Leo Frank. Hence Jacob Hirsch's obsession with his cousin the Horseman, who was himself reputedly obsessed with hunting down Josef Mengele. And hence Joshua Shapiro's decision to have a little fun with a visiting German industrialist at a WASPy party, where Joshua tells him about his latest business idea: "Tattoo credit cards. . . . Think of what you could do to cut down overhead if you were to tattoo the serial number on a client's arm. . . . Of course," an impish Joshua continued, "it would be necessary to test such an idea in the field. Germany, I think, would be ideal. You already have so many of the required technicians."[55]

It was in this spirit of sticking it to the proverbial goyim that Joshua and his Jewish friends created a memorial society dedicated to Canada's World War II–era prime minister, Mackenzie King, who not only prohibited Jewish refugees from entering Canada but met Hitler in 1938 and referred to him as a great man.[56] Once a year the memorial society would get together at King's former estate, now open to the public, have a champaign breakfast, and then proceed to the gravesite of King's beloved dog, where Joshua and friends would drunkenly sing "Safe in the Arms of Jesus"—but they would sing it entirely in Yiddish.[57]

Whereas the memory of antisemitism is an opportunity for mockery, its persistence provides Richler's scheming characters with an opening to exploit the fears of the Jewish community. Barney's friend Irv Nussbaum, a macher with the local branch of the United Jewish Appeal, was ecstatic anytime antisemitism loomed: "Seen this morning's *Gazette*? Terrific news. Big-time drug lawyer was shot dead in his Jaguar, outside his mansion on Sunnyside last night, and it's splashed all over the front page. He's Jewish, thank God. Name's Larry Bercovitch. Today's going to be a hummer. I'm sitting here going through my pledge cards."[58] "Seen this morning's *Gazette*?" exulted Nussbaum again on another occasion. "Some guys shat on the front steps of the B'nai Jacob synagogue. My phone's been ringing all day. Terrific, eh?"[59] And the burgeoning of Quebec nationalism merely heightened these anxieties.[60] Nussbaum was elated when opinion polls showed the separatists headed for a victory in the looming 1995 referendum—"there are bound to be more anti-Semitic incidents any day now. I feel it in my bones. Terrific!"[61] "I even hope their fucken Parti Québécois wins the referendum this time and scares the hell out of the Jews who still remain here," insists Nussbaum. "Only I want them going to Tel Aviv, Haifa, or Jerusalem this time."[62]

The tenacity of antisemitism in Quebec, coupled with the ubiquity of Zionism and Israel in twentieth-century Jewish politics, raises a perplexing question: Why did Richler not regard Zionism as the solution to the Jewish question? Why did his characters, who see their lives through the prism of Jewish persecution and fantasize about Jewish power, not make *aliyah*? Odessa had in fact served as a principal site for the gestation of Zionism before the Russian Revolution, with activists like Ze'ev Jabotinsky and Abraham T'homi embracing the negation of the diaspora through physical strength and violence. That they also expressed an admiration for the Jewish gangsters who served as prototypes for Isaac Babel's characters further suggests an important link between Odessa, Jewish rebellion, and Mordecai Richler.[63]

Richler did in fact flirt with Zionism as a youngster, joining Montreal's branch of Habonim, a Zionist youth group, shortly after his bar mitzvah in the mid-1940s.[64] And although he initially signed up in order to escape his strictly Orthodox household, so he could belt out "a song in praise of toil, the lyrics by Chaim Nachman Bialik," instead of reciting the hamotzi before every meal,[65] he was converted into "a zealot for Zion"[66] and envisioned making *aliyah* after college. "Meanwhile," Richler quips, "in the absence of Arab marauders, before retiring to our tent for the night I would climb the highest hill, searching for fishy-looking French Canadians."[67]

Richler never made *aliyah*, and few of his characters do either. Even Irv Nussbaum admits that "after all these years of fund-raising, and I must be personally responsible for at least fifty million squeezed out of here over the years, and I go over there and they tell me I'm a bad Jew because my children haven't settled there and don't serve on the front lines."[68] In this sense, Nussbaum's relationship with Israel mirrors Richler's, which he documents in his memoir, *This Year in Jerusalem*. Although Richler is taken with the place when he visits, he admits being "overcome by homesickness for my nearly empty, unspeakably rich, sinfully misgoverned country. I yearned for some Canadian homebrew farce rather than the daily death toll of Arab and Jew."[69]

Perhaps Richler thought Zionism's response to the Jewish question was too serious, lacking in the humor that fueled his writings even when he engaged with grave topics such as antisemitism and Jewish power. Quebec nationalism never engendered pogroms, just more comedic material, such as the province's notorious "language police" who combed Montreal searching out those who had the chutzpah to violate Bills 101 and 178, which severely constrained the public use of any language other than French in education, advertising, and signage. "There are actually grown men out here, officers of the Commission de Protection de la Langue Française, who go out with tape measures every day to ensure that the English-language lettering on outdoor commercial signs is half the size of, and in no brighter colour, than the French," indignantly states Barney's eldest son on a visit back to Montreal after living abroad.[70] The police were always on the prowl for violators. On one occasion, Richler recounts, they seized fifteen thousand Dunkin' Donuts bags because they were not bilingual.[71] On another occasion, a major scandal broke out in the Jewish community when the language inspector discovered unilingual-labeled matzoh boxes in a kosher grocery store and ordered them removed from the shelves.[72] But the government faced a major backlash, according to Barney's son in the novel's afterword: "The Jewish community was offered special dispensation: unilingually labeled Matzoh boxes were declared legal for sixty days of the year."[73] Even Nussbaum found humor in an incident that would normally propel him to ring the doorbells of frightened Jews: "Listen here," he said, "marijuana, cocaine, and heroin are banned here all year round, but, come Pesach, Jewish druggies are now a special case. Sixty days of the year we can munch matzohs without drawing the blinds or locking the doors."[74]

Nussbaum's likening of matzoh to drugs and his passing reference to Jews drawing their blinds and locking their doors are allusions to blood libel, to the collective memory of Christian violence against Jews that often occurred when the latter were accused of using Christian blood in Passover matzoh for ritual purposes. Blood libel jokes appear in at least three of Richler's novels, most graphically in *Solomon Gursky Was Here*, when Sir Hyman Kaplansky, a British Jewish notable of uncertain foreign origins whose true identity was likely that of one of the mysteriously vanished Gursky grandchildren, hosts a Passover seder for his upper-crust Gentile friends. Chaos ensues when the visiting lords and ladies are enjoined to eat "the bread of affliction" and "a thick reddish substance" bursts from the otherwise bland-looking matzoh. "We're all covered in ritual blood!" shrieked one of the guests before the practical joke became evident, thereby suggesting that well into the twentieth century the medieval charge of Jewish ritual murder persisted in popular consciousness even if it no longer incited deadly consequences.[75]

The legacy of antisemitism is fodder for Richler's comedy, much as it is for Lenny Bruce, Philip Roth, and Woody Allen, but for the Jews of Montreal trapped within a vice of exclusionary Quebecois nationalism it has greater immediacy, with the enduring collective memory of Old World violence provoking fantasies of vengeance but sprinkled with humor. It helps explain why Richler's characters look back to the thugs of Odessa as role models, as diasporic Jews who negated their exilic condition through brawn and brutishness, who used antisemitism as their justification for dipping their toes into the world of criminality.

Barney Panovsky and Joshua Shapiro may not exactly be Isaac Babel's gangsters, but they are their progeny, and they express admiration for their ancestors' response to antisemitism. Even a Zionist like Irv Nussbaum understood this, which is why he praised Barney as a wild Odessan Jew. But like most of Richler's Jews, they chose to remain in Montreal, their home in the diaspora, where they relished in expressing their Jewish indignation in a public sphere that had granted them unprecedented mobility yet retained a centuries-old mistrust of the proverbial Jew.

Richler's humor enjoins us to rethink what we mean by "Ashkenazi Jewish humor." The standard narrative takes us from the shtetl to the United States, from Sholem Aleichem through Woody Allen to Larry David. Given the mass exodus of European Jewry to America and the subsequent destruction of those left behind, this narrative is not surprising. If we were to quantify the production and dissemination of Ashkenazi humor in the second half of the twentieth century, New York and Hollywood would lead the way. This comedy expresses a Jewish identity transformed through American prosperity yet tinged by the collective memory of persecution and exile. But Mordechai Richler's Montreal is not identical to Woody Allen's New York, even though their connection is obvious: comedy built by descendants of Russian Jewish immigrants to the New World on the eve of World War I. Ashkenazi humor was not a monolith in Europe, nor is it on this side of the Atlantic, and it must be viewed through a more expansive lens. Richler's work globalizes post–World War II Ashkenazi Jewish humor.

Notes

1 Mordecai Richler, *Barney's Version* (New York: Washington Square Press), 351.

2 On Odessa, see Jarrod Tanny, *City of Rogues and Schnorrers: Russia's Jews and the Myth of Old Odessa* (Bloomington: Indiana University Press, 2011); Roshanna P. Sylvester, *Tales of Old Odessa: Crime and Civility in a*

City of Thieves (Dekalb: Northern Illinois University Press 2005); Charles King, *Odessa: Genius and Death in a City of Dreams* (New York: W. W. Norton), 2011.

3 On Odessan Jewish humor, see Tanny, *City of Rogues and Schnorrers*. On American Jewish comedy, see Lawrence J. Epstein, *The Haunted Smile: The Story of Jewish Comedians in America* (New York: PublicAffairs, 2001). Some of the themes in this chapter are touched upon by Michael Greenstein, "Mordecai Richler and Jewish-Canadian Humor," in *Jewish Wry: Essays on Jewish Humor*, ed. Sarah Blacher Cohen (Bloomington: Indiana University Press, 1987), 196–215. Greenstein, however, largely misses the Montreal angle, instead analyzing Richler's work through the larger Canadian prism. Greenstein argues that Richler is double alienated, once as a Jew in a sea of Canadian Gentiles and second as a Canadian engulfed a sea of American cultural hegemony. He mentions Isaac Babel only in passing.

4 Recent works on Jewish humor include Ruth R. Wisse, *No Joke: Making Jewish Humor* (Princeton: Princeton University Press, 2013); Jeremy Dauber, *Jewish Comedy: A Serious History* (New York: W. W. Norton, 2017); Jennifer Caplan, *Funny, You Don't Look Funny: Judaism and Humor from the Silent Generation to Millennials* (Detroit: Wayne State University Press, 2023).

5 Elliott Oring may have been the first to use the phrase "the people of the joke." See Elliott Oring, "The People of the Joke: On the Conceptualization of a Jewish Humor," *Western Folklore* 42, no. 4 (October 1983): 261–71.

6 See, for instance, David Gillota, *Ethnic Humor in Multiethnic America* (New Brunswick, NJ: Rutgers University Press), 2013.

7 See Epstein, *The Haunted Smile*; Stephen J. Whitfield, "Towards an Appreciation of American Jewish Humor," *Journal of Modern Jewish Studies* 4, no. 1 (March 2005): 33–48; Robert Cherry, *Why the Jews? How Jewish Values Transformed Twentieth Century American Pop Culture* (London: Rowman & Littlefield, 2021).

8 Sarah Blacher Cohen, "Introduction: The Varieties of Jewish Humor," in Sarah Blacher Cohen, *Jewish Wry*, 1.

9 Michael Wex, *Born to Kvetch: Yiddish Language and Culture in All Its Moods* (New York: St. Martin's Press, 2005), 6.

10 See, for instance, Martin Grotjahn, "Jewish Jokes and Their Relation to Masochism," in *A Celebration of Laughter*, ed. W. M. Mendel (Los Angeles: Mara Books, 1970); Theodor Reik, *Jewish Wit* (New York: Gamut Press, 1962). For a critique of this approach, see Dan Ben-Amos, "The 'Myth' of Jewish Humor," *Western Folklore* 32, no. 2 (April 1973): 112–31.

11 *Seinfeld*, "The Bizarro Jerry," October 3, 1996, NBC Network.

12 There is a rich historiography on the "whiteness" of non-Anglo-Saxon European immigrants in America—the Irish, the Jews, the Poles, the Italians, and others. On the Jews specifically, see Karen Brodkin, *How Jews Became White Folks and What That Says About Race in America* (New Brunswick, NJ: Rutgers University Press, 1998); Michael Rogin, *Blackface, White Noise: Jewish Immigrants in the Hollywood Melting Pot* (Berkeley: University of California Press, 1996); Eric Goldstein, *The Price of Whiteness: Jews, Race, and American Identity* (Princeton: Princeton University Press, 2008).

13 Michael Wex, *The Frumkiss Family Business: A Megilla in 14 Chapters* (Toronto: A.A. Knopf Canada, 2010), 1. Although Wex is Canadian, not American, he is not from Montreal and was not raised in Montreal's unique cultural context, which shaped Richler's comedy.

14 Mordecai Richler, *St. Urbain's Horseman* (Toronto: McClelland and Stewart Limited, 1985), 77.

15 Richler, *Barney's Version*, 315–20.

16 Richler, *Barney's Version*, 320–21.

17 Philip Roth, *The Plot Against America* (New York: Vintage Books, 2004), 18.

18 Richler, *St. Urbain's Horseman*, 286.

19 See, for instance, Robert J. Brym, William Shaffir, and Morton Weinfeld, eds., *The Jews in Canada* (Don Mills, ON: Oxford University Press Canada, 2010).

20 Richler, *Barney's Version*, 6.

21 On Jewish humor and the Silent Generation, see Caplan, *Funny, You Don't Look Funny*, chaps. 1–2.

22 Babel comes up frequently in Richler's novels, most notably in *St. Urbain's Horseman*, much as Richler himself had a strong interest, bordering on obsession, with Isaac Babel, as his biographers have documented. See Reinhold Kramer, *Mordecai Richler: Leaving St. Urbain*

(Montreal: McGill-Kingston, 2008), and Charles Foran, *Mordecai: The Life and Times* (Toronto: Vintage Canada Edition, 2011). In 1963, Richler adapted Babel's play *Sunset* for television. It was aired in the United Kingdom on the BBC, but CBC, Canada's principal network, showed little interest. Foran, *Mordecai*, 305–7.

23 Richler, *St. Urbain's Horseman*, 34.

24 Mordecai Richler, *Joshua Then and Now* (New York: Bantam Books), 8.

25 Richler, *Joshua Then and Now*, 9.

26 Richler, *Joshua Then and Now*, 290.

27 Richler, *Joshua Then and Now*, 290.

28 Richler, *Joshua Then and Now*, 148.

29 Richler, *Barney's Version*, 170–71.

30 Richler, *Barney's Version*, 170–71.

31 Il'ia Il'f and Yevgenii Petrov, *The Complete Adventures of Ostap Bender*, translated by John H. C. Richardson (New York: Random House, 1961). For an analysis of Ostap Bender, see Tanny, *City of Rogues and Schnorrers*, chap. 3.

32 On Canadian national identity, see Daniel Francis, *National Dreams: Myth, Memory, and Canadian History* (Vancouver: Arsenal Pulp Press, 1997).

33 Richler, *Barney's Version*, 329–30.

34 Mordecai Richler, *Oh Canada! Oh Quebec! Requiem for a Divided Country* (Toronto: Penguin Books, 1992), 10.

35 Mordecai Richler, *Home Sweet Home: My Canadian Album* (New York: Alfred A. Knopf, 1984), 142.

36 Richler, *Oh Canada!*, 10.

37 Richler, *Home Sweet Home*, 144.

38 Richler, *Barney's Version*, 6.

39 Mordecai Richler, *Solomon Gursky Was Here* (New York: Penguin Books, 1989), 327.

40 Richler, *Solomon Gursky Was Here*, 328.

41 Richler, *Solomon Gursky Was Here*, 328.

42 Richler, *Solomon Gursky Was Here*, 47.

43 Richler, *Home Sweet Home*, 107.

44 Richler, *Oh Canada!*, 2.

45 Mordecai Richler, *This Year in Jerusalem* (New York: Alfred A. Knopf, 1994), 41.

46 See Ira Robinson, *A History of Antisemitism in Canada* (Waterloo, ON: Wilfred Laurier Press, 2015); Gerald Tulchinsky, "The Contours of Canadian Jewish History," in Brym, Shaffir, and Weinfeld, *The Jews in Canada*, 5–21; Pierre Anctil, *A Reluctant Welcome for the Jewish People: Voices in Le Devoir's Editorials, 1910–1947* (Ottawa: University of Ottawa Press, 2019).

47 Robinson, *A History of Antisemitism*, 76.

48 Morton Weinfeld, "The Jews of Quebec: An Overview," in Brym, Shaffir, and Weinfeld, *The Jews in Canada*, 185.

49 Weinfeld, "The Jews of Quebec," 185.

50 Richler, *Joshua Then and Now*, 25.

51 Richler, *Oh Canada!*, 78.

52 Richler, *Home Sweet Home*, 37.

53 Richler, *Oh Canada!*, 77.

54 Mordecai Richler, *Belling the Cat: Essays, Reports, and Opinions* (Toronto: Alfred A. Knopf Canada, 1998), 122.

55 Richler, *Joshua Then and Now*, 28.

56 Richler, *Joshua Then and Now*, 137. On King and Hitler, see Robinson, *A History of Antisemitism*, 94–95.

57 Richler, *Joshua Then and Now*, 137–39.

58 Richler, *Barney's Version*, 22.

59 Richler, *Barney's Version*, 165.

60 On Quebec nationalism and the Jews in the 1980s and 1990s, see Robinson, *A History of Antisemitism*, 121–23.

61 Richler, *Barney's Version*, 140.

62 Richler, *Barney's Version*, 174.

63 See, for instance, Vladimir (Ze'ev) Jabotinsky, *Povest' moikh dnei* (Tel-Aviv: Biblioteka-Aliia, 1985); Abraham T'homi, *Between Darkness and Dawn: A Saga of the Hehalutz* (New York: Bloch Publishing, 1986).

64 Richler, *This Year in Jerusalem*, 4.

65 Richler, *This Year in Jerusalem*, 21.

66 Richler, *This Year in Jerusalem*, 32.

67 Richler, *This Year in Jerusalem*, 21–22.

68 Richler, *Barney's Version*, 174.

69 Richler, *This Year in Jerusalem*, 236.

70 Richler, *Barney's Version*, 352.

71 Richler, *Home Sweet Home*, 232.

72 "French Canadian Government Backs Off Matzah Ban," *Jewish News of Northern California*, April 19, 1996, accessed March 19, 2023, https://jweekly.com/1996/04/19/french-canadian-government-backs-off-matzah-ban/.

73 Richler, *Barney's Version*, 352.

74 Richler, *Barney's Version*, 353.

75 Richler, *Solomon Gursky Was Here*, 374–78.

Selected Bibliography

Anctil, Pierre. *A Reluctant Welcome for the Jewish People: Voices in Le Devoir's Editorials, 1910–1947*. Ottawa: University of Ottawa Press, 2019.

Ben-Amos, Dan. "The 'Myth' of Jewish Humor." *Western Folklore* 32, no. 2 (April 1973): 112–131.

Brym, Robert J., William Shaffir, and Morton Weinfeld, eds. *The Jews in Canada*. Don Mills, ON: Oxford University Press Canada, 2010.

Caplan, Jennifer. *Funny, You Don't Look Funny: Judaism and Humor from the Silent Generation to Millennials*. Detroit: Wayne State University Press, 2023.

Cherry, Robert. *Why the Jews? How Jewish Values Transformed Twentieth Century American Pop Culture*. London: Rowman & Littlefield, 2021.

Cohen, Sarah Blacher, ed. *Jewish Wry: Essays on Jewish Humor*. Bloomington: Indiana University Press, 1987.

Francis, Daniel. *National Dreams: Myth, Memory, and Canadian History*. Vancouver: Arsenal Pulp Press, 1997.

Oring, Elliot. "The People of the Joke: On the Conceptualization of a Jewish Humor." *Western Folklore* 42, no. 4 (October 1983): 261–71.

Richler, Mordecai. *The Apprenticeship of Duddy Kravitz*. Toronto: Emblem Editions, 2001. Kindle edition.

Richler, Mordecai. *Barney's Version*. New York: Washington Square Press, 1997.

Richler, Mordecai. *Belling the Cat: Essays, Reports, and Opinions*. Toronto: Alfred A. Knopf Canada, 1998.

Richler, Mordecai. *Home Sweet Home: My Canadian Album*. New York: Alfred A. Knopf, 1984.

Richler, Mordecai. *Joshua Then and Now*. Toronto: McClelland & Stewart, 1980. Kindle edition.

Richler, Mordecai. *Oh Canada! Oh Quebec! Requiem for a Divided Country*. Toronto: Penguin Books, 1992.

Richler, Mordecai. *Solomon Gursky Was Here*. Toronto: Penguin Group, 2005. Kindle edition.

Richler, Mordecai. *St. Urbain's Horseman*. Toronto: McClelland & Stewart, 1971. Kindle edition.

Richler, Mordecai. *This Year in Jerusalem*. New York: Alfred A. Knopf, 1994.

Robinson, Ira. *A History of Antisemitism in Canada*. Waterloo: Wilfred Laurier Press, 2015.

Roth, Philip. *The Plot Against America*. New York: Vintage Books, 2004.

Seinfeld. "The Bizarro Jerry," October 3, 1996. NBC Network.

Tanny, Jarrod. *City of Rogues and Schnorrers: Russia's Jews and the Myth of Old Odessa*. Bloomington: Indiana University Press, 2011.

Wex, Michael. *Born to Kvetch: Yiddish Language and Culture in All Its Moods*. New York: St. Martin's Press, 2005.

Wex, Michael. *The Frumkiss Family Business: A Megilla in 14 Chapters*. Toronto: A. A. Knopf Canada, 2010.

7

PARODY AS PASTICHE, PASTICHE AS PARODY

The Global Jewish Humor Cabal or the Cancellation of a Holocaust Joke in Japan

Jonathan A. Abel

In the age of globalization, we are told that the homogenization of ethnicity renders culture "odorless."[1] This is true not simply for cookie-cutter machine-made products and watered-down ethnic foods sold in the global marketplace but also for the creative arts more broadly. On the other hand, for cultural products whether global cinema, world literature, or ethnic culture to be successful, they need specific reference to historical and cultural details for a flavor of authenticity. Such details are necessary even as "reality effects" essentially emptied of deeper meaning, imbued only with structural difference qua difference, in other words, by simply embodying the category of otherness.[2] Indeed, the fact that bagels, chopped liver, or gefilte fish had become the grist (stand-ins for Jewish American identity) for a globalized Jewish humor is itself a token of conforming to global norms and genre conventions regarding ethnic culture. Likewise, where ethnic jokes may have once long ago hinged on such unique foods of a particular place and people, the odd-sounding proper names of minority characters, or the putative physical differences (often of appendages) of these others, these supposed vestigial signs of ethnic and racial difference have been systematically downplayed, removed, and cancelled out of the globalized humor that trades on the open market today. This loss of specific detail is why by the turn of the millennium, the kitschy *Seinfeld* television show (largely devoid of direct reference to Jewishness and yet somehow all about the Jews or displaying at least what Jarrod Tanny calls "implicit

Jewishness") had become both the end of Jewish humor and its globalized essence.[3] In short, when local culture travels, it is stripped of its particular essence, except for the minimum required hint necessary to conjure the local flair, itself a market-determined global necessity—especially in globally televised venues like the opening ceremony of the Olympics.

To understand the nuances of the cultural paradigm shift to a globalist humor, it is helpful to recall Frederic Jameson's distinction between parody and pastiche in global aesthetics: "Pastiche is, like parody, the imitation of a peculiar or unique style, the wearing of a stylistic mask, speech in a dead language. . . . Pastiche is blank parody, parody that has lost its sense of humor."[4] For Jameson, parody is making fun with a radical point, a political critique, whereas pastiche is an empty mimicry that has given up on the idea of comedy being transcendent, given up on the possibility of change. However, for Jameson, both parody and pastiche are imitations and "speech in a dead language," because, in spite of all of his description of the postmodern, Jameson forgets what the postmodern aesthetic perpetually reveals about cultural production—that there are no decisive origins and never have been. Jameson's explication of these kinds of mimetic reproductions of creative cultural production as dead presumes that there was a time when cultural productions spoke in a living language, as originals. But culture accrues through the grist of repetition and change in social behaviors over time. When we start to understand all cultural production as mere echoes of other products and times, we see this distinction fade. In contrast to Jameson, then, I would like to make the claim that parody is indeed alive, because its future orientation and radical possibilities are not tied to past relationships. Jameson's distinction between parody and pastiche can be usefully read to understand the recent scandal involving a Holocaust joke around the opening ceremony of the 2020 Olympics (about which more later), because it involves a shifting between a living ethnic parody with radical potential and global pastiche humor suited to the global networks of postmodern media content.

The new brand of global humor that emerges may indeed still be funny and may certainly appeal to more people; it may kill or slay, but it is not ethnic humor the way it has classically been imagined.[5] The time has long since come and gone when we could make tautological claims that Jewish humor is the humor of, by, and about Jews. Today, this may seem like an irrelevant point. But as recently as 2017, Jeremy Dauber's

384-page, five-thousand-year "serious history" of Jewish comedy makes just this laughable point. The book begins by setting two conditions for itself: "Jewish humor has to be produced by Jews" and "Jewish humor must have something to do with either contemporary Jewish living or historical Jewish existence."[6] On the contrary, this chapter argues that it is only in the liminal borderline cases (the cases of Jewish humor in absence or relative absence of Jews) that we can test the ontological viability of the subject—the form of Jewish humor. If Jewish humor is more than identity based (if it can outlive the Jews), then there is a there there. So there may be no better place to test the idea of Jewish humor than in a place where there are relatively few Jews—Japan.

Dauber seems to have an inkling of the gaping hole in his story when considering the whitewashing of Jewish humor by American Jews from Groucho through Jack Benny and Sid Caesar to Jerry Seinfeld, Larry Sanders, and Larry David. That is, Dauber acknowledges something structurally Jewish in jokes without reference to Judaism or Jewish culture. For him the sign of this is *Seinfeld*. He sees that there is still a trace of Jewish humor in characters like Elaine Benes and George Costanza despite what he sees as their surface Christianity. But he does not go far enough; jokes about Jews or Jewish subjects or the use of the structures of Jewish humor by non-Jews must clearly be considered part of Jewish humor. Of course, this opens up all manner of problems about reifying identity categorizations that can mean something different depending on the identity of the utterer of the joke. Since identity itself is a construct that transcends bloodlines, Jewish humor is a Möbius strip in which the in-group joke bleeds into the out-group and differing agendas blur into each other.[7] That is to say, Jewish humor may be a joke with at least two different kinds of laughter (laughing at and laughing with). In contrast to Dauber, I argue that this twentieth-century brand of American Jewish humor is the globalized pastiche form from Chaplin to Seinfeld that not only plays well with a *goyische* audience at home in the United States but also has a global tendency to travel well, such as on film or on the global stage of the Olympics.

Sketch

These questions were all part of the media frenzy around the swift removal of comedian Kobayashi Kentaro as director of the opening ceremony of the 2020 Tokyo Olympics (delayed until 2021 because of the COVID-19 pandemic) in the run-up to the games when a video of a sketch on the Holocaust he did in the 1990s surfaced. The offending online video is short, excerpted from a compilation released on VHS in 1998.[8] As the famous comedy duo the Rahmens,[9] Kobayashi and his partner Katagiri Jin adopt the roles of the two main characters of the popular Japanese children's television show *Can You Do It?* (*Dekirukana*, 1967–90). In that show, Gonta-kun (a man with a silly hat and brightly colored pants, played by Imura Jun) and Noppo-san (an anthropomorphic gopher) encourage kids to do arts and crafts projects at home using readily available materials and to use their imagination to play make-believe games. The skit starts off as a fairly conventional spoof of the TV show with the comic duo playing Noppo and Gonta; it is a meta-scene in which the two characters discuss proposing new bits to Mr. Toda, the producer of their show for children. Kobayashi as Gonta starts by recounting that Mr. Toda has said that *teaching* kids to make things is all well and good but that learning things by *doing* is the best. Then he suggests a kind of DIY baseball: It would be fun to roll up a newspaper and write the word "bat" on it, crush up some paper and write the word "ball" on it, and finally, for the crowd filling the stands, use paper cut into the shape of people and write the word "people" on it. His partner Katagiri as Noppo then responds, "We have a lot of paper cut into the shape of people. From that time when we said let's play Holocaust." Audience laughs. Then Kobayashi delivers the punchline, saying in deadpan: "Oh yeah, Toda-san [the producer] was really angry about that." Bigger laugh.

The skit supposedly makes light of the Holocaust, except it is not that simple. Appearing during a section of the videotape itself titled "We can't forgive you" (*Mō yurusanai*), the skit itself already contextualizes the offending reference to the Holocaust by incorporating a line that codes its offense as offensive—"Toda-san was really angry." Thus, the skit acknowledges the taboo on which it plays, incorporating and anticipating the delayed social outrage the joke itself would receive when taken in a new context (that of the Olympics) decades later. Even within the frame

FIGURE 7.1. The 1998 VHS cover from which the offending video was extracted for circulation on social media in the summer of 2021 (*Neta de shō jiten raibu*, vol. 4 [Tokyo: Nihon Columbia, 1998]).

of the zany skit's make-believe world about fictional characters proposing a make-believe bit to a TV producer for their show, children's play around atrocity is wrong and inappropriate. We are laughing at the idiots who would propose such a thing. Though it is not stated, the two characters clearly had been imagining the players (make-believers) in the roles of the Nazis, because the analogue of the baseball stadium crowd is the mass of people in "the great massacre of Jews" (the literal translation of the Japanese phrase for Holocaust, *yudayahito tairyō zansatsu*). The audience is not laughing at Toda-san the producer for becoming angry at the imbeciles. We laugh at the idiocy of the idea that the two goofballs had—not that they were wily and managed to make a Holocaust joke but that they would have even tried and, indeed, gone so far as to make paper cutouts of people for the make-believe in the first place.[10] Here this sociopathic play is the butt of the joke. Clearly the audience is laughing in the form of the nervous laughter of the discomfort around, and indeed the absurdity of, a children's television show advocating "make-believe of the large-scale massacre of the Jews" (*yudayahito tairyō zansatsu-gokko*, or what I've more simply translated above as "play Holocaust"). So, this immediate context should have made it clear that the entire joke is premised on the fact that the Holocaust is *not* something to be made light of—indeed, making light of it is the source of ridicule within the joke.[11]

But, of course, the Jewish organizations that took offense at the video when it surfaced in 2021 were not simply the bad readers of humor, as censors often get categorized. Rather, it is simply that their logic *advocating for cancelling or firing* originates in an entirely different context. For there is at least another context in which they work—the long history of Japanese Holocaust denial. One need not go back to the late nineteenth-century Japanese fascination with Judaism or to the Japanese importation of the rhetoric of discrimination against Jews through translation and circulation of the *Protocols of Zion* as part of the modernization and Westernization of the country, the Japanese reception of Hitler's association of Jews and Japanese as alternative modes of being non-white in the world in his *Mein Kampf*, and the Japanese postwar alignment of Hiroshima and Nagasaki with Auschwitz to have a sense of Japanese Holocaust denialism.[12] Instead, we can simply look at a more contemporary media history and the scandal that certainly would have been on the minds of the Japanese audience when the Rahmens performed their skit in 1998 to have a sense of this context.

In the February 1995 issue of the popular human interest magazine *Marco Polo*, with a cover featuring an image of actress Inamori Izumi, the controversial doctor and writer Nishioka Masanori published a nine-page article titled "The Greatest Taboo of Postwar World History: There Were No Nazi 'Gas Chambers,'" which claimed that typhus (and not Zyklon B) was the cause of mass death at the concentration camps.[13] On sale beginning January 17 (the same day as the Kobe earthquake), the magazine publication was timed to coincide with the fiftieth anniversary of the liberation of Auschwitz. But the magazine would soon be shuttered by the publisher because of a boycott by major advertisers (Mitsubishi, Volkswagen, Cartier, and Philip Morris) who wanted to avoid association with the scandal. Here global conglomerates worked in alignment with the anti-antisemitic Simon Wiesenthal Center's call to boycott the publisher, but by cancelling the magazine, the publisher, Bungei Shunju, reacted in a way that exceeded the expectations of the Center and the boycotters, who seemed to be after a retraction and the publication of some factual articles correcting the fallacies. On the one hand, the shuttering of the magazine was deemed by the foreign press to be a "very Japanese" form of falling on the sword for the greater good. On the other hand, the closing of the magazine provided the means by which the publisher could reassign the staff to other magazines. And the editor of the shuttered magazine, Hanada Kazuyoshi, would go on to try a similar stunt years later when he was involved in "comfort woman" denialism.[14]

Though it should be noted that there were powerful voices in Japan decrying the popularity of Jewish conspiracy theories even prior to the *Marco Polo* incident,[15] media scholar Tom Brislin writes about the significance of the scandal: "The extreme action of killing off of a magazine left a lingering question: Did it communicate the need for more tolerance, diversity and education in Japanese publications, or did it send the offending messages of conspiracism underground, to replenish and sprout anew?"[16] Even at the time, the press wondered if the magazine, as a scapegoat, was being made a martyr for precisely these kinds of conspiracy theories to proliferate elsewhere, a new piece of "evidence" of so-called Jewish media control.

Olympic Gaffe: Marketing the Global Jewish Conspiracy of Laughs

So, it is in the context of internationalist pressures and local right-wing nationalism that the comedian Kobayashi was removed from his role as director of the opening ceremony of the 2020 Tokyo Olympics in the summer of 2021. If we can understand that the dismissal of Kobayashi was less about the humor of the skit and more about the fact of mentioning the Holocaust at all within the context of humor and within the broader context of Japanese Holocaust denialism at a time when—and in a job for which—internationalism, amity, and peace were to have been prized, it may also be helpful to see that Kobayashi was likely chosen for the role of director of the opening ceremony precisely because he was thought to have that kind of worldly or universal sense of humor.

This assimilationist humor or humor devoid of local/ethnic flare is characteristic not of the older studies of Jewish humor that place the butt of such humor in the fun-sounding, now nearly universal Yiddish of *schmuck* and *putz* or in plays of stereotypical Jewish foods (bagels), body shapes (big noses), and habits (yarmulke wearing), but rather of the more neutered form of global humor that has circulated since the dawn of silent film, with a close affinity to the vaudeville and burlesque featured on the Lower East Side only miles away from Thomas Alva Edison's first film studios. It is an "assimilationist model" of humor that purposely removes proper name reference to anything obviously Jewish in order to become "universally applicable";[17] it is the Jewish American tradition of humor from Chaplin (neither a Jew nor an American, but more on this later) through the Marx Brothers, Sid Caesar, (some) Woody Allen, and (some) Mel Brooks. This was the tradition of humor into which Kobayashi had been fitting himself in the intervening years between his Holocaust joke and its resurfacing amid the Olympics.

Clearly Kobayashi was chosen as the artistic director in the first place because, as we shall see, he had a knack for such internationalist humor that could transcend local Japanese audiences. Besides his success in the Rahmens duo and on late-night Japanese TV in the 1990s and early 2000s, he famously starred as the cool Mac guy in the Japanese version of the Mac-versus-PC "Get a Mac" global ad campaign in 2006–9. While in the US version John Hodgman's nerdy heavy-set man in a business suit representing a PC was pitted against Justin Long's jeans-wearing cool dude representing a Mac, in Japan the Rahmens duo took on the roles, with Katagiri as the PC doofus and Kobayashi as the Mac slick dude. For reasons that will become apparent, the structure of the humor in the Apple ad and Kobayashi's place within it are key elements for thinking about his transition from Japanese humorist to globalist/Jewish comedian.

FIGURE 7.2. The Rahmens as PC and Mac in the "Get a Mac" ad campaign.

We should start by noting that the humor of the Mac ad series displays the traditionally defined forms of humor theory—superiority, relief, and incongruity.[18] If we had to say which of the two characters is the stereotypical Jew, there would be no simple answer.[19] On one hand, the Jew as the wily smart aleck, to be sure, is a stereotype—think of Bugs Bunny's mimetic rival Groucho. On the other hand, so is the assimilating businessman—the scapegoated guy trying to fit in, the guy saying, "See, we are the same," but who is clearly not the same. And this is as true in Japan (where books about Jewish business secrets still sell like hot *anpan*) as it is elsewhere in the world.[20] However, Jews are neither abundant and commonplace like PCs nor stereotypically aesthetically pleasing like a Mac. So, we are caught with an undecidable.[21]

Perhaps the key to understanding how Kobayashi's place in the humor advertisement works would be to see how such undecidability is entwined with how Jewish humor had been globalized in the twentieth century. In that sense, it will help to think about the work of another non-Jewish global humorist from a different era to whom Kobayashi has been compared and who enjoyed particular fame in Japan—Charlie Chaplin. But rather than first considering Chaplin the man, his career, and his links to both Japan and Judaism, a look at a poster on Japanese subway public service "manners" (*manā posutā*) can offer particular help in understanding the structure of the Mac-versus-PC ad campaign and its function in Japan (see fig. 7.3). A sort of public service announcement against what we now call "manspreading," the poster was featured in the Tokyo Station Gallery from February through April 2017 as part of the exhibition titled "The Doubled Voices of Parody: In and Around Japan's 1970s," focusing on parody and satire in Japanese pop culture from that era.[22]

Why was this poster funny to a Japanese audience in the 1970s? How could a then-decades-old film seem like a topical or eye-grabbing image worthy of hanging in subway cars? Part of the answer lies in the fact that Chaplin's *The Great Dictator* (1940) was not a wartime release in Japan because of a ban on "Jewish" productions transferred from other Axis powers. But, also, it is crucial here to remember that a ban on the film did not mean it was not known in Japan during the war. As one of the first global film stars, by 1939 Chaplin had long been a major celebrity in Japan, having solidified his success on-screen there during his well-publicized junket to Japan promoting *City Lights* in 1932. So, reporting news of the

独占者

FIGURE 7.3. One particularly striking work of public subway art featured in the Tokyo Station Gallery was the "Seat Monopolizer" poster designed by Kawakita Hideya, which was hung in Eidan subways (now Tokyo Metro) in 1976.

latest Chaplin film (even though banned) in 1939 was par for the course. Despite the ban on the film itself, newspapers, for instance, carried stories of the production of the film and its critical portrayal of Hitler and Mussolini at the time of its production and release in the United States.[23] This secondhand information about the film only increased the Japanese filmgoing community's desire to see the film. So, more directly important to the reception of the poster at hand was the warm reception the film received when it was finally given its first nationwide release in Japan in the summer of 1960.[24] This history means that the poster that appeared in the Japanese subway in the mid-1970s was not a throwback to a film of an older generation but rather a reference to a film poster in the recent memory of most adults—and likely more adults had seen the film's poster in the previous decade than even had seen the film. But to see what this parody image can tell us about humor and the Holocaust, the Japanese and the Jews, we need to look beyond the film's historical reception to see how the poster's humor functions structurally.

The poster title in Japanese—simply *Dokusensha* 独占者 (the monopolist)—is a play on words with *Dokusaisha* 独裁者 (meaning simply "the dictator," which was the Japanese translation of the title of Chaplin's famed opus). This poster title is then given the English language gloss of "The Seat Monopolizer" as a parody of a film poster for the English title *The Great Dictator* (1940). And the parody continues even down to the placement of a Tokyo subway logo in the lower right corner, which from a distance looks like the approval stamp of Eirin (the Japanese Ethics Bureau, which puts its imprimatur on every film projected in the country).

The structural humor of the poster can be best read in relation to Kobayashi's series of Mac-versus-PC advertisements in the composition of the three Chaplins riding a subway car. The poster presents Chaplin as both his famed, nebbishy Little Tramp and the comically puffed-up dictator Adenoid Hynkel, a thin parody of Adolf Hitler. Chaplin's Tramp character (often depicted as a poor immigrant), of course, was often considered a Jew (most famously by the Nazis), and in the fictional world of the film *The Great Dictator*, the tramp-like barber and former war hero who looks like the dictator is a Jew. Of course, in reality Chaplin's Tramp character, complete with the toothbrush mustache, preceded Hitler, opening the place for Chaplin to claim that the real-world dictator had been aping his style all along.[25]

What this means for "The Seat Monopolizer" poster is that, oddly, like Woody Allen's Fielding Mellish in *Bananas*, the dictator becomes the Jew. So Jewish tramps are the salarymen, and the authoritarian dictator is the outsider Jew. The dictator becomes the space for the out of place and scorned. A bossy boor. One who thinks they can occupy spaces (not Sudetenlands, not even Palestines, but the smaller stakes of the next seat over). The squeaky wheel. Or, in Japanese parlance, the nail that sticks up. By contrast, normal tramp-like wimpy salaryman citizens are left to squirm and gaze askance with reprobation. These posters thus interpolate their viewers to sympathize not with the dictator but with the tramp-like everymen who are forced to endure such unwieldy and irregular bodies in their space. It is an appeal to heed public messaging, to not be troublesome (*meiwaku*), to march together as a bundle of sticks, a *fascio*—through a kind of social fascism, one that is patrolled through whisper campaigns for cultured and civilized behaviors, for doing what is best for the public good. And this is why the Japanese Mac-versus-PC ads were less successful in Japan: The cool guy is an outsider to the everyday businessman. In a sense, the Japanese have become the Jewy tramps (businessmen), those pushed off to the side, while the Nazi has become the Jew—he who must assimilate. But, of course, here those pushed off to the side are the mainstream everyday citizens and not outsiders.

This confusion or slipperiness between the Jew and the dictator perfectly illustrates the problem and structure of Jewish humor and humor around Jews as they exist in Japan (and perhaps the world). Jews are funnier than we Japanese. Their humor is a key to their success in adversity. We should read books about their humor to become better businessmen.[26] Their outsider status, which among other things made them moneylenders in societies that would not have moneylending natural-born citizens, enabled their financial success. Their downtrodden lives—their status as somehow outside Western modernity—mimic our (Japanese) own, or rather we mimic theirs. We too can be successful like the Jews. We too can be a Japan that says no to Western (Jewish) capitalist interests.[27] We can stand up and make posters that will get this boorish (read Jewish) behavior encroaching on our space to stop. But, also, we can laugh at the taboos around Jewishness because they are not here, because they are foreign here. This sort of rationale gets us closer to the role of humor with and about Jews in Japan as a context for the recent Olympics scandal.

Globalized Humor and the Empty Shell of Ethnic Identity

To understand how the globalist conspiracy of pastiche Jewish humor functioned for the Olympics scandal in Japan, we do well to dive deeper into the above example of Charlie Chaplin and his opus *The Great Dictator*. Could anyone other than the non-Jewish global star often mistaken for a Jew have played Adenoid Hynkel? Even though Mel Brooks seems to think a Jew would have done just fine, he paid homage to the role only decades after Chaplin. But in the late 1930s, in that moment of antisemitic ultranationalism and totalitarianism, were there any Jews who could do it? Groucho Marx's performance in *Duck Soup* (1933) presaged and perhaps enabled Chaplin's taking on the specific guise of Hitler, but Groucho didn't quite become the historical dictator; instead, he played at being a generic one—Rufus T. Firefly. *You Nazty Spy!* (1940) of the Three Stooges nearly coincided with Chaplin's opus but (because of limited American interest) was destined not to have the global reach of either the Marx Brothers or Chaplin. Ernst Lubisch's *To Be or Not To Be* (1942) closely followed Chaplin's effort. But to be the first to use the global limelight conferred by celebrity to satirize Hitler during his reign perhaps took this particular goy, the one who got famous on a funny walk and a toothbrush mustache (which the real-world dictator himself would emulate). Indeed, it was a risk even Chaplin said he would not have taken had he known the full extent of the devastation being wrought on Europe.[28] So, it may have been the fact that he was not Jewish that allowed him to take on the very role for which he becomes an honorary Jew. Contrary to Sarah Silverman's recent protests, sometimes we need an actor in Jewface.[29]

To refer to a hallowed group of global humanists, Isaac Deutscher used the phrase "non-Jewish Jews," those who were Jewish by ethnicity and "optimism" about the universality of being human, "the relativity of moral standards," "vulnerable," and "rootless" rather than by religion.[30] Here I'd like to offer a corollary identity—the Jewish non-Jew or the honorary Jew who is a Jew because of a commitment to the cause of a truly universalist, global humanism that transcends (religious, national, ideological, corporeal, etc.) identities, that is, a person who is totally Jewish but for body, ethnicity, and religion.[31] This is why Kate McDonough could call Chaplin a "Jew not Jew."[32] Like actors such as Rachel Brosnahan in *The Marvelous Mrs. Maisel*, John Turturro in *The Plot Against America*, Kathryn Hahn, Zachary Levi, Adam Driver, and Justin Long in more recent years, Chaplin is one of these first globally relevant Jewish non-Jews. Kobayashi is another.

According to the standard narrative, Chaplin played at being a Jew from almost his first appearance onstage. And Jews have loved him for it, because it is a role even Jews could no longer inhabit fully. Chaplin signified a post-identitarian human Jew, one who could be popular everywhere, who could suffer the same fates as all human beings like Shakespeare's Shylock. But unlike Shylock, who was stigmatized for the unreasonable demand of a pound of flesh, Chaplin's Tramp is largely remembered as devoid of scoundrel behavior. The Tramp was not a perpetrator but a victim of modern times, a misunderstood outsider, like a Jew but also crucially just like everyone else in modernity. And it is in this simultaneous outsider status combined paradoxically with its broad appeal (because no one feels at home in modernity) that Chaplin found his global celebrity.

The history of Chaplin's entanglements with Jewishness and Japan has long been part of the biographical details of his celebrity, though they are rarely linked or thought of as contributing toward the inception of the idea that would become *The Great Dictator*. Charlie Chaplin did not suddenly become Jewish when he played a Jewish barber in *The Great Dictator* but rather had flirted with the identity for a long time. Long before he had endeared himself to audiences in roles like the one he played in *The Immigrant* (1917) that mimicked the Jewish American (as well as the Italian American and Irish American) experience, Chaplin as a boy, uncertain of his father's identity, at times considered if his father might have been Jewish because he thought of his half brother as Jewish.[33] Chaplin played the role of a Jewish comedian in one of his earliest stage appearances.[34] Upon returning to his neighborhood in London after he made his fame in the United States, he referred to the dwellers there as "my brother Jews."[35] It may even have been as one biographer wrote that "when it moved him, Charlie forthrightly claimed to be part Jewish. Or when it moved him—not."[36]

Of course, actual Jews know that identity is not only that which one claims about oneself, but rather is also (many times discouragingly so) that which others claim about you.[37] Beyond these myriad self-identifications with the race, he was considered a Jew by others. The press regularly tried to establish an "allegedly 'real' name" and the location of his birth.[38] But perhaps the most significant consideration of Chaplin's identity came from the Third Reich itself. Chaplin's friend Ivor Montagu famously sent him a copy of Nazi ideologue Johann von Leers's 1933 *Juden Sehen Dich An* (Jews Are Looking at You), which called the film star "the little Jewish tumbler, as disgusting as he is boring."[39] And the Nazi propaganda film *Der Ewige Jude* (The Eternal Jew, 1940) featured footage of Chaplin with voiceover:[40]

> The Jew Charlie Chaplin was welcomed by an enraptured crowd when he visited Berlin. Then the German public acclaimed the newcomer Jew. A deadly enemy. How could this happen? The phony dogma of human equality . . . had tricked the healthy instinct of the nation.

No matter the fallaciousness of his inclusion in such documents, these long-standing and complex relations with the Jewish identity perhaps helped lay a foundation for Chaplin's eventual openness to creating a film like *The Great Dictator*.

As tenuous as the above assertion about artistic influence is (and it is one intimated through various biographies), Chaplin's relation to Japan was just as complex and just as likely to contribute to the conditions for making the film, and yet it rarely figures as potentially relevant.[41] Chaplin was extremely popular in Japan, and Japanese culture was an important curiosity for Chaplin. During the decade from Chaplin's *Dough and Dynamite* (1914) debut in June 1916 at the Asakusa Denkikan Theater through the run of his *Idle Class* (1921) in Tokyo in October 1926, there was never a period longer than six months in which some Chaplin film or other was not advertised as being projected somewhere in Tokyo, according to a review of *Asahi Shimbun* and *Yomiuri Shimbun* indexes. And even after the production and circulation of his films slowed in the late 1920s, hundreds of articles on the celebrity of Chaplin appeared in the popular film magazines of the day as well as in the more general interest magazines and the daily newspapers.[42] In short, he was a global star whose films made him a lot of money in Japan.

In the opposite direction, Chaplin maintained a long and abiding interest in Japan. He was interested in Kabuki and tea ceremony and traveled to Japan for four visits spanning World War II. Though perhaps not his best friend (that was Douglas Fairbanks, a Jew), his personal valet was a Japanese immigrant to the United States. Kono Toraichi was responsible not only for the intimate job of cleaning up Chaplin's various sexual indiscretions, harassments, and abuses but also for acting as an intermediary when traveling to Japan to make deals on Chaplin's (and United Artists's) behalf. Kono also coordinated Chaplin's visit and press junket to Japan in 1932, which coincided with the peak of Japanese interest in the star. It was this 1932 visit that perhaps would have the biggest impact on the production of the film. The day after his arrival in Tokyo, Chaplin was nearly assassinated along with his host, Prime Minister Inukai Tsuyoshi, who died in what would become known as the May 15 Incident. This incident might have been one impetus for Chaplin becoming more overtly political in his films from *Modern Times* through *The Great Dictator*. Were it not for taking in an afternoon of sumo with Inukai's son Takeru (aka Ken), Chaplin would have been at the Inukai family home when a group of ultra-nationalists bearing guns slaughtered the international-minded politician. In 1933, a year after the incident, *Time* magazine reported that Chaplin was finally made aware of how close he had come to being assassinated through its reporting on the trial of the perpetrators:

> Sub-Lieutenant Seishi Koga rose to testify: "We thought that a war with America was needed to rehabilitate the Japanese national spirit. We planned to blow up Premier Inukai and Mr. Chaplin together. It was only when some of us were arrested and we had to hurry our preparations to kill Premier Inukai that we gave up our plan to kill the American too."[43]

Award-winning biographer Kenneth Lynn speculates that Chaplin realized that the plot against the politician included him because of his celebrity and that this mistake of his nationality as an American impacted the way in which Chaplin inhabited the role of dictator without giving specifics: "Half a dozen years later, memories of the political madness of Lieutenant Koga and his associates probably gave a boost to the demonism in his portrayal of Adolf Hitler in *The Great Dictator*."[44] However we interpret Lynn's hunch, it seems safe to at least speculate that the incident would have made Chaplin more sensitive to mistaken identity and the rise of global right-wing extremists than he might otherwise have been.

Such mistaken identity not only is a major plot point of the film *The Great Dictator* but also is the reason why Chaplin of all comedians was perfect for the role. We see this clearly in the paratextual, patently false disclaimer at the film's start: "Note: Any resemblance between Hynkel the dictator and the Jewish barber is purely co-incidental." The resemblance is the cause or at least the raison d'être for the film. The fact that he was a global star with the same toothbrush mustache as the German dictator did not make Chaplin's spoof inevitable. Indeed, *The Great Dictator* may not have been made were it not for two factors: that from the beginning of his career Chaplin willfully took on the role of a Jew and that Chaplin went to Japan. But the similarities provided the ground conditions for the film. As a generic critique of Naziism, the film was weak because accusing the dictator of looking Jewish or associating him with the object of his vitriol is not a great strategy with which to burst the boil of such vitriol—the logic of which still presumes there is something wrong with being Jewish. But as a specific mocking of Hitler, the parody was right on the philtrum.

Charlie Chaplin was many things to many people. He was a Jew to the Nazis. He was an American to the Japanese ultranationalists. He was

FIGURE 7.4. Modified from a promotional poster for the film, the cover image of Ono Hiroyuki's book *Chaplin and Hitler* (*Chappurin to Hitorā*, 2015) emphasizes the link between the historical personage of Hitler and the fictional persona of Chaplin's Tramp.

a Communist to the Americans. But above all, he was a comedic actor par excellence who was one of the first international global superstars of the silver screen, master of both pastiche and parody.[45] This sort of global everyman was precisely the role that Kobayashi sought to assume with his largely silent one-man act, Mr. Potsunen.

Potsunen: Post-Identity Pastiche Jewish Humor

Though Kobayashi began the century by producing video versions of Rahmens skits that spoofed Japanese cultural tendencies and manners through poking fun at and exaggerating the ways in which Japanese culture is policed in a series of shorts titled *The Japanese Tradition*, by the end of the decade he would transition to a global pastiche. But even some of *The Japanese Tradition* videos had more than local appeal. One joke in the shorts hangs on specifying the angle of back to legs bent in a particular kind of bow of excuse to be exactly thirty-five degrees. Another joke pokes fun at the Japanese proclivity for naming and numbering ways of behavior by providing seven styles for breaking apart and holding chopsticks.[46] Though perhaps intended as a sort of local in-joke on Japanese culture, when posted to the internet on still new platforms such as YouTube and Niconicodoga, these videos received broad global recognition both as oddly serious evidence of the ridiculousness of the rules of decorum in Japanese culture and as brilliant spoofs.

Over the course of the 2000s, Kobayashi grew into even more of a celebrity with his solo act as Mr. Potsunen (Mr. Lonely), a character that combines something of the vulnerability of Chaplin's Tramp, the mastery of communicative gesture associated with mimes, and the magic of visual gags and stage effects—an act more akin to the sensational global theatrical phenomena of the Blue Man Group and the TV magic of David Copperfield than to anything remotely smacking of the traditional Japanese arts. Developed over the course of more than a decade in over eleven different shows, Mr. Potsunen began as rather local and parodic, full of Japanese language puns and wordplays, but became more and more globalized and pastiche-like over time, in fact to the point where Potsunen was all but silent (using only a few internationalized Japanese words like *Ohayo* for "good morning").[47] And in so doing, the character followed the opposite

FIGURE 7.5. In an early version of Kobayashi's Mr. Potsunen, he donned Chaplin's bowler hat. Seen here dragging a pet. Screengrab from the "Me and Jon" segment of the 2008 DVD.

direction of Chaplin's Tramp, who went from sad generic everyman to the specific character of a Jewish barber and a particular fascist leader, from pastiche to parody.

In a sense, Kobayashi not only followed Chaplin's path to global stardom in reverse (moving from the specificity of ethnic humor, in *The Japanese Tradition*, to the global generic of miming) but also embraced the look of Chaplin's garb (which evoked early twentieth-century immigrant chic, which, if not explicitly Jewish, could be seen as Jewy or Jewish-esque)— from parody to pastiche, not in the explicitly Jewish mode of *The Great Dictator* but rather in the early Chaplin global pastiche mode.

And it is on the basis of success of the Mr. Potsunen shows, for which Kobayashi shed his Japanese identity and assimilated to the global Jewish conspiracy of pastiche humor, that he received the job of directing the opening ceremony for the Olympics in 2020. Seven years before Kobayashi would be named the director of the opening ceremony of the Olympics, Hatamoto Kōji, writing for the *Yomiuri* newspaper, wrote of the Mr. Potsunen performances: "It is refreshing to see him *earnestly taking on universal laughter* and enjoying himself doing it."[48] As if to emphasize the degree of Kobayashi's globalization, reviews of the later Mr. Potsunen performances consistently compared him to Chaplin. On the 2015 staging in Paris, the French theater magazine *TheatreOnline* called the influence of Chaplin's silent films on Kobayashi's performance "indéniable."[49] And

FIGURE 7.6. Later versions of Mr. Potsunen became more surreal, exaggerating the early twentieth-century European immigrant look. Kobayashi as Mr. Potsunen being taken for a walk by his pet. Promotional still from Kobayashi's run of *Mr Potsunen's Peculiar Slice of Life* (2015–17) in Leicester Square Theatre, London.

comparing his stature to that of two of the biggest comic actors of the French silver screen, *La Terrasse* explained the alter ego at the beginning of its review: "Chaplin had Charlie [the Tramp] . . . , Tati Mr. Hulot, and for Kobayashi Kentarō, it's Mr. Potsunen."[50] On the return of Mr. Potsunen to the London stage in 2017, Catherine Francoise for the *LondonTheatre1* wrote:

> Kobayashi is a Japanese comedian, manga artist, an award-winning playwright and plainly also an exceptionally gifted performance artist with an extraordinary imagination. His influences include Charlie Chaplin and Monty Python and his one-man show is an incredible mesh of comedic mime, animation, film, projection, magic, puppetry, movement and a fantastic imagination! It is also an incredibly polished

and nuanced performance, thought provoking, funny, engaging, constantly surprising and all done with masterful timing.[51]

That in Paris he was comparable to Tati, in London Monty Python, and in both cities Chaplin attests to the degree to which global humor as developed and disseminated by Chaplin had come to seem domestic, the degree to which global humor was localizable. And Kobayashi was its new master.

The 2017 *Mr Potsunen's Peculiar Slice of Life* onstage at London's Coronet Theatre and posted as a video to Facebook on the Coronet Theatre's website on June 17, 2020, in what would have been the run-up to the Olympics, seemed to reflect something that transcended language. Just like the early globally popular star of the silent silver screen who rose to fame via a sort of chameleonlike (or should we say Jewish-like) sensibility, Kobayashi assimilates global culture by becoming almost odorless or what has been referred to as nationless (*mukokuseki*) in recent musings on Japanese globalization. This is a globalization that needs (not so much subtitles as) intertitles, harkening back to a previous era of global cinema's "montage of attractions" before the droning, tedious excitements of bland action cinema of CGI mega blockbusters that unite us now. It brings us back perhaps even earlier to before the technological break of talkies, which is said to have divided the silent cinema's universal appeal into the Tower of Babel's constituent isolated cultures.

Though silent, one of Kobayashi's early linguistically dependent and, therefore, more localized versions of Mr. Potsunen included a scene titled "chapter 8 Anagram no Ana" (The Hole in Anagrams). The scene begins with Kobayashi as Potsunen sitting at a desk, stage left, with a camera over his shoulder with its image projecting live onto a big screen in the center of the stage. He places what looks like a cue card on the blotter of the desk in front of him. The audience can read on the big screen:

Anagram:
A form of word play. Breaking up a word or phrase into its constituent parts and rearranging them to form another meaning. This method is used for the creation of pennames and the proper names of people and places appearing in novels.
  [*He shuffles to the next card.*]

In random groups of words Creators find suitable combinations, and new meanings are born. If you think "Oh, well . . ." when reading one that is done quite well, the creators are happy.[52]

What follows is Kobayashi sitting at the desk pulling deck upon deck of cards from a stack, slowly turning them over to reveal not the numbers and suits of typical playing cards but rather letters from the Japanese phonetic script hiragana. In the first deck, he turns over the five cards for the word "anagram" (*a na gu ra mu*), and then Kobayashi quickly reshuffles to reveal *a, munagura*, meaning "ah, grabbing me by the collar." A small chuckle comes from the audience. Then Kobayashi says in a concerned voice, "So what? Do you have an objection? [*He grabs himself by his own collar and says*] Ah, grabbing me by the collar." The incongruity of the humorous moment gets its absurdist laugh. Then he collects the cards and starts again with a new deck. This time he deals out *tango no saikousei* ("rearrangement of words"), rearranging the cards to reveal *kono saisen ugoita* ("this rematch moved"). If all of this doesn't seem particularly funny, that is due to perhaps not only my inept translations of the Japanese but also the hyperlocalized language-dependent (ethnic) humor within which much of the early Potsunen performances were pitched. In other words, the lack of translatability is exactly my point about these early versions of a local ethnic humor, one that works for a community of Japanese speakers and is not easily translated for out-group (English-speaking or global) consumers. If such versions of Potsunen in the early 2000s were a bit too word based to export, this aspect had all but faded by the globalization of the character in the late 2010s.

During his transition to a more global brand of humor, Kobayashi was quoted in the *Yomiuri Shimbun* as saying, "My motto is laughter that requires no prior knowledge. I think first-timers will be able to enjoy the show without worry."[53] As if to confirm the complete crossover from parody to a pastiche brand of humor in the later Potsunen performances in 2015–17, the video version of his London performances of *Mr Potsunen's Peculiar Slice of Life*, which was distributed online for free in the run-up to the 2022 Olympics, begins with a silent intertitle that appears after the title and the name of the star are listed:

My solo performance "Mr Potsunen's Peculiar Slice of Life" was staged at the Coronet Theatre in 2017. It is a performance that depicts the world through a live picture book. You can enjoy it even if you do not understand Japanese. Thank you everyone. And have a fun everyday!

When words are used in the video, they are translated into English or at least function at the level of the global Japanese, like *domo arigato*. Consider the use of intertitles, which were projected on a backdrop screen for the staged performances and edited into the videos circulating on DVD and the internet. One of the early intertitles posted in Japanese with the English translation below reads: "Our imagination is not rich enough to make life as expected" (*Jinsei ga sōzō-dōri ni naru hodo, jinsei no sōzō-ryoku wa yutakade wanai*).[54] While the translated English captures the pathos of the predicament stated in the original Japanese, it misses the humor of the original, which in part comes from the repetition of *jinsei* ("human life") and *sōzō* ("imagination"). The original Japanese might better be translated as a sort of chiasmus: "The powers of imagination in human life are not so rich as we imagine human life to be." But such misprision did not prevent English-speaking audiences' enjoyment of the global slapstick and sight-gag humor between the segments. Whatever the failures of such global translations and transfiguration, his successful efforts at globalized humor through the Potsunen performances were clearly among the reasons for choosing Kobayashi as the director of the opening ceremony.

The Last Laugh: Morimura Yasumasa and the Ends of Parody and Pastiche

In Freud's view, humor is the means by which the superego (parent) goads the ego's (child's) distress saying, "It's nothing." This is a way of looking down on oneself from a meta-level. However, this is not the same thing as irony, which proudly shows the higher self that it can do so by disparaging the real pain or the self within pain—sometimes even to the point of death (as with Mishima Yukio). The reason is that while irony makes others uncomfortable, humor somehow also liberates others who hear it.[55]

FIGURES 7.7 AND 7.8. Two images from *A Requiem: Laugh at the Dictator* (2007), in which Morimura poses as Chaplin as Hynkel mocking Hitler. (Yasumasa Morimura, "A Requiem: Where Is the Dictator? 2," 2007, Color Photograph, 150 × 120 cm, courtesy of the artist and Yoshiko Isshiki Office, Tokyo; and "A Requiem: Where Is the Dictator? 3," 2007, Color Photograph, 150 × 120 cm, courtesy of the artist and Yoshiko Isshiki Office, Tokyo.)

With his installation project *A Requiem: Laugh at the Dictator* (2007) featuring a reproduction of Chaplin's Adenoid Hynkel, master impersonator and inspired portrait photographer Morimura Yasumasa marked yet another change in his career that had begun in a gender-bending mode, making perfect replica portraits of himself dressed as famous women in iconic poses—as Manet's Olympia nude reclined on resplendent bedding, as Marilyn Monroe in *The Seven Year Itch* with legs akimbo and skirt blowing, as Jodie Foster as an underage prostitute in Scorsese's *Taxi Driver*, as Frida Kahlo, and on and on. In a later more directly political mode, Morimura reproduced famous historical photographs, such as the photo of Lee Harvey Oswald being shot and Eddie Adams's Vietnam War photo of Police Commissioner Nguyen Ngoc Loan shooting Vietcong fighter Nguyen Van Lem in the street in 1968. In these photo recreations, Morimura poses both as victim and perpetrator. He would then go on to pose in the guise of political leaders around whom cults of personality accrued: Lenin, Mao Zedong, Trotsky, and Che Guevara. But it is in posing as Mishima Yukio posing as an ultranationalist and giving a speech before his suicide and as Charlie Chaplin dressed as Hynkel that Morimura truly blurs the lines between parody and pastiche.

In the same way that Morimura's "To my little sister: For Cindy Sherman" fixates on the fact that it is an homage to Sherman and not to the target of Sherman's critique (Morimura's reproduction is of Sherman's "Untitled #96," which classically parodied pornographic representations of young women), his reproduction of Chaplin as Hynkel (and not of Hitler directly) ought to make this a clear work of pastiche rather than parody, that is, a copy of a copy rather than a mocking of reality per se.[56] But this is not the case.

If Morimura's exhibition *A Requiem: Laugh at the Dictator* solely consisted of these images, we might conclude that it was only thin pastiche—a kind of cosplay homage to Chaplin. But the video running with the exhibition, which imitates but transforms and updates Chaplin's famous speech from the vantage point of the Jewish barber who switches places with the dictator, blurs any possibility of an easy distinction between pastiche and parody. Famously requiring hours upon hours of reshooting, Chaplin's speech is a kind of direct address to the audience for the kind of global humanism that would become the norm in the postwar world order as demarcated by the United Nations Charter for Human Rights:

> I don't want to be an emperor. . . . I should like to help everyone if possible. . . . Jew, Gentile, Black Man, White. . . . We all want to help one another, human beings are like that. . . . And this world has room for everyone, and the good Earth is rich and can provide for everyone. Dictators free themselves but they enslave the people! Let us fight to free the world—to do away with national barriers—to do away with greed.

Morimura alters this speech to make the claim that in today's globalized world, nations, large multinational corporations, and "newly invented information processing techniques" can all be a dictator who "manipulates many people . . . ignores people's advice . . . forces change to the system he doesn't like . . . [and] gets absorbed in amassing personal fortune." Morimura concludes by making the dictator more individualistic and personal: "Have you not been a dictator toward your family? Your lover? And your friends? . . . I myself am a dictator. You yourselves are dictators. The dictator of the twenty-first century does not have a face of a bad guy. The dictator of the twenty-first century is a ghost that nobody can see. I don't want to be a dictator."

Ban Yukie argues that Morimasa's work on Chaplin's dictator is more parody than satire. For Ban, Morimura's *A Requiem*, as a reproduction of a reproduction, critiques not only Hitler but also Chaplin's spoof of Hitler.[57] While I agree that Morimura's portrayal adds a layer of critique, its added distancing from reality that is filtered through yet another reproduction (Chaplin's) seems closer to what Jameson called pastiche (or what Karatani labels irony) than parody, which is thought to be liberating or transcendental. And yet pastiche as the apolitical opposing term to parody does not quite fit the bill either. In other words, Morimura's work reveals any binary schema between parody and pastiche itself to be problematic:

Parody	Jameson's Pastiche (Karatani's Irony)
Late Chaplin	Early Chaplin
Early Kobayashi	Late Kobayashi
Radical potential, liberatory, transcendental	Complicit/complacent
Ethnic	Empty
Local/communal/in-group	Global/inclusive
Real-world reference	Inter-referential to other art
Modern	Postmodern
Alive	Dead

Ban's dismissal of Linda Hutcheon's categories of parody and satire to do justice to Morimura may be right, but Hutcheon's notion of a pastiche that is not simply complacent or complicit can be more apropos here because it names a kind of humor that is powerful even as it is pastiche—it names the power of humor by the powerless or less powerful, a Jewish kind of humor. Of just this sort of mimicry by those without power, Hutcheon writes:

The assumption seems to be that authenticity of experience and expression are somehow incompatible with double-voicing and/or humor. This view seems to be shared, not only by Marxist critics, but also by some feminist critics. And yet it is feminist *writers*, along with blacks, who have used such ironic intertextuality to such powerful ends—both ideologically and aesthetically (if the two could, in fact, be so easily separated). . . . It is one of the major ways in which women and other eccentrics both use and abuse, set up and then challenge male traditions in art.[58]

Rather than simply writing off the efficacy of pastiche humor, Hutcheon persuasively argues that those out of power can use humor to upend the center. Indeed, for the male Marxists whom Hutcheon critiques, the power of humor lies in the ability to step back outside of the childlike silliness and to see it as humor from the position of an adult or parent. Analyzing the performance of humor as a doubled divide between subjective thinking (self-centered [internal]) and objective thinking (object oriented [external]), Karatani Kōjin, as an example of one such Marxist, finds Freud's parent-child relation of humor in literary practice as being radical. But in the historical transition from specific ethnic humor (subjective) to general global humor (objective), we lose that doubling tension and, therefore, lose the radical edge.[59] We see this both in the move from humor to irony in Karatani's terminology and in Jameson's move from parody to pastiche. Jameson and Karatani want for the politics of the distinction between pastiche (or irony) and parody to be clear and fast—alive or dead, the Hutcheon theory of feminist pastiche (a minority pastiche?) and Morimura's art suggest that pastiche has the power of global capital or even (as Hitler's "original" performances were already performatives empty of power other than their performance) that there is no viable distinction, that everything is pastiche because there never was an original.

Though her focus is clearly on feminist and, by proxy, African American humor, Hutcheon's notion can also be applied to Jewish humor. The duality/indeterminacy of the ambivalent politics of Jewish humor indeed also straddles the bridge between ineffectual pastiche and radical parody. For the same reason that Lacanian psychoanalyst Saitō Tamaki considers Morimura a "a phallic mother" (a woman with the power of men), we can see Jewish humor as precisely situated in the vexed position of the minority using the ephemeral culture (putatively useless humor) to garner power through in-group identification.[60] Although classically its self-deprecating tendency is taken to be its charm and power,[61] Jewish humor also, of course, can clearly reify the very categories it seeks to undo.[62] As Chase observes about the development of Jewish humor in the nineteenth century, "Humorous utterances always represent unstable moments that disrupt established patterns of significance. On the other hand, humor also partakes of stability."[63] And in this stability, we can begin to articulate the structure of perhaps a late-stage or latent Jewish humor that need not be by or about Jews or Jewish things (from bagels to holocausts) but lies more in an awareness that humanity is bound together by its exile, its incessant rootlessness on a cruel earth, that putative origins and rightful places are simply nationalist and fascist myths. In short, this is a postmodern, post-identitarian Jewish humor that would be as much encompassing of Jerry Seinfeld and Taika Waititi as it would of Kobayashi and Morimura.

What then is "Jewish humor" here? It transcends the Jew and the Jewish topos. A Japanese can do it. And it does not need to be about Jewish themes like the Holocaust. Jewish humor is precisely that humor that is desired by the global public to evoke our collective self-centered feeling of victimhood and outcastness, our shared sense of not belonging, having been scapegoated, as well as our responsibility for making others feel as though they don't belong, for scapegoating others. In short, Jewish humor can be read in the global mix as an ethical humanist sort of humor that, like Kobayashi's Holocaust joke from the 1990s, implores its audience to reflect on prejudice and to rise above it.

Notes

1 Koichi Iwabuchi, *Recentering Globalization: Popular Culture and Japanese Transnationalism* (Durham, NC: Duke University Press Books, 2002).

2 Roland Barthes, "The Reality Effect," *The Rustle of Language*, trans. Richard Howard (New York: Hill and Wang, 1986), 141–48.

3 *Seinfeld* aired in Japan as *Our Neighbor Seinfeld* (*Tonari no Sainfuerudo*) on the Wowwow network for five seasons. All seasons were available in Japanese on DVD, with seasons 6–9 available on streaming platforms such as Amazon Prime. See Jeremy Dauber, *Jewish Comedy: A Serious History* (New York: W. W. Norton, 2017), passim, and Jarrod Tanny,

"Decoding *Seinfeld*'s Jewishness," in *A Club of Their Own: Jewish Humorists and the Contemporary World*, ed. Gabriel N. Finder and Eli Lederhendler (New York: Oxford University Press, 2016), 53–74.

4 Fredric Jameson, "Postmodernism and Consumer Society," in *The Anti-Aesthetic: Essays on Postmodern Culture*, ed. Hal Foster (Port Townsend, WA: Bay Press, 1983), 114.

5 Ofra Nevo, "What's in a Jewish Joke?" *Humor*, no. 2 (January 1991): 251–60. On nostalgia, see Frederic Jameson, *Postmodernism, or, the Cultural Logic of Late Capitalism* (Durham, NC: Duke University Press, 1983), and Koichi Iwabuchi, "Nostalgia for a (Different) Asian Modernity: Media Consumption of 'Asia' in Japan," *Positions: East Asia Cultures Critique* 10, no. 3 (2002): 547–73.

6 Actually, it begins with something equally asinine. These baseline conditions for Jewish comedy were set by Dauber, whose very book on the subject of Jewish humor starts not with a joke but with the false claim that "you can't start a book on Jewish Humor without a joke." What he meant was that *he* couldn't start a book on Jewish humor with a joke. For his claim to not ring false, we have to consider the claim part of the joke that follows. But for Dauber, signs don't float; jokes are clearly defined; and only Jews can make Jewish jokes. Where a joke begins and ends is a tough thing to define. Yet Dauber misses the point as he misses the heart of what makes Jewish humor Jewish—the "-ish." Jeremy Dauber, *Jewish Comedy: A Serious History* (New York: W. W. Norton, 2017), xii.

7 In short, Lenny Bruce's relational definition of Jewishness obtains: "If you live in New York or any other big city, you are Jewish. It doesn't matter even if you're Catholic; if you live in New York, you're Jewish. If you live in Butte, Montana, you're going to be goyish even if you're Jewish." Lenny Bruce, *How to Talk Dirty and Influence People: An Autobiography* (New York: Hachette Books, 2016), 5.

8 *Neta de shō jiten raibu*, vol. 4 (Tokyo: Nihon Columbia, 1998).

9 Though Rahmens sounds like the food ramen, Kobayashi has claimed that the name was formed because "when Rahmen, which means 'frame' in German, is gathered together, you can put it in a box. And in Japanese box (hako) also means theater." "Moji shūruna warai de kaisō 'geijutsu-teki konto' no rāmenzu," *Asahi Shimbun*, February 19, 2002, evening edition.

10 In terms of content and structure, the Rahmens' joke is analogous to a Mitchell and Webb sketch that similarly deals with the Holocaust at

a meta-level by raising the possibility about doing a sketch about opening a snack shop near the gift shop at Auschwitz. After discussing the possibility of an "Arbeit Macht Fries" chips stand at Auschwitz, the punchline comes: "Do you think there's a sketch in that?" "No." Ultimately both the Mitchell and Webb version and the Rahmens version are less concerned with the Holocaust than they are ironic about the taboos around joking about the Holocaust.

11 Here it is analogous with what Anat Feinberg argues about Tabori's *Mein Kampf*; namely, "it is a pained laughter—biting, terrifying, macabre. For many spectators, critics, opponents, and admirers alike, this tastelessness, this crudeness, is the hallmark of Tabori's 'theater of embarrassment.'" Anat Feinberg, "The Joy of Breaking Taboos," *Jews and Theater in an Intercultural Context* (Boston: Brill, 2012), 290.

12 "Japanese relieved their sense of war guilt by identifying with the Jews." Miyazawa Masanori and David G. Goodman, *Jews in the Japanese Mind: The History and Uses of a Cultural Stereotype* (Lanham, MD: Lexington Books, 2000), 12. Goodman also sees Hiroshima as a means to "trump" the Holocaust; see 178 and also 182. See also Ran Zwigenberg, *Hiroshima: The Origins of Global Memory Culture* (Cambridge: Cambridge University Press, 2014). In addition to the excellent bibliography of Japanese books about Jews created by Miyazawa Masanori, which ends in 1988, there continues to be a steady stream of publications in Japan (as elsewhere) that exhibit a Japanese fascination not only with Jews and Judaism but also with antisemitic conspiracy theory and racism. Miyazawa Masanori, *Nihon ni okeru Yudaya Isuraeru rongi bun kenmokuroku 1877–1988* (Tokyo: Shin izumi-sha, 1990). See also Jacob Kovalio, *The Russian Protocols of Zion in Japan: Yudayaka/Jewish Peril Propaganda and Debates in the 1920s* (New York: Peter Lang, 2009). Meron Medzini, *Under the Shadow of the Rising Sun: Japan and the Jews During the Holocaust Era* (Boston: Academic Studies Press, 2019).

13 This mimicked the structure of denial of reality that was Nishioka's initial cause célèbre in the press when he advocated "studies" that purportedly showed that AIDS caused HIV and not the other way around. See Nishioka Masanori, "HIV wa hontōni eizu no gen'in ka?" *Nihon Ijishinpō* 3619 (1993): 70–72.

14 Rotem Kowner, "The Strange Case of Japanese 'Revisionism,'" in *Holocaust Denial: The Politics of Perfidy*, ed. Robert S. Wistrich (Boston:

De Gruyter and Magnes, 2012), 181–94. Rotem Kowner, "Tokyo Recognizes Auschwitz: The Rise and Fall of Holocaust Denial in Japan, 1989–1999," *Journal of Genocide Research* (August 2010). Mark Schreiber and William Wetherall, "Tabloid Nationalism and Racialism in Japan," in *Press Freedom in Contemporary Japan*, ed. Jeff Kingston (London: Routledge, 2016).

15 See, for instance, Yabe Takeshi, "Nihon no 'Yudaya inbo-setsu' no kokkei-sa—honto no sabetsu-sha ga mienai nihonjin" (The ridiculousness of Japanese "Jewish Conspiracy Theories": Japanese who don't see the real discrimination), *Ekonomisuto* 34, no. 71 (August 1993): 81–83.

16 Tom Brislin, "David and Godzilla: Anti-Semitism and Seppuku in Japanese Publishing," http://www2.hawaii.edu/~tbrislin/David_Godzilla.htm.

17 Lawrence J. Epstein, *The Haunted Smile: The Story of Jewish Comedians in America* (New York: PublicAffairs, 2008), 51.

18 John Morreall, *Taking Laughter Seriously* (Albany: State University of New York Press, 1983). John Morreall, ed., *The Philosophy of Laughter and Humor* (Albany: State University of New York Press, 1987). Victor Raskin, *Semantic Mechanisms of Humor* (Dordrecht: Reidel, 1985), 30–41, and D. H. Monro, "Humor," in Paul Edwards, ed., *The Encyclopedia of Philosophy*, vol. 3 (New York: Macmillan and The Free Press, 1967), 90–93.

19 Of course, both Looney Toon characters were voiced by Lithuanian Jew Mel Blanc.

20 The rhetoric around the scandal was hyperbolic. Around the scandal, we find common justifications for prejudicial hate speech: because the history and culture of Jews is little known in Japan, if instances of hate speech, conspiracy theory, and lies occur in public mainstream discourse, it is simply because of lack of knowledge. The inexperienced and unknowing are simply repeating the vitriol they hear from the ether, and because there are no Jews to whom it applies, there is no real harm. Indeed, this is how the appeal by Rabbi Abraham Cooper, the associate dean of the Simon Wiesenthal Center, appeared when submitted as an open letter to Takakazu Kuriyama, the Japanese ambassador to the United States: "For the survivors of the Holocaust, the Marco Polo article is akin to a public denial of the dropping of the A-bomb on Hiroshima and the death and suffering which is wrought on the Japanese people. . . . We hope that the government of Japan will publicly condemn through

the appropriate Japanese governmental agency, the views expressed by these hate mongers" (qtd. in Brislin, "David and Godzilla"). Here the comparison of gas chamber denialism was related directly to denying the atrocities of Hiroshima. In the summer of 2021, the *Asahi* newspaper quoted the vice president of the Weisenthal Center making a similar comparison, but now to the less incendiary and more topical Japanese abductions by North Koreans—a hot topic in Japanese news during the previous decade: "Abraham Cooper, the center's vice president, told the Asahi Shimbun that Kobayashi's dismissal was 'an appropriate move. We want the Japanese people to understand what the families of Nazi victims are feeling,' he said. 'How would the people of Japan feel if a comedian made a joke about people abducted by North Korea? . . . There are basic norms about human dignity. Those who continue to suffer should not be the target of "jokes" ' " ("Horokōsuto keishi ni sekai kara hanpatsu, hitei suruto keibatsu no kuni mo," *Asahi shimbun dejitaru*, July 22, 2021).

21 And this undecidable is evidenced in the misperceptions about the actor Justin Long, who plays the Mac in the American ads. Though he was raised Catholic, he has been called an honorary Jew, acting the part of a Jew, for instance, in 2020's *After Class*. See also Dorri Olds, "Justin Long—An Honorary Jew," YouTube, https://youtu.be/GvpDcnDMHL8.

22 Placards feature quotations about parody from famous leading figures in the culture industry, including philosopher Tsurumi Shunsuke, copyright lawyer Koizumi Naoki, gag manga artist Akatsuka Fujio, and controversial visual artist Akasegawa Genpei. The quotations, though cognizant of the global history of parody, did not reference Jewishness or humor directly. However, they gave color to the exhibit on parody. The quotation by legal scholar Koizumi Naoki referred to the US Supreme Court's ruling on "Pretty Woman" and 2 Live Crew's appropriation of the song; he calls parody the "devil's child" (*onikko*) of the world of copyright law, since distinguishing what is a comment on an original means that the original work must be visible through the change that parody brings. And juxtaposed with the Chaplin poster, the quotation implied that, to understand the social commentary and joke, one needed to know both who Chaplin's Tramp was and who his depiction of Hitler (as Adenoyd Hinkel) was. The quotation from gag manga artist Akatsuka Fujio argued that maintaining the freedom to parody was a core of artistic freedom, even when we disagree with the parody; indeed, he goes so far as to argue

that parody is a guarantee of freedom of expression. Tsurumi's quotation on a single large panel, though, put these comments on democracy and legality into historical context.

23 "Izure ichi mondai? Chapurin Shinsaku 'Dokusai-sha,'" *Asahi Shimbun*, February 9, 1939, 2, evening edition.

24 See, for instance, "Tsūretsuna 'Chappurin no dokusai-sha' 20-nenme, yatto kōkai, sukoshi mo furu-sa o kanji sasenai" (Chaplin's Scathing *The Great Dictator* Finally Opens After 20 Years, and It Doesn't Feel a Bit Old), *Yomiuri Shimbun*, August 23, 1960, 5, evening edition. The film was also given wide release in following decade.

25 I thank Indra Levy for this note from Chaplin's autobiography: "Vanderbilt sent me a series of picture postcards showing Hitler making a speech. The face was obscenely comic—a bad imitation of me, with its absurd moustache, unruly, stringy hair and disgusting, thin, little mouth." Charles Chaplin, *My Autobiography* (New York: Penguin Books, 1964), 316.

26 Books on the business acumen of Jews abound in Japan. Just to give an inkling of the broad market for such books, here is a brief list of the top Japanese business books purporting to give Jewish secrets since the turn of the millennium: Māvuin Tokeiyā, *Jewish Business Law* (Tokyo: Nihonkeiei gōri-ka kyōkai shuppan-kyoku, 2000); Teshima Yūrō, *Yudayahito no bijinesu kyōhon—kyūyaku seisho no chie o yomitoku* (Taiyō shuppan, 2005); Honda Ken, *Yudayahito daifūgō no oshie shiawasena kanemochi ni naru 17 no hiketsu* (*The Millionaire's Philosophy for a Happy Life*) (literally, Teachings of the Jewish Millionaire: 17 Tips for Being Happy and Rich) (Tokyo: Yamato bunko, Yamato shobō, 2006) (published in three volumes total between 2006 and 2013); Honda Ken and Imatani Tetchū, *Komikku yudayahito daifūgō no oshie* (Tokyo: Yamatoshobō, 2011); Takeda Tomohiro, *Sekai o kaeta Yudaya shōhō* (Tokyo: Bijinesu-sha, 2019); Taki-nai Kyōkei, *Naze sekai no o kanemochi no 35-pāsento wa yudayahitona no ka? Yudaya no kami o mikata ni tsukereba kigyō wa kanarazu seikō dekiru!* (Tokyo: Sanraizu paburisshingu, 2019); Ishizumi Kanji, *Yudaya-shiki essensharu gakushū-hō* (Tokyo: Nihon Nōritsu kyōkai manejimento sentā, 2016). And more than simply praising Jews as businessmen, Jewish joke books have been published widely in Japan since the 1960s. Consider the blurb on one such Jewish joke book that stereotypically links such humorous sensibility with

business acumen: "Jews are well aware of the benefits of humor. They make great use of jokes during negotiations. Their laughter is full of humanity and pathos, and they are intelligent and witty. Sometimes, they make jokes about their own people who have a strong commercial spirit. . . . This book introduces a number of humor stories that I have collected independently in the field of international business. This book introduces a number of humorous stories collected from the field of international business, and shows the cleverness of the Jews who never let anything happen to them!" Ugaya Yasahiro, *Atama ga yoku naru yudayahito jōku-shū* (Tokyo: PHP kenkyūjo, 2008). Other similar books include *Yudaya jōku jinsei no shioaji*, ed. Mirutosu henshū-bu (Tokyo: Mirutosu, 2010); *Yudayajōku: warai no kessaku-sen* (Tokyo: Rokkōshuppan, 1978); Kase Hideaki, *Yudaya jōku no eichi: gyakkyō mo kyūchi mo, warai de kirinukeru* (Tokyo: Kōbunsha, 2003); Kase Hideaki, *Jinsei saikyō no buki warai (jōku) no chikara: yudayahito no eichi ni manabu* (Tokyo: Shōdensha shinsho 216, 2010); Harupen Jakku, *Jōkujōku yudayahito no warai meisaku-sen* (Tokyo: Ryū shobō, 1983); Jack Halpern, *Totte oki no Yudaya jōku: Yudayahito to nihonjin no bunka ni miru chigai* (Tokyo: Besutoserāzu, 1992); Salcia Landmann, *Yudaya saikō no jōku*, trans. Wada Tsutomu Hiroshi (Tokyo: Mikasa shobō, 1994), a translation of Salcia Landmann, *Der judische Witze* (Deutscher Taschenbuch Verlag, 1960); Jakku Harupen, *Totte oki no Yudaya jōku: Yudayahito to nihonjin no bunka ni miru chigai* (Tokyo: Wani bunko, 1992); and Ugaya Yasahiro, *Tsūkai! Amerikan jōku bijinesuman hikkei komatta toki ni kanarazu yakutatsu yudayabito no chie* (Tokyo: Gogatsu shobō, 2004).

27 Morita Akio and Shintarō Ishihara, *The Japan That Can Say "No": The New U.S.-Japan Relations Card* (Tokyo: Kobunsha Kappa-Holmes, 1989).

28 "Had I known of the actual horrors of the German concentration camps, I could not have made *The Great Dictator.*" Chaplin suggests that at the time of making the films, the greater risk was being accused of being communist rather than anti-fascist. Chaplin, *My Autobiography*, 387–88.

29 Although Jewface has historically referred to both non-Jews and Jews playing stereotypically (even kitschy) Jewish characters from minstrelsy through vaudeville and the early silver screen, the term has come to mean non-Jews donning Jewish roles in more recent years (and especially since the comedian Sarah Silverman's not so ironic critique that

Hollywood has been giving more and more Jewish roles to non-Jews). This shift of definition, which has been increasingly more suspicious of non-Jewish bodies inhabiting the role of Jew, has oddly made Jewface less and less a critique of identity as such or even a place of free play (inhabitable of course by those in power) and more and more a simple marker of an increasingly static sense of identity. One need only to consider the now perhaps impossible role of Eddie Murphy's brilliant Saul (the Jewish customer in the barbershop in *Coming to America*) to garner a sense of the loss for identity critique in the overly rigid policing of such borders. Like Kobayashi playing Potsunen, Murphy is never closer to Chaplin's global limelight than when he (like Charlie) pretends at Jewishness. See Jody Rosen, "The Long History of Jewface," *New Yorker*, October 7, 2023, https://www.newyorker.com/culture/the-weekend-essay/the-long-history-of-jewface; Hannah Schwadron, *The Case of the Sexy Jewess: Dance, Gender, and Jewish Joke-Work in US Pop Culture* (New York: Oxford University Press, 2018); "Jewface: 'Yiddish' Dialect Songs of Tin Pan Alley," YIVO Institute for Jewish Research, n.d., accessed August 14, 2024, https://yivo.org/Jewface.

30 Isaac Deutscher, *The Non-Jewish Jew: And Other Essays*, ed. Tamara Deutscher. (New York: Verso, 2017). Also available at https://www.marxists.org/history/etol/newspape/amersocialist/deutscher01.htm.

31 Just as for "many Jewish socialists, being an internationalist meant not being Jewish at all," being a Jew meant for some non-Jews the possibility of being an internationalist. See Yuri Slezkine, *The Jewish Century* (Princeton: Princeton University Press, 2004), 155.

32 Lisa Stein Haven, *Charlie Chaplin's Little Tramp in America* (New York: Palgrave Macmillan, 2016), 59.

33 Richard Carr, *Charlie Chaplin: A Political Biography from Victorian Britain to Modern America* (New York: Penguin, 2017), 19.

34 Chaplin's first appearance as a Jew is referenced as "a disastrous and humiliating one-night appearance as a Jewish comedian" in Dan Kamin, *The Comedy of Charlie Chaplin: Artistry in Motion* (New York: Scarecrow Press, 2008), 6. And he kept up the ruse later in life: "Here he is in 1924, in a meeting with production executives planning a big-budget life of Christ. Charlie wanted the lead. 'I'm the logical choice. I look the part, I'm a Jew, and I'm a comedian.' Did he envision himself doing shtick

while walking on water? He didn't get the part." Sid Fleischman, *Sir Charlie: Chaplin, the Funniest Man in the World* (New York: Greenwillow Books, 2010), 186.

35 Carr, *Charlie Chaplin*, 19.

36 See Fleischman, *Sir Charlie*, 185.

37 Dauber is curtly dismissive of consideration of Chaplin's as an example of Jewish comedy: "Anyone who defines themselves as Jewish in any way is potentially part of our subject; others, even if sometimes mistaken for Jews (Charlie Chaplin, looking at you), are out." Dauber, *Jewish Comedy*, xii. But, indeed, as the above paragraph should show, Chaplin himself at times defined himself as Jewish. Werner Sollors discusses these aspects of ethnicity to be uniquely American. That is, in his telling, America is a place where ethnicity by consent (chosen relations) came to mean more rhetorically than ethnicity by descent (heredity). And, yet, clearly America is also the place where affiliations do not and cannot always rescue one from filiation. Werner Sollors, *Beyond Ethnicity: Consent and Descent in American Culture* (New York: Oxford University Press, 1986), 6.

38 Carr, *Charlie Chaplin*, 18.

39 See Simon Louvish, *Chaplin: The Tramp's Odyssey* (London: Faber & Faber, 2009), 268, and Kamin, *The Comedy of Charlie Chaplin*, 154.

40 Louvish, *Chaplin: The Tramp's Odyssey*, 267

41 Miriam Silverberg, who sees a Japanese influence on *Modern Times*, does not mention a potential connection to *The Great Dictator*.

42 Miriam Silverberg, *Erotic Grotesque Nonsense: The Mass Culture of Japanese Modern Times* (Berkeley: University of California Press, 2009), 1–2 and 212–15.

43 "Foreign News: Chaplin & Assassins," *Time*, August 7, 1933, http://content.time.com/time/subscriber/article/0,33009,745838,00.html. See also Louvish, *Chaplin: The Tramp's Odyssey*, 254.

44 Kenneth S. Lynn, *Charlie Chaplin and His Times* (New York: Cooper Square Press, 2002), 256. Though Miriam Silverberg speculates that Chaplin's visit to a Japanese prison may have had direct influence on his *Modern Times* four years later, she marks no analysis of what impact or influence the attempted assassination may have had on *The Great Dictator*. *Modern Times* features not only a jail scene but also a famous

scene in which Chaplin's Tramp inadvertently ends up carrying a red flag leading a march. But though one could reasonably doubt the relation of Japan to this sort of kitschy engagement with politics, it is harder to do so with the experience of having nearly been assassinated. See Silverberg, *Erotic Grotesque Nonsense.*

45   But identity is not only what you claim it to be (no matter how much you claim it); identity sadly is also what people claim you to be, what is thrust upon you. See Dan Kamin, "Split Personality: *The Great Dictator*," in *The Comedy of Charlie Chaplin*, 154; Carr, *Charlie Chaplin*, 18–19; Lita Grey Chaplin and Jeffrey Vance, *Wife of the Life of the Party: A Memoir* (Lanham, MD: Scarecrow Press, 1998), 91. "I was accused of being Jewish when 'The Great Dictator' came out, but you don't have to be Jewish to be anti-Hitler. And when 'Verdoux' opened, the Daily News said, 'Charlie Chaplin slings Communism at us.' I've never read Karl Marx in my life! I've never been what people wanted me to be." Haven, *Charlie Chaplin's Little Tramp in America*, 23n20 and 69.

46   Jan Bardsley and Laura Miller, *Manners and Mischief: Gender, Power, and Etiquette in Japan* (Berkeley: University of California Press, 2011); *Motion Blur: Graphic Moving Imagemakers*, ed. Onedotzero (London: Laurence King Publishing, 2004), 197. *Nihon no katachi*, DVD, ed. Namikibashi (Tokyo: Asumikku hanbai, Kadokawa Entateinmento, 2006).

47   Kobayashi was not the first Japanese comedian to pick up on Chaplin's screen presence. During the peak of Chaplin's success in Japan, comedians such as Enomoto Ken'ichi and Yokoyama Endatsu both picked up on Chaplin's style and gestures (Yokoyama going so far as to sport a toothbrush mustache for a while).

48   Emphasis added. Hatamoto Kōji, "[BS shisha-shitsu] 'Kobayashi Kentarō terebi raibu potsunen in yōroppa,'" *Yomiuri Shimbun*, September 23, 2012, 34.

49   "La petite vie étrange de Monsieur Potsunen," Theatreonline.com, January 31, 2015, https://www.theatreonline.com/Spectacle/La-petite-vie-etrange-de-Monsieur-Potsunen/49070.

50   Eric Demey, "La petite vie étrange de Monsieur Potsunen," *La Terrasse*, December 17, 2014, https://www.journal-laterrasse.fr/la-petite-vie-etrange-de-monsieur-potsunen/.

51 Catherine Francoise, "Kentaro Kobayashi's *Mr Potsunen's Peculiar Slice of Life*," LondonTheatre1, July 6, 2017, https://www.londontheatre1.com/reviews/kentaro-kobayashis-mr-potsunens-peculiar-slice-of-life/.

52 25:36, Potsunen, "Potsunen: Anagram no ana," accessed July 2, 2025, https://www.youtube.com/watch?v=xcxQwWgpx2M.

53 "Rahmens Kobashi kokkyō koeru warai nōmen tsukatta shinsaku mo," *Yomiuri Shimbun*, September 10, 2012, 11, evening edition.

54 6:25 / 1:09:23. This sort of chiasmus also appears elsewhere in the intertitles. "When you consult your Encyclopedia of Insects you still don't understand it, it's either a new species of insect or it's not an insect." 14:25

55 Karatani Kōjin, "Hyūmoa toshite no yuibutsuron," [1992] *Hyūmoa toshite no yuibutsuron*, Kōdansha gakujutsu bunko 1359 (Tokyo: Kōdansha, 1999), 140–41. Citing Jameson, Karatani writes about "humor" (rather than parody), which has radically transformative powers as opposed to irony (rather than pastiche).

56 Ayelet Zohar, "The Elu[va]sive Japanese Portrait: Repetition, Difference and Multiplicity," *Trans-Asia Photography Review* 2, no. 1 (Fall 2011). What differs from his impersonations of Mao and Che Guevara, in Morimura's taking on the guise of Chaplin taking on the guise of Hitler, is that in the first he parodies the iconic images of the strong masculine leaders of communist struggle while in the second he pays pastiche homage to Chaplin's parody of Hitler. One is miming real-world dictators and strongmen, and the other is miming a mime of such people. On Morimura's shift from copy to copy of a copy, Zohar sees a transition to emphasize process over result in this shift from parody to pastiche: "Morimura was able to both extract the theatrical quality of the political game, and simultaneously keep the bitter laugh and haunting spirit of Chaplin's film, indicating how this work is actually 'realer than real', a simulacrum that positions political reality within Judith Butler's notion of 'a copy of a copy.' . . . Through the act of copying Chaplin who, in turn, mimics Hitler, a chain of signifiers is constructed, indicating the collapse of the hunt for truth or reality." But more than Butler's emphasis on performativity, the categorical difference between a copy and a copy of a copy is probably best theorized by Baudrillard's notion of simulacrum.

57 Ban Yukie, "Morimura yasumasa no 'dokusai-sha o warae' ni okeru parodi no ito," *Nisho gakusha daigaku jinbun ronso* 92, no. 3 (2014): 149–73.

58 Linda Hutcheon, *A Poetics of Postmodernism: History, Theory, Fiction* (New York: Routledge, 1988), 134.

59 In short, humor of the political nature (parody) is a way out or a way through modernity as opposed to "irony" (pastiche), which for Karatani is a complacent and complicit part of the system of modernity. In these stark views, Karatani is of a mind with Adorno, who similarly remarks on the totalization of the field of culture that most laughter falls within.

60 Dan Ben-Amos's data-driven folklore study of recordings of jokes by (mostly) Jews uncovers what he will call the "myth" of Jewish humor as self-deprecating. But in comparing the broadly culturally accepted view of Jewish humor as being self-deprecating with the reality of the recordings of Jews telling jokes to other Jews, Ben-Amos reveals that there are at least two Jewish humors: those told by Jews to Jews (which are not self-deprecating) and those told by non-Jews to non-Jews about Jews (which are Jew deprecating). What he does not do is give evidence for the kinds of jokes Jews make about Jews in the company of non-Jews, and it is likely here in wider society/community where in fact the reason why so many of the Jews quoted in the early part of the argument (Freud, Howe, Roth, etc.) believe in the "myth." They are concerned not with the insular jokes Jews tell Jews but with the public-facing Jewish jokes in the world. Dan Ben-Amos, "The 'Myth' of Jewish Humor," *Western Folklore* 32, no. 2 (1973): 112–31, especially 123. More generally, we can see Ben-Amos's argument to illustrate the broader (dare I say universal) point in the superiority and inferiority theories of humor that some group is likely being ridiculed and scapegoated and some group elevated and brought together through humor.

61 See Martin Grotjahn, *Beyond Laughter: Humor and the Subconscious* (New York: Blakiston Division, 1957), 22–25.

62 Jarrod Tanny makes the argument that it is kvetching rather than self-deprecation per se that is characteristic of eastern European Jewish humor. He makes the case that this incessant complaining stems from the contradictions of maintaining the idea of being chosen by God for ascension to heaven and the reality of everyday discrimination and life of struggle. In this way, what may appear to the unknowing as self-deprecation is actually a means by which Jews recommit to their chosen status. See Tanny Jarrod, *City of Rogues and Schnorrers: Russia's Jews and the Myth of Old Odessa* (Bloomington: Indiana University Press, 2011), 14–17.

63 Jefferson S. Chase, *Inciting Laughter: The Development of "Jewish Humor" in Nineteenth Century German Culture* (New York: de Gruyter, 2000), 8.

Selected Bibliography

Bruce, Lenny. *How to Talk Dirty and Influence People: An Autobiography.* New York: Hachette Books, 2016.

Dauber, Jeremy. *Jewish Comedy: A Serious History.* New York: W. W. Norton, 2017.

Deutscher, Isaac. *The Non-Jewish Jew: And Other Essays.* Edited by Tamara Deutscher. New York: Verso, 2017.

Iwabuchi, Koichi. *Recentering Globalization: Popular Culture and Japanese Transnationalism.* Durham, NC: Duke University Press, 2002.

Kovalio, Jacob. *The Russian Protocols of Zion in Japan: Yudayaka/Jewish Peril Propaganda and Debates in the 1920s.* New York: Peter Lang, 2009.

Kowner, Rotem. "Tokyo Recognizes Auschwitz: The Rise and Fall of Holocaust Denial in Japan, 1989–1999." *Journal of Genocide Research* (August 2010).

Masanori, Miyazawa, and David G. Goodman. *Jews in the Japanese Mind: The History and Uses of a Cultural Stereotype.* Lanham, MD: Lexington Books, 2000.

Medzini, Meron. *Under the Shadow of the Rising Sun: Japan and the Jews During the Holocaust Era.* Boston: Academic Studies Press, 2019.

Nevo, Ofra. "What's in a Jewish Joke?" *Humor* 2, no. 1 (January 1991): 251–60.

Rosen, Jody. "The Long History of Jewface." *New Yorker*, October 7, 2023. https://www.newyorker.com/culture/the-weekend-essay/the-long-history -of-jewface.

Schwadron, Hannah. *The Case of the Sexy Jewess: Dance, Gender, and Jewish Joke-Work in US Pop Culture.* New York: Oxford University Press, 2018.

YIVO Institute for Jewish Research. "Jewface: 'Yiddish' Dialect Songs of Tin Pan Alley." Accessed August 14, 2024. https://yivo.org/Jewface.

Zohar, Ayelet. "The Elu[va]sive Japanese Portrait: Repetition, Difference and Multiplicity." *Trans-Asia Photography Review* 2, no. 1 (Fall 2011).

8

OF JEWS AND CATS

Joann Sfar and North African Jewish Humor

Jennifer Caplan

"Jewish humor," as used by English-speaking and especially American observers, almost exclusively implies eastern European, Ashkenazi humor.[1] Although no one has been able to offer a complete and coherent definition of what Jewish humor is, when you look at the numerous vague attempts, you see the Ashkenormative implications. In *Jewish Comedy*, Jeremy Dauber began by asking what makes a certain joke Jewish. "Is it the syntax," he asks, "with its faint Yiddish overtones? . . . Or is it just a joke about herring?"[2] Elliot Oring was more explicit. He argued, "The Jewish joke and Jewish humor more generally spring from the soil of Eastern Europe."[3] Joseph Telushkin argued that two of the defining characteristics of Jewish humor were anxiety around antisemitism (and especially the Holocaust) and anxiety around American Jewish assimilation, both of which assume the eastern-Europe-to-America migration pattern so common in late nineteenth- and early twentieth-century America.[4] In *No Joke*, Ruth Wisse describes the "geographically and linguistically divergent communities this book explores," but an examination of the book reveals that "divergence" still only covers the same eastern European Jewish diaspora we find in all these examples.[5] Mel Brooks himself, luminary of Jewish comedy, has long argued that what we call Jewish humor is a misnomer. "You got it wrong," he once said. "It's not really Jewish comedy—there are traces of it, but it is really New York comedy, urban comedy, street-corner comedy. It's not Jewish comedy—that's from Vilna, that's Poland."[6]

Over and over in attempts to define the indefinable qualities of Jewish humor, people gesture to language (but always Yiddish), the immigrant experience (but always from eastern Europe to America), antisemitism (but always in the form of European violence and persecution), or the foods, holiday observances, ritual habits, and clothing that are specific to Ashkenazi Jewish culture. That makes it difficult to analyze non-Ashkenazi-based Jewish humor because either we are trying to fit a square peg into a round hole or we are removing things from their unique cultural setting in order to try to make oranges into apples. The analysis I am going to undertake in this chapter is made both easier and more difficult by the fact that Joann Sfar, best known as a graphic novelist, claims both Ashkenazi and Sephardic cultural heritage. His mother was Ukrainian, but she died when Sfar was very young. He was raised primarily by his father, who was Algerian, so Sfar's home life had much stronger North African influences. He was born and raised in France, however, which further complicated his Jewish cultural identity as a European Jew, but he was part of a European Jewish community heavily influenced by the legacy of Francophone colonization of North Africa.[7]

This is an identity still fraught with the legacy of both colonialism and antisemitism, as was seen in August 2022 when French President Emmanuel Macron announced his intention to include Haïm Korsia in his delegation on a visit to Algeria. Korsia is the chief rabbi of France and is the child of Algerian Jews, but the announcement of his inclusion in the delegation was immediately decried as an act of Zionist infiltration by many right-wing Algerians, and Korsia's eventual removal from the delegation (after testing positive for COVID-19) was seen by some as capitulation to antisemitic pressure.[8] Additionally, Sfar is working with a fragmented history. Aomar Boum has written of North African Jewish history that is "a web of discourse emanating from three distinctive voices: that of the French colonial vulgate, an edited post-independence national historical narrative, and local oral traditions and memories."[9] Although Boum is specifically discussing Morocco, not Algeria, the same loss of a historical record and recreation of a narrative from partial sources plague Algerian, Tunisian, and other Francophone African Jews trying to reconstruct their colonial past.

Sfar's early novels dealt primarily with European and Ashkenazi topics, in particular his popular graphic novel *Klezmer*, but in recent years his work has taken more of a Sephardic/Mizrachic turn, including *Les Olives*

Noir, about a Jewish child in Jesus-era Palestine, and *Le Chat du Rabbin*, or *The Rabbi's Cat* as it is titled in English. While he has written many more volumes of *The Rabbi's Cat* in French (eleven at the moment) than have been translated into English, the first five volumes were collected into a two-part set and published in English in 2005 (French issues 1, 2, and 3) and 2008 (French issues 4 and 5).

To contextualize and understand Sfar's North African–inflected Jewish humor I will begin with a discussion of the muddled racial and cultural identities of North African Jews. A useful example is the work of Albert Memmi, specifically his autobiographical novel *The Pillar of Salt*. Memmi is not a humorist, yet *The Pillar of Salt* is marked throughout with a biting satiric wit that gives some insights into what may be different about Sephardic Jewish humor. Ashkenazi Jewish humor is often said to be self-deprecating, while Memmi's protagonist, and to a certain extent Sfar's as well, saves his sharpest barbs for those around him, especially those who are part of or colluding with the colonial European bureaucracy. Additionally, Memmi's and Sfar's novels both involve the way North African Sephardic Jews see themselves as different from (and potentially inferior to) an idealized image of the European, Ashkenazi Jew. Using Memmi as a satiric baseline will allow for greater contextualizing of Sfar's *The Rabbi's Cat*, which is the work in which he situates his humor and identity most strongly in a non-Ashkenazi milieu.

A brief comparison between *The Rabbi's Cat* and Art Spiegelman's *Maus* offers additional insights into some of the ways in which Sfar's work does not precisely mimic even another graphic novel about Jews using animal metaphors.[10] I will not belabor the argument that Sfar's work is humor. The novels, as we will see in more depth below, are suffused by an ironic tone that makes the experience of reading them often quite funny, but Sfar's style of humor is ephemeral in a way that makes trying to pin down a precise moment of comedy unnecessarily pedantic. As E. B. White once said, "Humor can be dissected, as a frog can, but the thing dies in the process."[11] Importantly, the characters in Sfar's novels do not think they are being funny, but they are funny primarily because they are so serious. By reading Sfar's depiction of colonized Algerian Jews through the lens of Memmi's depiction of colonized Tunisian Jews, we can draw some conclusions about what is distinct about North African Jewish humor and what it may share with its eastern European counterpart.

Albert Memmi and the Question of North African Jewish Identity

They say that everything old becomes new again and that history repeats itself. That certainly seems to be true for questions about Jews and race. Throughout the nineteenth century, as the pseudoscience of race developed, many groups we now consider "ethnicities" were classified as races. The United States Census had separate racial categories for Chinese and Japanese for decades, and many European groups were designated as white subraces, including Italians, Roma, and Jews. In most parts of Europe, Jews were characterized as their own racial category as soon as modern racial categories were developed, and that bled into the European colonial settings, where it became more complicated in Jewish communities that blended European Jews and Jews native to the colonized area. Because so much humor by (and about) Jews involves interactions between Jews and their non-Jewish neighbors, the different valances of these regional classifications may have bearing on how and why Jewish humor looks subtly different in different areas. This classification of Jews into their own race was obviously one of the things that allowed the Nazi eugenic arguments to function, but it was not initially created by the Nazis or developed as a tool of antisemitism. Many Jewish doctors and scientists in the nineteenth and twentieth centuries wrote in support of the idea of a Jewish race (although many also argued against it). In most cases, this was a way to assert Jewish exceptionalism and collect data that "proved" the Jewish race had a lower criminality rate, for example, or contracted syphilis less often.[12]

For obvious reasons, this all changed after World War II, and Jews in many places became simply "white." Much has been written about this phenomenon in its American context, from Karen Brodkin's *How Jews Became White Folks and What That Says About Race in America* to Eric Goldstein's *The Price of Whiteness*, but the consensus for more than half a century was that American (and therefore, in most people's minds, Ashkenazi) Jews are white. In the American context, Jews were always legally white while being seen as racially other in an unofficial or cultural context. In other nations, where Jewish occupied their own specific racial category, the change sometimes took different forms, but there was an overall move toward Jews becoming part of the racial majority in most places. Recently, however, the rise of white nationalism and antisemitism on both the left and the right has people asking the question again: Are Jews white? This question has a direct impact on figures like Joann Sfar, whose identity as the son of a North African father and a Ukrainian mother spans this gap between the assumption that "Jewish" means Ashkenazi and (often incorrectly assumed) white and the reality that many Jews, including Ashkenazi Jews, hold non-white identities. This, then, overlaps with the question of how to evaluate Sfar's humor. Can we evaluate it in a similar manner to other European or Ashkenazi Jewish comedians, or does the African setting of *The Rabbi's Cat* in particular mean that we cannot use the same rubrics for determining whether it qualifies as "Jewish humor"? To put it another way, are the struggles of colonized Jews in North Africa similar enough to the struggles of eastern European Jews that we can assume those populations would develop humor that looked similar? Can we use those ways in which Sfar's humor looks different from the bulk of Jewish humor to claim enough basis for a discrete non-Ashkenazi form of Jewish humor?

To add contextual framework to Sfar's categorization as a North African Jew, let us first explore the way Jews were categorized in a colonial North African context. By examining the way Jews move into, out of, and through ethnic categories depending on context, we can gain some additional insights as to why Sfar's work has been so difficult to categorize within the existing canon of Jewish humor. Albert Memmi's *The Pillar of Salt* is about Tunisian Jews finding their place in the colonial context. While *The Pillar of Salt* is a novel, it is deeply autobiographical and is Memmi's primary literary exploration of his childhood and young adulthood, including his experiences in a Nazi forced labor camp during World War II. Memmi was born in 1920 in Tunisia, which was then under French colonial control. His parents were both Jewish, but his mother was a Berber Jew while his father was native Tunisian and Italian. Memmi grew up on the edges of the Jewish ghetto of Tunis, speaking the Tunisian dialect of Judeo-Arabic. His awareness of his own intersectionality happened in stages and came to define his relationship both to his African surroundings and to the white Europeans he idolized as a young man.

The protagonist of the novel is named Alexandre Mordechai Benillouche. As a simulacrum for Memmi, Alexandre speaks with preternatural intelligence and awareness, but early in the book he describes his name and with it his complicated identity:

Alexandre: brassy, glorious, a name given to me by my parents in recognition of the wonderful West and because it seemed to them to express their idea of Europe. . . . I was furious at my parents for having chosen this stupid name for me. Mordechai (colloquially I was called Mridakh) signified my share in the Jewish tradition. It had been the formidable name of a glorious Maccabee and also of my grandfather, a feeble old man who never forgot the terrors of the ghetto. Call yourself Peter or John, and by simply changing your clothes you can change your apparent status in society. But in this country Mridakh is as obstinately revealing as if I shouted out: "I am a Jew!" More precisely: "My home is the ghetto," "my legal status is native African," "I come from an Oriental background," "I'm poor." But I had learned to reject these four classifications.[13]

Alexandre chafes at his ghetto life. His mother is an illiterate tribeswoman. His father works a trade and expects Alexandre to do the same. Alexandre wants to study medicine and later philosophy and be worldly and accepted in European circles. The contempt in which his peers and teachers hold Jews, he seems to believe, is because the Jews are poor and clannish and backward. The French government placed Jews in their own category, below the French but slightly higher than the other native African populations, and Alexandre thought that he would transcend that by becoming educated. Throughout the novel Alexandre sees himself as clever, witty, educated, and able to demonstrate his superiority to others through his biting sarcasm at their expense. But when World War II breaks out, the teachers who Alexandre thought respected him turn their back on him. He believed that because he spoke fluent French and read Camus he would be spared, but he ends up in a Nazi-controlled prison camp because in the end he was African, and Jewish, and the Reich did not care that he spoke French.

This is a novel about a move from feelings of ethnic superiority to feelings of ethnic confusion. Alexandre always knew he wasn't European, but because Jews had an actual legal category that placed them above other native Africans and because he danced the French colonialists' dance, he believed he had transcended his Jewishness, his Africanness, his Orientalness, and his poorness. He had not, and while the prison camp to which he was sent was not the nightmare that European Jews were experiencing, it nevertheless caused him to understand that he could never be European, even when he left Tunisia at the end of the book. Memmi wrestles with the place of Jews in North Africa, both those who are part of white settler colonialism and those who are native African Jews. The book establishes that while the social and ethnic place of African Jews is complicated, one thing that often sets them apart from both their native African and white colonial neighbors is their reliance on wit and sarcasm.

Sfar, *The Rabbi's Cat*, and Jewish Humanity

Sfar, as a European-born child of immigrants raised in the late twentieth century, is of course very different than Memmi. Sfar is, in some ways, a combination of who Alexandre was and who Alexandre wanted to be in that Sfar's mother was an eastern European immigrant to France, but the parent who raised him was a native African Jew. Sfar grew up in France, not Africa, so his identity and background are similar to that we might imagine for Alexandre's children, were he to have any. Nevertheless, the context of Memmi's world and identity is helpful primarily because the characters Sfar is writing about in *The Rabbi's Cat* would have been Memmi's colonized contemporaries. So while Sfar's identity matters because he is the humorist (if we wish to call him that), it is also the identity of the characters that shapes the way *The Rabbi's Cat* functions as North African Jewish humor. In addition to Sfar's identity as an Algerian Jew being ethnically complicated, *The Rabbi's Cat* itself complicates the boundary between human and nonhuman animals, and much of the humor of these novels comes from this blurring of the lines between species. On its own this is a funny conceit, but when viewed in the context of the preceding discussion, this can also be read as one more way of establishing the liminal categorical existence of North African Jews.[14]

Mark Twain once said, "Man is the only animal that blushes. Or needs to."[15] Western civilization has spent much of our history trying to distance ourselves from our own animal nature, and there is little controversy in saying that Western religious traditions have been instrumental in allowing ourselves to forget that we are animals. Judaism has, of course, the troublesome legacy of Genesis, in which Adam is given "dominion" over the other animal species, but the scriptural denigration of nonhuman animals doesn't end there. Throughout rabbinic literature are examples of the use of animal metaphors as the sharpest and most biting insult you could bestow upon another human being. Many of these are read as being sort of tongue in cheek, but they nevertheless show a commitment to hierarchical thinking. Additionally, however, these examples show a history of Jewish thought about humans, animals, and humans as animals that can lend some clarity to why the trend of Jewish writing about humanlike animals is so often humorous.[16] In the Talmud Tractate Berachot 25b, for example, we are told that gentiles are considered less than human and are compared to donkeys, all to explain why we need to be specifically told not to pray in front of a naked gentile (because, apparently, that is a problem that often arises?). Obviously, you cannot pray in front of a naked human, but gentiles are beasts, are lesser, and therefore it must be clarified that their nakedness is similar to human nakedness.

Lest you think this an insult the rabbis reserved only for non-Jews, however, there is also Tractate Pesachim 49b. In this tractate an "*am ha'aretz*,"[17] a common Jew, is compared to all manner of beasts, and we are told it is permitted to stab such a man, even on the holiest of days, but not to slaughter him ritually because he is an unclean animal, unfit for ritual sacrifice. One may "tear him like a fish," meaning you can rip his spine out through his back, and like a gentile he is said to be like a donkey who will bite you and break your bones. Although it is doubtful that anyone actually took these Talmudic injunctions literally, they are nonetheless part of a long, hallowed tradition of hierarchical thinking in Jewish tradition that has placed some people above other people and all humans above all nonhuman animals. While it is dangerous to assume people a millennium and a half ago found the same things funny that we do, it is nevertheless possible to see in these animal comparisons a sort of hyperbolic humor that continues to be an identifiable trend in the way Jewish humor from a variety of geographical regions and cultural contexts addresses the relationship between Jews and others (including other Jews). Because much of the humor—and meaning—of Sfar's novel rests on the intersection and overlap of human and nonhuman animals, it may be helpful to read portions of *The Rabbi's Cat* alongside some notable sequences from *Maus*. This will offer further data points to support the idea that North African Jewish humor has distinct differences from Ashkenazi Jewish humor.

In addition to being one of the most critically acclaimed graphic novels of all time, Art Spiegelman's *Maus* is also looked at as one of the best and most innovative explorations of post-Holocaust Jewish thought and in particular the psychology of the children of survivors (of which Spiegelman is one). Because *Maus* has been so influential and so written about, I am not going to go through a detailed context for the novel.[18] What is important for this chapter are the ways in which Spiegelman hints at slippage in our belief that we have a stable species identification and also that our interpersonal relationships are much more ruled by our animal nature than by any highfalutin notion of "humanity." Because *Maus* established a framework for Jewish graphic novels exploring animals-that-are-people-that-are-animals, *The Rabbi's Cat* is able to explore similar questions about what makes us human while also injecting more humor into the concept. Because Sfar isn't dealing with the specific gravitas of the Holocaust, he is able to poke fun at his characters in a broader way than Spiegelman could.

There is a notable sequence of panels on the final pages of the first volume of *Maus* in which Spiegelman's parents, Vladek and Anja, are hiding from the Nazis in a dark basement. These panels acknowledge the metaphorical nature of the book and fight back against a simple, allegorical reading of the story. Throughout the book Jews are represented as mice, but here we learn the mice are not really mice. Anja is frightened of the rats in the dank cellar in which a group of Jews are hiding from the Nazis. To put her at ease, Valdek tells her they are mice. So the human mice and the nonhuman mice are discrete species. But it nevertheless remains important to Spiegelman's story that the human mice *are* mice, as opposed to Sfar's cat, who is perhaps a person but isn't a human.

The Rabbi's Cat is not about Sfar's actual family but is nevertheless also autobiographical in ways. *The Rabbi's Cat* not only allowed Sfar to engage more in the North African history and settings he learned from his father's side of his family but also let him probe many of the same ethical considerations Spiegelman was working through almost two decades previously while engaging in the same kind of dark humor we saw in Memmi. Both *Maus* and *The Rabbi's Cat* ask the question "What makes someone a Jew?," although they do it in different ways. For *Maus* it comes down to what animal we are. Can a frog become a mouse? Are we humans in mouse masks? Is our human nature really that separate from our animal nature? *The Rabbi's Cat*, on the other hand, is literally a cat. A skinny, hairless, big-eared pet cat who loves the Rabbi's daughter and enjoys spending time with the Rabbi while he works. In the first few pages of the book, the cat eats a "tiresome" parrot and—voilà!—he gains the ability to speak.[19]

The power to speak appears to be the dividing line between animal and human for the Rabbi, because as soon as the cat speaks the Rabbi begins to push human, and specifically Jewish, ethics on the cat. Early in the book the cat narrates by saying, "He wants me to study the Torah and the Talmud—the Mishnah, the Gemara. He wants to put me back on the straight and narrow. He tells me that I have to be a good Jew, and that a good Jew does not lie. I answer that I am only a cat. I add that I don't know if I am a Jewish cat or not."[20] As above, the immediate Jewish response to understanding the relationship between human and nonhuman animals is to consult the Torah and the Talmud and the Jewish ethical tradition. Can a cat be a Jew? Furthermore, can a cat be a good Jew? The Rabbi seems unsure, so he goes to consult *his* rabbi, and the cat and the Rabbi's rabbi enter a lengthy theological discussion about the nature of God and the nature of humanity, which shows the Rabbi's rabbi to be rigid and inflexible in his thought and the cat to be quite a clever little theologian. Sfar's humor throughout much of the book is very dry, and it is the humor generated by those who are depicted as being completely in earnest as they do ridiculous things. Although the boundaries between types of humor are quite porous, this element of Sfar's work has much in common with the techniques often identified with British humor and less with what we traditionally identify with Ashkenazi Jewish humor.[21] The novels are funny throughout, but it would be unnecessarily pedantic to try to isolate individual moments that prove the humor.

In the end, of course, the cat is ultimately denied a bar mitzvah, which he believes means he cannot be a Jew, so the Rabbi forbids the cat to be around his daughter any longer. While this oversimplification of what makes one Jewish—and the conflation of all Jewish identity-affirming and life cycle–promoting rituals into the singular event of the bar mitzvah—could be seen as just a misunderstanding of Judaism on Sfar's part, it is, in fact, emblematic of his humor and represents the dry, satiric tone his humor takes throughout the books. It also, like Spiegelman, offers an opportunity to think about what makes humanness so special and to question whether humans really are superior to nonhuman animals if the animals are capable of much richer and more sophisticated thought.

A second image from *Maus* further demonstrates the framework Spiegelman established that Sfar then both reinforces and subverts. Spiegelman's wife, Francoise, is French and converted to Judaism after they married. On the first page of the second volume of *Maus*, we find Art trying to decide how to visually depict his wife. The French are, naturally enough, depicted as frogs in the few places where we encounter French soldiers. But what to do with Francoise? Is she a frog? A poodle (Americans are dogs, so that would reflect her new citizenship)? We know the answer because we are looking at mouse Francoise next to Art, but we're nevertheless watching Art struggle with this question. To Francoise it is simple; he is a mouse so she is a mouse; she converted to Judaism so now she is a mouse. End of story. Art sees identity as more difficult to explain than that. Mousehood, perhaps, must be achieved over years of struggle. If Francoise can be a mouse simply by taking it on, what does it mean for his parents and the other Holocaust victims who could not take their mousehood off? Is it fungible, or is it not?

During a dream sequence in which the Rabbi becomes a cat, on the other hand, he has *become* a cat; he is not a human who temporarily looks like a cat. During this sequence the cat describes the things he and his master do, including eating from the trash cans of nonkosher butchers, being chased—but not caught—by dogs, and sexually assaulting female cats. The cat says that there are "female cats that meow. I grab one by the neck and teach her a thing or two."[22] The Rabbi, on the other hand, does not want to force himself on the female cats that way. The text in English and French is very similar, but the French is perhaps marginally funnier when the cat tries to understand the Rabbi's refusal by saying, "Des restes d'humanite, ou de judiasme, ou alors il est vieux," alongside a speech bubble in which the cat Rabbi pushes away a female cat saying, "Non, non, mademoiselle."[23] The English edition translates the explanation as "Perhaps some remnant of his humanity, or Judaism, or just that he's old" and then "No, no miss." While the two versions do carry the same meaning, there is a subtle rhythm to the original French that carries the humor of the sequence a bit better. In English it feels more melancholy. In addition, the rhythm of "Non, non, mademoiselle" is arguably a funnier beat than "No, no miss."

Sfar's cat is truly a cat, and the Rabbi, while he may have traces of humanity remaining that keep him from behaving entirely as the cat does, is fully a cat as well. The original French, especially in the dream sequence, also harkens back to Jacques Derrida's discussion of his difference from his cat in *The Animal That Therefore I Am*. Just as Derrida finds his essential difference from his cat within his own discomfort at being naked in his cat's presence, the Rabbi's essential cat-ness is felt in his lack of discomfort at his nakedness and the ease with which he engages with (most) feline activities that his human self could never do. Sfar is more interested in nonhuman personhood, which is both another reason he can mine the concept for more humor and a potential site for differentiating his North African humor from Ashkenazi sensibilities. For obvious reasons (at least according to Joseph Telushkin and others), a great deal of Ashkenazi Jewish humor comes out of lingering Holocaust anxieties. Spiegelman, therefore, like many other post-Holocaust writers, is trying to reclaim Jewish humanity from the Nazis, who had denied it. Sfar, on the other hand, is more comfortable with dehumanizing his Jewish characters in order to establish the connection his Jews have to their natural, native environment. As we saw in *The Pillar of Salt*, the discrimination of the French colonial government wasn't the same as Nazi anti-Jewish legislation, so for Sfar and Memmi it is more important to stake a claim to Jews' belonging as Africans and as part of their surroundings in order to establish difference between them and the colonizers. The Rabbi can *truly* be a cat, while Spiegelman's animals are always really humans, most clearly illustrated in the final example from *Maus*.

The Rabbi's rabbi argues that it is a love of God that makes one a Jew, and since the cat loves only the Rabbi's daughter, he cannot be a Jew. The cat himself seems to think that it is more of a general moral orientation to the world that makes him a Jew or not and that he is every bit the Jew the Rabbi's rabbi is. The cat, like Francoise in *Maus*, sees Jewishness as something that is built (at least in part) on relationships with those around you, while the rabbi rejects that approach in favor of a strict theological view. The cat struggles with Jewish teachings; he cannot take the story of Adam and Eve or Creation literally because he claims carbon dating and genetics prove they are absurd. The Rabbi tells him he is being blinded by Western thought, which "puts names to things, labels, as if to say 'These things are part of my system, I have understood them.' But by the time you've finished naming a thing it has already changed and the name you gave it no longer defines it exactly, so you end up with empty words in your mouth."[24] The analogy is clear; Western thought makes "cat" and "human" incommensurate categories, but the conversation between the cat and the rabbi belies the fact that labels are not stable and that to expect things to forever conform to one paradigm is to set yourself up for failure. Although there are many Jews who are part of the "Western" philosophical canon, Jewish thought and "Western" thought are not identical categories. Nevertheless, this separation of "Western" from Jewish in this instance is a clear delineation of the way these North Africans see themselves as differentiated from European traditions.

At the end of this story arc (which is the first issue of the French publication), the cat proves capable of self-sacrifice to a degree that sets him apart from the humans around him. This is, of course, nothing surprising. There are dozens—or probably even hundreds—of stories of pets putting themselves in danger or in harm's way to protect their humans. The cat's willingness to put himself on the line for the Rabbi is not, in and of itself, remarkable. It is the reasoning behind it, and the way he puts himself on the line, that gives this scene weight. The Rabbi has been the rabbi to his community of Algerian Jews for decades. But the French government is instituting literacy tests, in French, to certify which rabbis are fluent enough. Our Rabbi is not. He studies, but he simply does not know French well enough. The cat is watching the test go poorly and in a moment of panic realizes they need divine intervention. "I don't care if it's forbidden," the cat says. "I invoke the name of God. Adonai. Adonai. Adonai. Adonai. Adonai. Adonai. Adonai. Meow."[25] The cat did what he knew was taboo, but his concern for the Rabbi was so great that he didn't care what the consequences might be. He invoked the name of God to demand a miracle on behalf of the Rabbi, and in doing so his power of speech is taken from him.

Did the cat get his miracle? We don't really know. The Rabbi thinks he did poorly on the test, but when the results come, he did well enough, and he is allowed to continue on as rabbi. Maybe that was divine intervention, or maybe the Rabbi had succeeded all on his own. Regardless, the cat returns to functional muteness, which frustrates him even more than before he could speak. As the Rabbi once told him, "Once you leave the Garden of Eden you can never go back."[26] The cat knows what it was to be able to share his thoughts with those around him, and his inability to do it anymore plagues him. Yes, he can still speak to other animals, but he finds their conversation lacking. The old hierarchy of the animal kingdom seems to be reified by the cat, despite his experiences having shown him that he is every bit the scholar and thinker that any human is. But without the power of speech he feels diminished and no longer sees himself as an equal to the humans. And, yet, there is a moment early on where the cat and the Rabbi share a dream. They travel the city together, and at the pivotal moment the Rabbi tells the cat he "can't understand why I want to be human when he would so much like to be a cat." So, the two of them become cats together and finally find some peace. A final image that shows Spiegelman's difficulty with stable species identifications comes midway through volume 2 of *Maus* and is possibly the most famous series of panels in the entire work. In these images we find Art at his drafting table. The most commonly discussed feature of these panels is that as the shot resolves to a wide angle we can see that Art is literally working on *Maus* on a pile of mouse corpses. He clearly struggled with his own commodification of so much death and with the success he had found on the backs of a sea of dead bodies. But if you look closely you see a second important detail of these images. In these panels and throughout the next couple of pages as Art talks to his psychiatrist, he is depicted as a human wearing a mouse mask. Art is questioning whether he even deserves to be a mouse or if he is, in fact, a lowly human masquerading as a mouse. Hamida Bosmajian has an essay about *Maus* in which she writes that "children of Holocaust survivors experience a sense of having been 'too late' acutely, and it is not unusual for such children to express the insane wish to have been with their parents at Auschwitz 'so I could really know what they lived through,'" which Art actually articulates in volume 2.[27] If Francoise's mousehood had to be earned, perhaps Art's did as well. And because he was born after the Holocaust he can't ever truly be a mouse and must instead remain a person who only pretends to be a mouse.

The second volume of *The Rabbi's Cat* focuses more on the humans of this community and in doing so demonstrates much more about the ways in which Sfar sees Algerian Jewish identity as different from that of European Jews. The Algerian Jews receive a large crate meant to be full of books from Europe and find a Russian Jew hiding in the box. He is depicted as physically very different from the Algerians, with his light skin, blond hair, and blue eyes. He speaks Yiddish and Russian, while our

Algerian Jews speak Arabic, Ladino, French, and a bit of Spanish. Their different histories and cultures are represented by their lack of any language in common, because while they both know prayerbook Hebrew neither has been exposed to the recreation of Hebrew as a spoken language. The cat, as it happens, can understand and speak to this newcomer, but as no one else can understand the cat anymore, he cannot act as translator. There is a Russian (not Jewish) in town, and they use him as a translator to find out why the Russian Jew is there. It turns out he was trying to get to Addis Ababa, because he is a Zionist and believes there is a long-lost country full of Black Jews in Ethiopia, who are the descendants of Solomon and Sheba. He is, in essence, coming to the same conclusions Rastafarianism has come to, albeit from the Jewish side. He is also a painter, and they communicate largely through visual means.

A conversation in the early part of the volume demonstrates the liminal racial identity of these Algerian Jews when the Rabbi rejects the idea that there could be Black Jews. Of African Jews he claims, "That's us, son. We're the African Jews," but when pushed to imagine *Black* African Jews, he says it is impossible.[28] "The proof is, look: blacks, they have slavery; Jews, they have pogroms. It's a lot to bear. Now imagine a people that had both at the same time. It just can't be."[29] Notice that the Rabbi says of Jews that "they" have pogroms, not "we." He is contrasting Black African communities with white, European Jewish communities to make his comparison. His identity as an African Jew is to be neither of these two persecuted groups.

The remainder of the volume is an adventure story. The Russian Jew, the old expat Russian, the Rabbi, and the cat head out to Ethiopia to find a mythical kingdom of Aramaic-speaking Black Jews. Not the Falasha of contemporary Ethiopia; the Russian Jew is aware of them but claims there is also a kingdom of separate Jews who have been hidden since biblical times. Along the way they pick up a Muslim cousin of the Rabbi, the expat Russian is killed in a duel, and the Russian Jew falls in love with a formerly enslaved Black African waitress. At the end of the second volume of *The Rabbi's Cat* (and issue 5 of *Le Chat du Rabbin*), the Russian Jew and his Black African wife finally find the lost kingdom of Black Jews. These Jews, however, speak Amharic, and neither the Russian nor his wife can understand them, nor can they understand any of the languages our protagonists speak.[30] The cat, on the other hand, can understand the Amharic and the elephants can understand our protagonists. The two types of Jews may as well be entirely different species (and in truth the Ethiopians send our protagonists away because, in a callback dripping with irony, they say they do not believe white Jews exist), but the nonhuman animals can bridge the communication divide. Once again, in Sfar we see a similar but slightly tweaked approach to Spiegelman's schema, which shows Sfar to be more willing to create equivalencies between Jews and animals.

Conclusions

The Rabbi's Cat illustrates the work that some contemporary Jewish artists are doing to use humor through graphic novels as a way to ask hard questions about the relationship between the Jewish ethical tradition, Jewish identity, and the modern world. Questions like "What does it mean to be a human?" and "What does it mean to be a Jew?" take on great significance in the racially and politically charged world of interwar French-occupied Algeria. Sfar is illustrating a part of his family history, so these are not idle questions to him but real existential explorations of who he is, and he uses humor as part of his processing mechanism. Humor is a popular medium for tackling difficult topics for many reasons, but one of the key reasons is its ability to defuse or deescalate fraught topics. By writing these stories through humor, as well as by placing them nearly a century ago, Sfar can mask his most trenchant commentary on contemporary life in bright colors and funny animals. Sfar follows not only Ashkenazi Jews like Spiegelman but also his fellow North African Jews like Memmi in using an unexpected slippage between the self and the other, whether human or nonhuman, to highlight the ways in which traditional hierarchical thinking leads to (in some instances catastrophic) societal failures. What does it mean to wear your mouse mask over your humanity? And how can one be a good Jew if one is only a cat? Sfar's approach to identity is subtly different than his entirely Ashkenazi counterparts because his background, like Memmi's, involves an identity that is African, Oriental, and colonized. His sense of Jewish relationships to place differs from that of those Jews who share the "shtetl to America" narrative, and his humor reflects these subtle differences in ways that make it impossible to understand his work without thinking of it in an African context.

If we return to the question of whether "Jewish humor" is humor done by Jews or is humor done by Jews that contains certain elements, then *The Rabbi's Cat* could be used to confirm the former definition or complicate the latter. It is humor, and it is both done by a Jew and about Jewish topics, so if your definition of Jewish humor is simply based on identity and subject matter, then *The Rabbi's Cat* qualifies. If, as we saw at the beginning of this chapter, your definition is based on certain shared elements, almost all of which stem from eastern European linguistics or the shtetl experience, then *The Rabbi's Cat* may not qualify, employing as it does more absurdism than language play and more concern about the experience of being a colonized other than anxiety over immigration or antisemitism. The answer could be, perhaps, that just as we have come to acknowledge distinct Jewish food cultures and distinct Jewish languages and distinct Jewish clothing styles that all represent the different cultural and geographic regions Jews have inhabited, we should speak of Jewish humors that can coexist without diminishing the unique qualities of each variety.

Notes

1 I will use "Ashkenazi" and "eastern European" interchangeably, although they are not truly synonymous. The overlap between the two concepts has influenced the way Jewish humor is seen as monolithic, however, so the interchangeability is part of my argument. Using "Sephardic" and "North African" synonymously is much more complicated, so there I will try to be more precise in using North African to refer to reality and Sephardic when what I mean is to invoke the (often imagined) sense of difference between those Jews and Ashkenazi Jews or between that culture and Ashkenazi culture.

2 Jeremy Dauber, *Jewish Comedy* (New York: W. W. Norton, 2017), ix–x.

3 Elliott Oring, *Joking Asides* (Logan: Utah State University Press, 2016), 166.

4 Telushkin, Joseph, *Jewish Humor* (New York: William Morrow, 1998), 15–26.

5 Ruth Wisse, *No Joke: Making Jewish Humor* (Princeton: Princeton University Press, 2015), 7.

6 Danielle Berrin, "Mel Brooks and Philip Roth on Jewishness and Love," *Jewish Journal*, January 15, 2013, accessed July 21, 2023, http://www
.jewishjournal.com/hollywoodjew/item/mel_brooks_and_philip_roth
_on_jewishness_work_and_love.

7 An excellent recent example of these conflicting identities is Aomar
Boum's graphic novel *Undesirables* (Stanford: Stanford University Press,
2023). Boum is a Moroccan scholar who is the chair of Sephardic studies
at UCLA, and the novel does an excellent job of demonstrating the cultural conflict that continues to cloud the identity of Francophone North
African Jews and their descendants. *Undesirables* is not comedic at all,
and interestingly neither the author nor the illustrator (Nadjib Berber) is
Jewish, so it is not an additional example of North African Jewish humor
but is a very striking novel.

8 Algérie Part, "Le grand rabbin de France souhaite le retour de tous les
juifs nés en Algérie," accessed July 28, 2023, https://algeriepart.com/
le-grand-rabbin-de-france-souhaite-le-retour-de-tous-les-juifs-nes
-en-algerie/; Algemeiner, "Algerian Islamists Slam Macron over Presence of French Chief Rabbi in Official Delegation," accessed July 28,
2023, https://www.algemeiner.com/2022/08/24/algerian-islamists-slam
-macron-over-presence-of-french-chief-rabbi-in-official-delegation/.

9 Aomar Boum, "Southern Moroccan Jewry between the Colonial Manu-
facture of Knowledge and the Postcolonial Historiographical Silence,"
in *Jewish Culture and Society in North Africa*, ed. Emily Gottreich and
Daniel Schroeter (Bloomington: Indiana University Press, 2011), 75.

10 It is also worth pointing out that neither *Maus* nor *The Rabbi's Cat* broke
entirely new ground in their Jews-as-animals motifs. One could argue
Maus owed much to Kafka's "Josephine the Singer, or the Mouse Folk,"
while *The Rabbi's Cat* imagines cat-Jews as I. L. Peretz did a century earlier in "Di Frume Katz."

11 Although this quotation is often attributed to Mark Twain, there is no
citational proof that he ever said or wrote it. Many people have said versions of it, but the earliest attribution is to E. B. White (together with his
wife, Katherine) in the October 1941 *Saturday Review of Literature*.

12 For a complete history of this debate see Mitchell Hart, *Jews and Race*
(Waltham, MA: Brandeis University Press, 2011).

13 Albert Memmi, *The Pillar of Salt* (Boston: Beacon Press, 1992), 94.

14 In *Laughter* Henri Bergson argues that we can only laugh at human things, so when we laugh at things animals do, it is because we are ascribing to them some human characteristics or behaviors. Following Bergson's argument, the very concept of things like *The Rabbi's Cat* and *Maus* contains intrinsic humor because we are naturally inclined to laugh at talking animals and animals performing human activities.

15 Mark Twain and Walter G. Chase, *Following the Equator: A Journey Around the World* (Hartford, CT: American Publishing Company, 1897), ch. 27 epigraph.

16 In addition to *The Rabbi's Cat* and *Maus*, we can look to earlier examples such as Kafka's "A Report to an Academy" or Malamud's "The Jewbird" to see this trend of Jewish animal humor.

17 See also Mark Leuchter's chapter, this volume.

18 Some good sources for additional background include Spiegelman's *MetaMaus*, the collection *Considering Maus*, and Victoria Aarons's work on second-generation Holocaust graphic novels.

19 Joann Sfar, *The Rabbi's Cat* (New York: Pantheon Books, 2005), 6–7.

20 Sfar, *The Rabbi's Cat*, 9.

21 For example, the techniques of Mr. Bean, Monty Python, and Black Adder, all of whom rely on this technique of generating humor through the absurdity of the characters' earnest devotion to their actions and cunning plans.

22 Sfar, *The Rabbi's Cat*, 32.

23 The pagination of the French and English translations is the same, so this is also p. 32 in the French edition.

24 Sfar, *The Rabbi's Cat*, 24–25.

25 Sfar, *The Rabbi's Cat*, 66.

26 Sfar, *The Rabbi's Cat*, 20.

27 Hamida Bosmajian, "The Orphaned Voice in Art Spiegelman's *Maus*," in Geis, *Considering Maus*, 33.

28 Sfar, *The Rabbi's Cat*, 83.

29 Sfar, *The Rabbi's Cat*, 84.

30 Brian Boomhower, "Heteroglossia and Polyphony in *Le Chat du Rabbin* by Joann Sfar" (master's thesis, University of South Carolina, 2016). Retrieved from https://scholarcommons.sc.edu/etd/3542.

Selected Bibliography

Aarons, Victoria. *Holocaust Graphic Narratives: Generation, Trauma, and Memory.* New Brunswick, NJ: Rutgers University Press, 2020.

Bosmajian, Hamida. "The Orphaned Voice in Art Spiegelman's *Maus.*" In *Considering Maus: Approaches to Art Spiegelman's "Survivor's Tale" of the Holocaust,* ed. Deborah Geis. Tuscaloosa: University of Alabama Press, 2007.

Dauber, Jeremy. *Jewish Comedy.* New York: W. W. Norton, 2017.

Geis, Deborah, ed. *Considering Maus: Approaches to Art Spiegelman's "Survivor's Tale" of the Holocaust.* Tuscaloosa: University of Alabama Press, 2007.

Hart, Mitchell. *Jews and Race.* Waltham, MA: Brandeis University Press, 2011.

Oring, Elliott. *Joking Asides.* Logan: Utah State University Press, 2016.

Sfar, Joann. *The Rabbi's Cat.* New York: Pantheon Books, 2005.

Spiegelman, Art. *Maus: A Survivor's Tale.* New York: Pantheon Books, (1986) 1991.

Telushkin, Joseph. *Jewish Humor.* New York: William Morrow, 1998.

Wisse, Ruth. *No Joke: Making Jewish Humor.* Princeton: Princeton University Press, 2015.

9

IS IT A WONDERFUL COUNTRY?

Holocaust Satire in the Israeli Satirical Show Eretz Nehederet

Liat Steir-Livny

Holocaust humor has gone through major changes in Israel since the 1990s, from being a total taboo to being an integral part of Israeli culture and TV. The satirical television program *The Chamber Quintet* (*Hahamishia Hakamerit*) (Matar Productions, Channel 2-Tela'ad, Channel 1, 1993–97), which is considered a milestone in Israeli TV, presented skits on Holocaust commemoration that broke the taboo for the first time.[1] *It's a Wonderful Country* (*Eretz Nehederet*) (Keshet Productions, Channel 2-Keshet, 2003–present) made it official that Holocaust humor and satire are part of mainstream Israeli TV. Unlike *The Chamber Quintet*, which addressed this topic in several (albeit seminal) skits, *It's a Wonderful Country* has made Holocaust satire an integral part of its narrative. This popular TV show, the only satiric program that has been broadcast on prime time for more than twenty years with consistently high ratings, was voted the "most Israeli" entertainment show in 2016. Its numerous Holocaust skits have thus legitimized Holocaust humor in the eyes of the public.

This chapter looks at the two main thrusts of Holocaust humor on *It's a Wonderful Country*. The first consists of using humor and satire to criticize forms of Holocaust commemoration in Israel. The second examines the use of Holocaust humor, satire, and parody to draw attention to other burning issues in Israeli culture. Based on scholarship dealing with Holocaust awareness in Israel, as well as the role of aggressive humor and satire in society and TV, this chapter shows that even though the program has

contributed to legitimizing Holocaust humor and making it more mainstream, it still stirs up controversy and prompts violent reactions. This,
however, has not stopped the producers from continuing to criticize Holocaust commemoration and other topics through humor and, in so doing,
championing the importance of satire as a potent form of social critique.

Introduction: Holocaust Memory in Israel, Satire, and TV

The memory of the Holocaust has not faded over the years in Israel.
On the contrary, Holocaust representations and the public discourse on
the Holocaust have intensified since the 1980s for a combination of social,
political, chronological, and technical reasons.[2] This upswell of feelings
emanates both from below (such as the massive contribution of second-
and third-generation artists to efforts to preserve yet innovate forms of
commemoration) and from the top as the byproduct of the efforts of collective memory agents who encourage the acting out of the trauma and
the framing of the Jewish people as the targets of unending victimization.[3]
Scholars have shown that the Israeli media, school system, and culture, as
well as public discourse in Israel, frame the Holocaust as a current-day,
ongoing local trauma rather than an event that came to an end in Europe
in the 1940s.[4] Israel is a post-traumatic society, whose ongoing security
problems fuel even more constant anxiety. The past is construed not as a
series of remote events that are long gone or distant memories but as reoc-
curring instances of the same attempts at annihilation of the Jewish people
that are experienced as integral and explicative of the present.[5]

Jewish Israelis are often said to suffer from "secondary traumatic
stress"; that is, indirect exposure to trauma affects those who were not
involved in the original traumatic events themselves. Secondary traumatic
stress can manifest in friends and relatives of traumatized individuals as
well as in wider circles. Studies have suggested that indirect exposure to
a trauma through intense cultural and media coverage (television, radio,
journalism, internet, etc.) can affect people who were not involved.[6] The
result is what researchers refer to as the constant "victimization discourse"
or a "religion of trauma."[7]

Over the past 120 years, numerous theories regarding humor, satire,
and parody have been developed. This chapter addresses those theories

that pertain to the development of Holocaust black humor in Israel. In his book *Laughter: An Essay on the Meaning of the Comic* (1900), French Jewish philosopher Henri Bergson laid the foundations of what would later be known as the social theory of humor and laughter. He saw laughter and the comic as sociological tactics used by society to punish individuals who deviate from its norms.[8] More recent research suggests that laughter can change the behavior of institutions and societies as a whole and is not restricted to the individual level. When humor ridicules ugly human phenomena, it may do so in a laudable attempt to eradicate misconduct. Laughter evoked by presentation of the absurd may be aimed at rectifying the world, by drawing attention to the injustices that exist in society. Humor can often convey a message more forcefully than when using overtly didactic methods.[9] People laugh when they grasp that the humoristic target is what needs improvement or rectification.[10] The arts and mass media frequently harness humor for this purpose.

Satire has the same function of reforming society. It showcases the negative side of certain events, people, and perceptions. The aggressive bitterness of satire constitutes a call for change. Because satire deals with situations specific to a given society and period, the audience can only identify the target by having some knowledge of the society in question. In this sense, satire can only rarely be transferred from one society to another.[11]

Satiric discourse typically combines three major functions of humor that it delivers simultaneously: the intellectual function, the social function, and the aggressive function. The intellectual function gives the satirist a feeling of superiority. The social function helps reinforce intra- and intergroup bonds, strengthens the cohesiveness of interpersonal relationships, and is crucial to opposition groups.[12] The aggressive function is a safe outlet for anger and resentment. Freud argued that people turn their physical aggressiveness into (more acceptable) aggressive humor. Since society criticizes physical aggressiveness, people developed another way to release their aggression through humor. This kind of humor allows individuals to express hostility and to vent their frustrations without risking punishment. Satire takes on various forms, from direct, blunt insults to sophisticated and nuanced wordplays.[13] Although aggression may be hardwired in evolution, expressing aggression through humor is a way to let off steam that does not threaten the structure of social relations.[14] Aggressive

humor motivated by the need to feel superior allows for the expression of
hostility toward those of equal and higher status. Thus, humor fulfills its
aggressive function and provides its authors with a fleeting though enjoy-
able feeling of superiority. It is the laughter of the helpless, which releases
feelings of vengeance and contempt, that allows the powerless to rise
momentarily above their oppressors.[15] For a short while, humor can make
feelings of anger, depression, and anxiety disappear and can strengthen
social cohesion among those who share these feelings.[16]

Television in Israel only dates back to 1968. Since the 1990s it has
become a dominant arena in the battle over Holocaust memory.[17] Given
that television is owned and managed by power groups in society, it makes
sense that it would try to bulwark its hegemony and immobilize the margins. The three main channels in Israel (11, 12, and 13) still attempt to
preserve a kind of tribal campfire to shore up national pride and endorse
Jewish and Zionist values. This is particularly noticeable in televised broad-
casts at times of crisis and during Jewish and national holidays.[18] However,
television also provides opportunities for change. Horace Newcomb and
Paul Hirsch consider television to be a "cultural forum": an arena in which
controversial, diverse issues and points of view can be openly discussed
without repercussions and in which a multiplicity of meanings rather than
a monolithic point of view can be presented.[19]

The role of television as a guardian of the hegemony, but also as a
venue for certain subversive content, becomes more complex with respect
to humorous skits, given the polysemic nature of humor.[20] The hegemony
can use humor to preserve the narrative it seeks to promote, but television
has the subversive potential to present positions contradicting national
myths and to deconstruct these positions.[21] On the one hand, humorous
skits can be perceived as a way to depict superficial stereotypes and to
strengthen hegemonic control.[22] On the other hand, the comic dimension
may leave room for criticism by creating a carnivalesque reversal enabling
a temporary release from inflexible hierarchies.[23]

The most successful TV satire shows in Israel since the 1990s that
tap into Holocaust humor and satire and subvert hegemonic voices are
The Chamber Quintet, It's a Wonderful Country, The Nation's Back (*Gav
ha'uma*) (Channel 10, 2015–20, formerly *The State of the Nation* [*Matzav
ha'uma*], Keshet Productions, Channel 2, 2010–15), *The Chosen People*
(*Am S'gula*) (Keshet Broadcasting, Channel 2, 2011), and *The Jews Are*

Coming (*HaYehudim Ba'im*) (Yoav Gross Productions, Channel 11, 2014–22).[24] They articulate the powerful position of the Holocaust as a constituting event in the consciousness and identity of Jewish Israelis and promote a new intellectual, ideological, and esthetic point of view of the collective memory of the cataclysm. They create social cohesion among groups who oppose the way Israeli collective memory agents like politicians, the educational system, the media, and public figures have appropriated the memory of the Holocaust. In a society that looks upon reality through the prism of the Holocaust, they also criticize other phenomena by using Holocaust associations.

A survey conducted in 2016 by the Panels Research Institute, on the country's sixty-eighth Independence Day, reported that *It's a Wonderful Country* was voted the "most Israeli" of all entertainment programs in the history of Israeli TV.[25] It is "the most prominent satirical show in Israel," declared *Haaretz* newspaper in 2013,[26] and in 2020 journalist Lucy Aharish claimed that "when you think about satire in the last twenty years, the first program you think of is *It's a Wonderful Country*."[27]

Muli Segev (b. 1972), the chief editor of *It's a Wonderful Country*, clearly states his agenda and is aware that his show is considered a left-wing satire. In interviews, he has criticized Prime Minister Benjamin Netanyahu many times, has called him "a crook" and "an instigator,"[28] and has claimed that the Jewish settlers in the occupied territories have held the state hostage for forty years: for example, "They are the mad boy that everybody is afraid to upset. This is an absurd situation which I find unacceptable."[29] He often proclaims that he prefers satire "with teeth": "In the beginning it was an entertainment show," he says, "until we dared produce skits that were less funny and more shocking."[30] Segev is not afraid of producing very controversial skits about ongoing military operations in which he questions whether they are justified. He and other satirists on the show have received explicit physical threats.[31] Segev is, of course, aware of the show's power: "Our strength lies in our ability to make an impact by thrusting a javelin in the entire country's living room."[32] He is also aware that many of the show's viewers are right-wingers who must endure his repeated attacks on the Right. "The public is willing to see things that make it laugh even if it goes against the dominant opinion," he claims.[33] He has stated that Israelis like to argue and enjoy sharpening their positions and constantly engaging in self-definition: "There is no nation that deals as much with its self-definition as the Israeli nation, and that is also our main occupation." In his view, the show is aimed not at attacking the right wing but rather at attacking the government. "No matter what the government does, we will attack it—that is our job." Since it is a right-wing government, they are on the receiving end, but left-wing politicians and public figures are not off the hook.[34]

The First Thrust: Criticizing Holocaust Commemoration in Israel

The satirical skits broadcast on It's a Wonderful Country protest the way collective memory agents commemorate the Holocaust and use it to ignite fear and anxiety. These skits employ aggressive humor to vent the frustration of groups who feel that Holocaust memory is being manipulated to create a sense of constant victimization for personal and collective gain. The skits also strengthen the social cohesion among groups that are opposed to this type of manipulation of memory because these skits create a series of code words, forming their own forbidden language of Holocaust humor in a society that sanctifies it.

Holocaust Memory in the School System

"We deal a lot with the Holocaust, but mainly with the political uses by the prime minister—the way he uses it in his foreign policy, and the fears he tries to instill in everyone from a very young age," says Segev.[35] In 2014 Shai Piron, the minister of education at the time, mandated a committee to prepare educational guidelines for kindergarten and elementary school teachers when preparing for Holocaust Martyrs' and Heroes' Remembrance Day. Prior to that time, kindergarten teachers presented the Holocaust in class in unscripted ways, which he wanted to unify.[36] The publication of the plan kindled a stormy debate in Israel. It also prompted a response in the form of a skit on It's a Wonderful Country

In the skit, "Danit the Victim" (in Hebrew: Danit Ha-korbanit) (season 11) actress Liat Har-Lev plays a children's star doing a children's show. With a big smile on her face she joyfully enters a stage set that includes a large banner with the words "Arbeit macht frei" written in large letters. She is dressed in a striped concentration camp prison uniform with the Star of

David on it. Actor Roy Bar-Natan plays Shai Piron, who is sitting on the set and helps her explain the Holocaust to children by using a big yellow Star of David hand puppet whom they call "Patchy the Patch" (in Hebrew: Tuly hatlay). Instead of talking to the kindergarteners about childish issues, she discusses the Holocaust and sings children's songs but changes the words so that they deal with the Holocaust (e.g., instead of "What a happy day I have today" she sings, "What a Holocaust commemoration day I have today, what a happy day, day of intimidation"). Patchy the Patch asks Danit to tell the children what happened during the Holocaust, and she begins it as though it is a fairy tale: "Once upon a time, in a land far far away, but not too far, a long time ago, but not that long ago, bad people lived." "What were their names?" asks Patchy. "They were called lalala Nazis and their helpers," she sings to the tune of another children's song, "and these Nazis wanted to annihilate all the Jews." "What is annihilate?" asks Patchy. "Annihilate is to kill," she responds. "What is to kill?" asks Patchy. "To kill is what I should have done to my agent, who promised me that doing children's shows would not ruin my career in adult shows." The actress uses extreme body language and facial expressions, speaks in an altered voice, continually displays a large fake smile, and evidences the unflappable cheerfulness of many children's show stars.

The scriptwriters not only criticize the new initiative but refer to another issue that was often criticized on *The Chamber Quintet*, another satire show, as well as in serious debates, namely, the "Zionist lesson" of the Holocaust and contentious efforts by right-wing figures to brand Arabs as the new Nazis. Danit, who previously highlighted the fact that the Holocaust was not such a distant event, now tells Patchy that if the Israel Defense Forces (IDF) had existed during the Holocaust "it would have destroyed the Nazis within an hour" and that the IDF will protect "us" from a second Holocaust that "people like the Arab grocer Mustafa are secretly hoping for." The children's song "Grandpa Tuvia" is turned into "Adolf Hitler" using phraseology that clearly associates past and present, Hitler and the Arabs as the new Nazis ("Hitler will come back with a kef-fiyeh"[37]). She sings "now go to sleep" and ends with yet another big fake cheerful smile. The dissonance between the childish context and the horrific theme highlights the absurdity of teaching the Holocaust to preschool children and the constant attempt by right-wing governments to instill constant fear and Holocaust-related anxiety. This topic is very important for Segev. In his puppet collection in his office, he showcases Patchy, the yellow badge.[38]

Fighting the Politicization of Holocaust Memory

As the right wing has strengthened its hold on Israel since the late 1970s, the left wing has intensified its critiques in various cultural fields. Satire is one of them. *It's a Wonderful Country*'s skits have connected various politicians with Holocaust humor and satire, but the most vilified politician is Netanyahu. This is a response to Netanyahu's constant use of the Holocaust when discussing the Israeli–Palestinian conflict, the Israeli–Arab conflict, or the Israeli–Muslim conflict. In the past decade, he has often made parallels between Arabs and Nazis, Palestinians and Nazis, and equated the nuclear threats of Iran's former President Mahmoud Ahmadinejad with Hitler's goal of exterminating the Jewish people. Netanyahu has repeatedly promoted the impression that Iran would be responsible for a second Holocaust.

Segev has commented that Netanyahu's constant dealing with the Holocaust "[has] turned it into a card that Israel flashes in front of the world, even when criticized for actions that deserve criticism. Instead of reinforcing a sense of humanity, his daily trivial use of the subject reinforces victimhood."[39] During the 2012 Purim holiday, for example, Netanyahu held a series of meetings with President Barack Obama in the United States to discuss, among other things, the nuclear threat from Iran and whether Iran should be preemptively attacked. Netanyahu found it appropriate to give Obama the Book of Esther (Megillat Esther),[40] which relates how in the fifth century BC, the ancient Persians set out to exterminate the Jews and how their plans were ultimately foiled. In his speech to Obama, he also produced a historical document, dating from World War II, in which Jewish American representatives asked the American government to bomb Auschwitz. Netanyahu hinted that this time the Jews would not wait for the United States to refuse this request and would handle matters themselves. In the vast majority of his speeches and in particular on the eve of Holocaust Martyrs' and Heroes' Remembrance Day at Yad Vashem, he compared the Holocaust to the future Iranian second Holocaust.

In an episode screened on Purim in 2012, *It's a Wonderful Country* presented a skit called "Remembrance Day for Shushan and Heroism" (in Hebrew: Yom ha-zikaron la-shushan vela-gvuran), which satirized the political connections between ancient Persia and modern-day Iran by creating a take on the Israeli Holocaust Martyrs' and Heroes' Remembrance Day in Israel.

The skit depicts employees (Mariano Edelman and Eli Finish) at a nuclear reactor in Iran during "Remembrance Day for Shushan."[41] In this skit, the ceremonial hallmarks of Israel's Holocaust Martyrs' and Heroes' Remembrance Day are reversed by referring to Iran. The phrase "and these are the names of the fallen," intoned during observance of Holocaust Martyrs' and Heroes' Remembrance Day in Israel, is used in the skit in tribute to Haman's murdered sons.[42] The two-minute siren that is sounded throughout Israel on Holocaust Martyrs' and Heroes' Remembrance Day is here replaced by shaking a rattle (the noisemaker that is shaken every time Haman's name is uttered during the reading of the Scroll of Esther).

In the skit, the master of ceremonies speaks of the downtrodden Persians who, under the rule of Ahasuerus (the ancient Persian ruler), went like "sheep to the slaughter."

This references an attitude in Israel's first decades when survivors were sometimes criticized for having gone to their death in the Holocaust "like sheep to the slaughter." On Holocaust Martyrs' and Heroes' Remembrance Day in Israel, the TV schedule is modified to broadcast programs dealing solely with the Holocaust and its memory, and sad songs are played throughout the day on Israeli radio.[43] In the skit, the TV program schedule in Iran has also been changed, and the radio plays songs of "good old Iran" while the Israeli "Zionists" who stuck to their usual schedules that day are slandered by the Iranian nuclear reactor employees as "Purim deniers" (a satirical pun on the term "Holocaust deniers"). The skit also depicts a well-known phenomenon in Israel when people find it difficult to stifle their (nervous) laughter during the two-minute siren. Here, an Iranian reactor employee cannot keep himself from laughing during the ceremony. The role switching in the skit ridicules Netanyahu's attempts to represent the Israelis as eternal victims. By deconstructing the behavioral patterns of Holocaust Martyrs' and Heroes' Remembrance Day, the writers showed the ease with which memory can be manipulated politically.

Thou Shalt Not Compare

"Nobody claims that there are extermination camps here, but racism and xenophobia certainly exist," Segev states.[44] This view was made clear in a skit entitled "International 'This Is Not a Holocaust Day' Day" (January 29, 2018),[45] depicting a "This Is Not a Holocaust Day" ceremony that satirizes the general attitude that it is forbidden to compare other events to the Holocaust and by extension criticize right-wing policies and performances. The skit illustrates how racism toward left-wingers, Palestinians, and asylum seekers is completely accepted by the right wing in Israel because "this is not the Holocaust." The skit is based on a stormy debate at the time in Israel: poet Yonatan Geffen's post on his Instagram account that week in which he compared Anne Frank to Ahed Tamimi, a Palestinian teenager who was filmed resisting an Israeli soldier and became a symbol of the Palestinian resistance to the Israeli occupation of Gaza and the West Bank. Avigdor Lieberman, who was then minister of defense, suggested banning Geffen's songs from the IDF radio channel. The legal adviser to the government said it would be illegal. Geffen finally apologized, and Lieberman withdrew his demand.[46]

In the skit, Geffen repeats lines from his post and says, "On the day the story of the struggle will be told, you [Tamimi] will be mentioned in the same breath as Joan of Arc and Hannah Szenes." The satirists added, "And Donald Duck" (in Hebrew this line rhymes). In the skit, right-wingers Lieberman and Minister of Culture Miri Regev attack Geffen and others. Whenever a left-winger tries to point to the suffering of other people or groups, they begin to sing, "This is not a Holocaust," a paraphrase on the chorus "It is not too bad" from a famous Israeli ditty of the same name by the Triplet Twins. The crowd sings along and cheers every time one of them begins to sing. The music was based on Geffen's famous children's album *The Sixteenth Lamb*. The skit made reference to a performance by Aviv Geffen, Yonatan's son, calling Netanyahu "a tyrant," which was banned by Regev (who denied this was the reason). Eyal Kitzis, the moderator, noted that Holocaust survivors support the asylum seekers and tried to discuss the Africans' misery but was interrupted brutally by another chorus of "This is not a Holocaust." The skit showed that instead of learning the consequences of racism from history, right-wingers draw strength from victimization and are unable to accept others' suffering, display racism and hate toward "the other," and refuse to see the similarities.

A heated debate broke out after the skit was aired. Miriam Indig, a ninety-year-old Holocaust survivor, called the Ministry of Communication. The phone call was filmed by her caregiver, who uploaded it to Facebook, where it went viral. In the call she said she had been insulted by the skit, which, in her opinion, mocked Holocaust survivors and Szenes, "with whom I was imprisoned." In tears she said, "We suffered so much there and here people are making fun of it like it didn't happen." Prime Minister Netanyahu shared her post on his social media and wrote, "I guess there is no limit to cynicism and the loss of values."[47]

The Second Thrust: Using Holocaust Humor to Criticize Other Issues in Israel

In the last twenty years, Holocaust humor on TV has used the Holocaust to criticize other topics. In a society saturated in Holocaust awareness, *It's a Wonderful Country* harnesses Holocaust associations to target the shortcomings of Israeli society by satirizing the siege mentality, popular culture, attitudes toward "the other," and social issues.

Criticizing the Siege Mentality

The problematic security situation, the constant struggle between Israel and the Palestinians, and the multiple wars, operations, and terror attacks have produced a post-traumatic society in which it is very easy to ignite fears. In 2004, a skit on *It's a Wonderful Country* was broadcast after a terror attack in the Sinai Desert (a popular vacation spot for Israelis) and at a time when official warnings were in place against traveling there and other hot spots. In the skit, a travel agent (Tal Friedman) tells a couple (Orna Banai and Dov Navon) who are worried about traveling to dangerous places that they should consider going on vacation to a concentration camp memorial site. When they get to the site, the woman notes that she feels safe because of the watchtowers and the electrified fence. Numerous complaints were filed to the Israel Television and Radio Authority as well as to Yad Vashem. Keshet, the show's production company, responded that there had been no intention to ridicule the Holocaust or use its memory as entertainment. Its spokesperson pointed out that *It's a Wonderful Country* is a satire whose skits are intended not only to provoke laughter but also to take issue and even to shock. He claimed that the skit was an allegory for the state of fear in Israel after the recent terror attacks in the Sinai and warnings about overseas travel, which added to the sense of siege.[48] The skit criticized the "industry of fear" in Israel[49] that feeds off recurrent warnings about the likelihood of terrorist attacks. The criticism was directed not only at the threats but also at the hysteria engendered by the media.

Fighting Right-Wing Politics on National Issues

It's a Wonderful Country uses Holocaust satire to protest its view of the misappropriation of the Holocaust by the right wing to create constant victimization. However, the show itself uses Holocaust (satire) to portray right-wing politicians and public figures as Nazis. In other words, those who use satire to protest the politicization of the Holocaust sometimes use satire in which they themselves politicize the Holocaust.

For example, in 2006, Knesset member Avigdor Lieberman made statements about exchanging territory with the Palestinian Authority and transferring Arab citizens of Israel to the Palestinian Authority in return and then compared members of the Yesh Gvul movement (a human rights, anti-occupation movement) to Kapos in the Nazi extermination and concentration camps. He became the focus of a controversial *It's a Wonderful Country* skit in December 2006. Each time Lieberman's character appeared on the skit, he was greeted with "Heil Lieberman!" and a right-arm salute. The skit was making the statement that there are nationalistic and violent perceptions among members of the right wing that resemble Nazism. In reaction to the skit, right-wingers distributed a picture of Segev on the internet wearing an SS uniform; thus, the vicious circle of using Holocaust associations to protest contemporary politics continued unabated.

The Attitude Toward "the Other": Fighting for Social Justice

It's a Wonderful Country's satirists also use Holocaust associations to claim that the universal lesson from the Holocaust has not been learned in Israel and that Israeli leaders treat minorities with dangerous racism. One of the main issues in this context is the debate over refugees and migrant workers from Africa.

Since 2000, when Africans began entering Israel through the border with Egypt in growing numbers, particularly from Sudan and Eritrea, the subject of refugees and asylum seekers has created controversy and violent debates. Most immigrants came to the country between 2007 and 2012, before a wall was built between Israel and Egypt. Currently, roughly thirty-seven thousand Africans reside in Israel, whose population in 2020 was about nine million.[50] The debate over these Africans is primarily manifested in the choice of words used to describe their status. According to the left-wing narrative, the vast majority are refugees and asylum seekers who should be integrated into society, whereas according to the right-wing view, the vast majority are infiltrators, illegal immigrants, and job seekers who must be deported. These, however, are popular perceptions, which differ from the legal definitions.[51] Since the Africans' arrival, right-wing governments have engaged in numerous social and judicial maneuvers that have not yet yielded a clear policy defining "infiltrators" and "asylum seekers,"[52] and they have tried to facilitate a policy of mass deportation. This culminated in an announcement on April 2, 2018, in which Netanyahu reported that the state of Israel had reached an agreement with the United Nations whereby sixteen thousand asylum seekers would be transferred to Canada, Italy, and Germany. Another sixteen thousand were supposed to be sent to various kibbutzim, moshavim (a type of cooperative agricultural communities), and other areas. Several hours later, Netanyahu canceled the plan under pressure from right-wing political parties and right-wing public debate.[53]

It's a Wonderful Country's satirists have criticized right-wing stands on this issue several times. For example, in March 2010, right-wing Knesset member Yaakov Katz circulated a memorandum calling for African asylum seekers who had entered Israel through Egypt to be grouped together in a "distant city" that they would build themselves through "workfare."[54] Paying homage to the opening sequence of *Inglorious Basterds* (Quentin Tarantino, 2009), a skit addressed the theme of the right wing's persecution of refugees and illegal migrant workers. It showed Katz, depicted by the actor Tal Friedman, as Nazi officer Colonel Hans Landa, who hunted down Jews in occupied France in the original film. In the skit, Katz is shown going from house to house dragging out asylum seekers and foreign workers. Several of Friedman's statements also repeated memorable lines from the film. This skit thus used the Holocaust to claim that the historically

victimized had become the present-day perpetrators, a well-known perception among left-wingers.[55]

In December 2013, following the refusal of African asylum seekers to
be sent to the Holot detention facility, a government paper was published
in which the asylum seekers were not mentioned by name but rather given
numbers. Many respondents compared the numbers to those tattooed
by the Nazis on the arms of Jewish prisoners in Auschwitz-Birkenau. A
photograph uploaded to the Facebook page of *It's a Wonderful Country*
presented former Minister of Interior Gideon Sa'ar getting ready to tattoo an anonymous refugee. The photograph caused turmoil and received
mixed responses, with some utterly appalled and others in favor. A day
later, in response to the turmoil, the image was deleted from the program's
Facebook page.

Popular Culture

It's a Wonderful Country uses Holocaust associations not only to protest
politics and social issues but also to point to the deterioration of Israeli
public life in general by exposing the domination of popular culture in
contemporary society. A good example is the skit "The Camp" (2011).
In this skit the screenwriters used the Holocaust to criticize the idiocy of
reality shows and Israelis and to take issue with the level of brutality on
Israeli television.[56] In "The Camp," actor Yuval Semo plays a casting director auditioning actors for a new, barbarian reality show. The candidates
(who did not know that they were actually being filmed for a satirical
program) are shown in the format of "a German reality show" called "The
Camp—Only One Person Wins." The format resembles that of *Survivor*,
and the big prize is—symbolically—six million new Israeli shekels. Semo
tells the prospective participants who come to audition that the participants will be divided into two tribes who inhabit two exotic islands and
need to compete against each other for tribal immunity: the two groups are
called "the Germans" and "the Jews."[57] The candidates were asked whether
they would agree to be on the show and what they would agree to do
during the shooting; their responses showed that they would do anything
for fifteen minutes of fame and were unconcerned with the show's clear
Holocaust associations. They said they would fight to the finish and con-
sented up front to anything the production staff told them to do, including
getting married, giving birth, striking an old woman, or throwing their

mothers out of the program. The casting agent showed the potential contestants a model of the camp and explained that the Germans were housed
in a hotel and the Jews in "crumbling" huts. When asked which side they
wanted to be on, the majority choose the Germans. Even when the interviewer asked questions making it impossible to ignore the parallel between
the new program and the Holocaust, the contestants stuck to their positions that, in order to win and to appear on a reality show, they would do
anything and everything. This time only ten complaints were sent to the
television authority about the comparison between the Holocaust and a
reality show.[58] The production team of *It's a Wonderful Country* said that
the skit was intended to illustrate the spirit of the era in which we live,
where the desire to be famous and a TV star at all costs outweighs personal
and national values: "Our goal when we produce a satirical program is
to trigger public debate, and to hold up a mirror to Israeli society even if
what it reflects back is very disturbing." The television authority responded
that *It's a Wonderful Country* is a satirical show, even though it did ask its
producers to be extra careful when dealing with such sensitive subjects.[59]

Conclusion

TV satire is a guarantor of social engagement: It promotes social processes,
such as increasing group cohesion and relieving stress within the group. It
boosts the group's morale and strengthens the bonds between its members,
helps generate consensus within the group, and minimizes the distance
between its members. Humor also contributes to social cohesion by creating a common language, an environment that emphasizes the group's
uniqueness. When the individual laughs along with the group, it means
that they agree with the group's state of mind and thoughts. While laughing, the individual is reinforced by the laughter of the other members, and
the individual's own laughter reinforces the other members of the group.[60]
Humor as social cohesion helps people who belong to the political opposition feel part of a larger group.

In the political and social Holocaust satire and parody of the left
wing, humor gives the opposition left wing a sense of power and is used
not only to vent frustration but also to create social cohesion. However,
the satirical use of the Holocaust by the left wing to protest Holocaust

commemoration, political and social injustice, and the deterioration of society reveals that even those who want to avoid politicizing the Holocaust and its domination over Israelis' everyday lives find themselves recreating politicization and highlighting its dominance over Israelis, albeit with the opposite narrative.

Notes

1 Eyal Zandberg, "Critical Laughter: Humor, Popular Culture and Israeli Holocaust Commemoration," *Media, Culture & Society* 28, no. 4 (2006): 561–79; Liat Steir-Livny, "Beyond the Chamber Quintet: Holocaust Humor on Israeli TV in the 2000s," in *Israeli Television: Global Contexts, Local Visions*, ed. Miri Talmon and Yael Levi (New York: Routledge, 2021), 235–46.

2 Dalia Ofer, "The Past That Does Not Pass: Israelis and Holocaust Memory," *Israel Studies* 14, no. 1 (Spring 2009): 1–35; Idit Gil, "The Shoah in Israeli Collective Memory: Changes in Meanings and Protagonists," *Modern Judaism* 32, no. 1 (February 2012): 76–101; Yechiel Klar, Noa Schori-Eyal, and Yonat Klar, "The 'Never Again' State of Israel: The Emergence of the Holocaust as a Core Feature of Israeli Identity and Its Four Incongruent Voices," *Journal of Social Issues* 69, no. 1 (2013): 125–43.

3 See, for example, Iris Milner, *A Torn Past* (Tel Aviv: Am Oved, 2004); Nurith Gertz, *A Different Choir: Holocaust Survivors, Aliens, and Others in Israeli Cinema and Literature* (Tel Aviv: Am Oved and Open University, 2004); Yosefa Loshitzky, *Identity Politics on the Israeli Screen* (Austin: University of Texas Press, 2002), 32–71; Liat Steir-Livny, *Remaking Holocaust Memory: Documentary Cinema by Third-Generation Survivors in Israel* (Syracuse: Syracuse University Press, 2019).

4 Oren Meyers, Motti Neiger, and Eyal Zandberg, *Communicating Awe: Media Memory and Holocaust Commemoration* (Basingstoke, UK: Palgrave Macmillan, 2014).

5 Amos Goldberg, "Introduction," in Dominick LaCapra, *Writing History, Writing Trauma* (Baltimore: Johns Hopkins University Press, 2000), 7–28 [Hebrew].

6 Charles Figley, "Compassion Fatigue as Secondary Traumatic Stress Disorder: An Overview," in Charles Figley, ed., *Compassion Fatigue: Coping with Secondary Traumatic Stress Disorder in Those Who Treat the Traumatized* (New York: Brunner-Routledge, 1995), 1–20.

7 Alon Gan, *From Sovereignty to Victimhood: An Analysis of the Victimization Discourse in Israel* (Jerusalem: Israel Democracy Institute, 2014) [Hebrew], 104–13; Adi Ophir, *Working for the Present: Essays on Contemporary Israeli Culture* (Tel Aviv: Hakibbutz Hameuhad, 2001) [Hebrew], especially 29–51, 256–80.

8 Henri Bergson, *Laughter: An Essay on the Meaning of the Comic* (London: Macmillan, 1911).

9 Avner Ziv, *Personality and Sense of Humor* (Tel Aviv: Papyrus, 1996) [Hebrew].

10 Avner Ziv, "Humor as a Social Corrective," in *Writing and Reading Across the Curriculum*, ed. Laurence Behrens and Leonard J. Rosen, 3rd ed. (Glenview, IL: Scott, Foresman, 1988), 356–60.

11 Ziv, "Humor as a Social Corrective."

12 Paul Simpson, *On the Discourse of Satire: Towards a Stylistic Model of Satirical Humor* (Amsterdam: John Benjamins Publishing, 2003).

13 Sigmund Freud, *Jokes and Their Relation to the Unconscious*, standard edition (New York: W. W. Norton, 1990).

14 Elliott Oring, *Engaging Humor* (Champaign: Illinois University Press, 2008); Ziv, *Personality and Sense of Humor.*

15 Haya Ostrower, *Without Humor We Would Have Killed Ourselves* (Jerusalem: Yad Vashem, 2009) [Hebrew], especially 105–20.

16 Ziv, *Personality and Sense of Humor.*

17 Dalia Ofer, "The Past That Does Not Pass: Israelis and Holocaust Memory," *Israel Studies* 14, no. 1 (Spring 2009): 1–35.

18 Noam Yuran, *Channel 2: The New Statehood* (Tel Aviv: Resling, 2001) [Hebrew].

19 Horace M. Newcomb and Paul Hirsch, "Television as a Cultural Forum: Implications for Research," *Quarterly Review of Film Studies* (1983): 45–55.

20 John C. Meyer, "Humor as a Double-Edged Sword: Four Functions of Humor in Communication," *Communication Theory* 10, no. 3 (2000): 310–33; Owen. H. Lynch, "Humorous Communication: Finding a Place

for Humor in Communication Research," *Communication Theory* 12, no. 4 (2002): 423–45; Limor Shifman, *Televised Humor and Social Cleavages in Israel, 1968–2000* (Jerusalem: Magnes Press, 2008) [Hebrew], 1–9.

21 Shifman, *Televised Humor and Social Cleavages in Israel*, 1–9.

22 Vincent Brook, *Something Ain't Kosher Here: The Rise of the "Jewish" Sitcom* (New Brunswick, NJ: Rutgers University Press, 2003).

23 Michael Bakhtin, *Rabelais and His World* (Bloomington: Indiana University Press, 1993)

24 Holocaust humor has been used since the 1990s in many sitcoms and comedy shows, for example, *Traffic Light* (*Ramzor*) (Keshet Broadcasting, Channel 2, 2008–14), *Miller's Junction* (*Tzomet Miller*) (Keshet Broadcasting, Channel 2, 2016), *My Successful Sisters* (*Ha'ahayot hamuzlahot sheli*) (Guri Alfi, Yes, 2016), *Mother's Day* (*Yom haem*) (Dana Eden Productions, Channel 2 Keshet 2012, 2016), *50* (Yes, 2019), and more.

25 Li-Or Averbuch, "There Was No Prime Minister Who Dealt So Much with the Conflict," *Globes*, May 14, 2016 [Hebrew], accessed May 14, 2016, https://www.globes.co.il/news/article.aspx?did=1001123689.

26 Doron Halutz, "Election Season of Muli Segev and *It's a Wonderful Country*," *Haaretz*, February 2, 2013 [Hebrew], accessed February 2, 2013, https://www.haaretz.co.il/magazine/1.1918617.

27 "Muli Segev in an Interview with Lucy About Satire, Politics and Public Opinion in Israel," DemokraTV, YouTube, June 16, 2020, accessed June 16, 2020, https://www.youtube.com/watch?v=5yBaPFxis1Q.

28 Raz Schechnik, "I Said to Netanyahu, 'If You Bring Peace, I'm Ready to Leave Everything and Be the Author of Your Speeches," *Yediot Ahronot*, May 9, 2018 [Hebrew], accessed May 9, 2018, https://www.yediot.co.il/articles/0,7340,L-5255730,00.html.

29 Dafna Yudovitz, "We Took Off Lital Ma'atuk Because Instead of a Message About Hell in Schools We Created Che Guevara of the Disturbed Students," *Globes*, May 16, 2010 [Hebrew], accessed May 16, 2010, https://www.globes.co.il/news/article.aspx?did=1000559880.

30 Halutz, "Election Season of Muli Segev and *It's a Wonderful Country*."

31 Rutha Kupfer, "Muli Segev: The Creator of *It's a Wonderful Country* Does Not Saddle for Jokes," *Haaretz*, May 15, 2009 [Hebrew], accessed May 15, 2009, https://www.haaretz.co.il/gallery/1.3345060.

32 Dafna Yudovitz, "We Took Off Lital Ma'atuk."

33 Ella Levi Weinriv, "Muli Segev: 'We Do Not Think About How to Reverse the Regime,'" *Globes*, July 9, 2018 [Hebrew], accessed July 9, 2018, https://www.globes.co.il/news/article.aspx?did=1001245141.

34 Li-Or Averbuch, "There Was No Prime Minister Who Dealt So Much with the Conflict"; Halutz, "Election Season of Muli Segev and *It's a Wonderful Country*."

35 Li-Or Averbuch, "There Was No Prime Minister Who Dealt So Much with the Conflict."

36 Dan Michman, Sergio DellaPergola, Paul Burstein, and Adam S. Ferziger, "A Reply to Ian Lustick's Article," *Contemporary Jewry* 37 (2017): 171–81; see 177.

37 Traditional Arab headdress.

38 Itay Stern, "Muli Segev: 'We've Not Been in Such a Funny Mood Lately,'" *Haaretz*, March 6, 2016 [Hebrew], accessed March 6, 2016, https://www.haaretz.co.il/gallery/television/.premium-1.2873321.

39 Halutz, "Election Season of Muli Segev and *It's a Wonderful Country*."

40 Megillat Esther is one of the five scrolls in the Writings (*ketuvim*) part of the Jewish Tanakh (the Hebrew Bible). The Megillah is read in synagogues during the Jewish festival of Purim.

41 Shushan was the capital city of ancient Persia.

42 Haman plotted to kill the Jews, but, in the end, he and his sons were executed.

43 See, for example, Oren Meyers and Eyal Zandberg, "The Sound-Track of Memory: Ashes and Dust and the Commemoration of the Holocaust in Israeli Popular Culture," *Media, Culture & Society* 24, no. 3 (2002): 389–408.

44 Li-Or Averbuch, "There Was No Prime Minister Who Dealt So Much with the Conflict."

45 "International This Is Not a Holocaust Day," *Mako* [Hebrew], accessed May 2, 2023, https://www.mako.co.il/tv-erez-nehederet/770e3d99ade16110?subChannelId=5e99894bf8d21610VgnVCM2000002a0c10acRCRD&vcmid=796fdd1ff7341610VgnVCM2000002a0c10acRCRD.

46 Ran Boker, "Jonathan Geffen on the Comparison Between Ahad Tamimi and Anne Frank: 'Apologies with All My Heart,'" *YNET*, January 28, 2018 [Hebrew], accessed January 28, 2018, https://www.ynet.co.il/articles/0,7340,L-5077093,00.html.

47 "Holocaust Survivor Against *It's a Wonderful Country*: How Can You Laugh at It?," *YNET*, February 1, 2018 [Hebrew], accessed February 1, 2018, https://www.ynet.co.il/articles/0,7340,L-5079458,00.html.

48 Roy Holler, "Eretz Nehederet Hurt Holocaust Survivors," *YNET*, November 10, 2004 [Hebrew], accessed November 10, 2004, https://www.ynet.co.il/articles/0,7340,L-3002314,00.html.

49 Idit Zertal, *The Nation and Death* (Tel Aviv: Dvir, 1993) [Hebrew]; Daniel Bar-Tal, *Living with the Conflict* (Jerusalem: Carmel, 2007) [Hebrew].

50 "Statistics Foreigners in Israel," *Population and Immigration Authority*, April 2018 [Hebrew], accessed April 2018, https://www.gov.il/BlobFolder/reports/foreign_workers_stats_0118/he/%D7%A8%D7%91%D7%A2%D7%95%D7%9F%201.pdf.

51 "Statistics Foreigners in Israel"; Levi Uriel, "Searching for a Policy," *Davar Rishon*, June 20, 2017 [Hebrew], accessed June 20, 2017, https://www.davar1.co.il/72906/.

52 Tali Kritzman-Amir, ed., *Where Levinsky Meets Asmara: Social and Legal Aspects of Israeli Asylum Policy* (Tel Aviv: Hakibutz Hameuhad, 2015) [Hebrew].

53 Moran Azulay and Amir Alon, "Natanyahu Folded: Pauses the Application of the Infiltrators' Agreement," *YNET*, April 3, 2018 [Hebrew], accessed April 3, 2018, https://www.ynet.co.il/articles/0,7340,L-5217730,00.html.

54 Arik Bender, "Ketzale's Solution for Foreigners: A Work Camp," *NRG*, March 23, 2010, accessed May 20, 2012 [Hebrew], accessed May 20, 2012, https://www.makorrishon.co.il/nrg/online/1/ART2/085/436.html.

55 Liat Steir-Livny, "From Victims to Aggressors: Cultural Representations of the Link Between the Holocaust and the Israeli-Palestinian Conflict," *Interactions: Studies in Communication and Culture* 7, no. 2 (September 2016): 123–36.

56 Sahara Blau, "Hitler Is Looking for a Parking Place," *Tzav Piyus*, April 28, 2011 [Hebrew].

57 Yossi Nissan and Li-Or Averbuch, "The Second Authority Will Scold Holocaust Skit with Keshet," *Globes*, April 3, 2011 [Hebrew], accessed April 3, 2011, http://www.globes.co.il/news/article.aspx?did=1000635720.

58 Nissan and Averbuch, "The Second Authority."

59 "The Camp Skit in *It's a Wonderful Country*," *City Mouse Online*, April 4, 2011 [Hebrew], accessed August 30, 2025, https://www.haaretz.co .il/gallery/television/2011-04-05/ty-article/0000017f-f85f-d47e-a37f -f97fe3130000.

60 A. Sover, *Bedarco shel haadam hazohek* [The Pathway to Human Laughter] (Jerusalem: Carmel, 2009); see especially 23–25, 55–57.

Selected Bibliography

Brook, Vincent. *Something Ain't Kosher Here: The Rise of the "Jewish" Sitcom.* New Brunswick, NJ: Rutgers University Press, 2003.

Figley, Charles. "Compassion Fatigue as Secondary Traumatic Stress Disorder: An Overview." In *Compassion Fatigue: Coping with Secondary Traumatic Stress Disorder in Those Who Treat the Traumatized*, ed. Charles Figley, 1–20. New York: Brunner-Routledge, 1995.

Gertz, Nurith. *A Different Choir: Holocaust Survivors, Aliens, and Others in Israeli Cinema and Literature.* Tel Aviv: Am Oved and Open University, 2004.

Gil, Idit. "The Shoah in Israeli Collective Memory: Changes in Meanings and Protagonists." *Modern Judaism* 32, no. 1 (February 2012): 76–101.

LaCapra, Dominick. *Writing History, Writing Trauma.* Baltimore: Johns Hopkins University Press, 2000. [Hebrew]

Loshitzky, Yosefa. *Identity Politics on the Israeli Screen.* Austin: University of Texas Press, 2002.

Meyers, Oren, Motti Neiger, and Eyal Zandberg. *Communicating Awe: Media Memory and Holocaust Commemoration.* Basingstoke, UK: Palgrave Macmillan, 2014.

Milner, Iris. *A Torn Past.* Tel Aviv: Am Oved, 2004.

Ofer, Dalia. "The Past That Does Not Pass: Israelis and Holocaust Memory." *Israel Studies* 14, no. 1 (Spring 2009): 1–35.

Ostrower, Haya. *Without Humor We Would Have Killed Ourselves.* Jerusalem: Yad Vashem, 2009. [Hebrew]

Shifman, Limor. *Televised Humor and Social Cleavages in Israel, 1968–2000.* Jerusalem: Magnes Press, 2008. [Hebrew]

Steir-Livny, Liat. *Remaking Holocaust Memory: Documentary Cinema by Third-Generation Survivors in Israel.* Syracuse: Syracuse University Press, 2019.

Yuran, Noam. *Channel 2: The New Statehood.* Tel Aviv: Resling, 2001. [Hebrew]

Zandberg, Eyal. "Critical Laughter: Humor, Popular Culture and Israeli Holocaust Commemoration." *Media, Culture & Society* 28, no. 4 (2006): 561–79.

Ziv, Avner. *Personality and Sense of Humor.* Tel Aviv: Papyrus, 1996. [Hebrew]

10

DI YIDN KOMEN / HAYEHUDIM BA'IM

The Jews Are Coming . . . to Laugh Off the Trauma of the Holocaust

Avinoam Patt

In the aftermath of the Holocaust, survivors in postwar Europe deployed humor as a way to process the recent traumas of the war, to cope with the enormity of the destruction, and to endure the seemingly absurd nature of continued Jewish life after the Holocaust. Humor helped survivors to maintain a sense of psychological advantage while also serving as an outlet for subversive and cynical observations on the postwar world.[1] After the war, humor directed at non-Jewish audiences often focused on using humor as a weapon, to minimize and belittle Nazis (most famously in the work of Mel Brooks). In recent decades, however, as the place of the Holocaust has only grown in contemporary Jewish culture and identity, references to the Holocaust in Jewish humor have grown more frequent, although the function and deployment of such Holocaust humor are substantively different in form and agenda. Rather than deploying humor as a psychological coping mechanism or weapon against Nazis, Holocaust humor has taken on a decidedly more political tone, often used as a means of critiquing the place of the Holocaust in contemporary Jewish society, politics, and culture. In my chapter in *Laughter After: Humor and the Holocaust*, I compare the deployment of Holocaust humor in recent Israeli and American Jewish sketch comedy to assess what humor can teach us about the place of the Holocaust in contemporary Jewish life.[2] I focus on several examples from Israel and the United States, including the shows *Eretz Nehederet (It's a Wonderful Country)*, *Hahamishia Hakamerit (The*

Chamber Quintet), and *HaYehudim Ba'im* (*The Jews Are Coming*) in Israel, as well as the work of Larry David, Sarah Silverman, Amy Schumer, and Nathan Fielder in America. Unlike Holocaust humor used as a weapon to attack Nazis and Nazism or humor used to alleviate suffering, these more contemporary instances of humor often use the Holocaust as a backdrop for jokes precisely in order to reinforce or emphasize the absurdity of the joke. Most frequently, these jokes employ the motif of the Shoah as a means of satirizing the current political climate, memorial practices, Holocaust education, and more, while also reflecting the prominent place of "remembering the Holocaust" in contemporary American and Israeli Jewish identity. In many ways, Holocaust-inflected (sketch) humor has played a similar function in both Israel and the United States: to make fun of the tendencies in both countries to sacralize and, by the same token, to trivialize the Holocaust. Most recently, however, Holocaust-inflected humor in Israel has been deployed to draw attention to abuses of power in Israeli politics and society; on the other hand, in the United States, Holocaust-inflected humor has increasingly drawn attention to the current and mounting powerlessness of American Jews, reflecting a cautionary tale of a different sort.

And yet, while Holocaust humor in an American context must be sensitive to rising levels of antisemitism and the dangers of misinterpretation, walking a fine line between what might be funny and what might seem taboo, Shoah humor in Israel plays to another audience with other concerns. The Israeli context, it seems, enables Israeli comedians and performers to tell jokes that would be deemed taboo before an audience of non-Jewish Americans, while also expecting a much deeper knowledge of the historical subject in order to get the jokes.

While I only touched on the Israeli sketch comedy show *HaYehudim Ba'im* (*The Jews Are Coming*) briefly in my previous research on the topic, a question posed to me at the "No Respect: Jewish Humor Around the World" conference at the University of North Carolina Wilmington in February 2020 drove me to take an even deeper dive into the remarkably successful (and funny) Israeli series about Jewish history. As one participant at the conference asked me, "Are the show's creators, Natalie Marcus and Asaf Beiser, themselves the descendants of Holocaust survivors?" To what extent does their frequent invocation of the Shoah (in a humorous context on the show) constitute "insider humor" created by descendants of survivors? Or does their humor reflect a deeper truth about the centrality of Shoah memory (and the ability to laugh about it) in Israeli society? What can the frequent invocations of the Nazi symbols and Holocaust history on the show teach us about the place of the Shoah in Israeli comedy?

The Israeli sketch comedy series *HaYehudim Ba'im* is a satirical TV show (2015–24) devoted to sketches that target the entire history of the Jewish people from biblical times to the 1990s through a humorous lens, including sketches on World War II and the Holocaust. The show's creators are indeed both descendants of Holocaust survivors (all four of Marcus's grandparents and Beiser's father).[3] From a Zionist perspective, while the show focuses primarily on biblical and Israeli history, it also integrates Israeli history into the broader scope of Jewish history. If the show works hard to tackle all of the sacred cows in both Israeli and Jewish history, then it is worth considering how the show approaches the Shoah and what it reflects about the sensibilities of its creators and their relationship to the post-memory of the Shoah. This chapter will consider what the Holocaust-inflected humor on the show can tell us about the place of the Shoah in Israeli society, how the Holocaust is used as a prism for critiques of contemporary Israeli society, whether this humor translates to a broader non-Israeli audience, and what, in turn, this might tell us about the role that descendants of survivors play in the creation of Shoah-inflected humor in Israel. *HaYehudim Ba'im* takes the state to task for trivializing the Shoah as part of a broader critique of the ways in which history and historical education have become politicized. Above all, it continues a tradition of self-deprecating Jewish humor that encourages Jews not to take themselves too seriously. At the same time, it points to important differences in the function of "insider humor" for an audience of mostly Israeli Jews who identify in personal ways with the legacies of survivors.

The show was first broadcast on Israel's historic Channel 1—for many years the only TV channel in the country—and now on the KAN network and its app. Unlike the satirical news program *Eretz Nehederet* (*It's a Wonderful Country*), which like the American program *The Daily Show* tends to focus on politics and current events, *HaYehudim Ba'im* analyzes central moments in Jewish history and culture through a comedic lens, combining a Mel Brooks *History of the World* approach with a deep dive into Jewish and Israeli history. The show features one of the foremost veterans of Israeli sketch comedy, Moni Moshonov (star of *Zehu Zeh*), along with newer stars Yossi Marshak, Yael Sharoni, Ido Moseri, and Yaniv Biton, among others. In addition to presenting skits on the Bible—think sketches that form humorous midrashim, or forms of biblical commentary, on the binding of Isaac, Moses having to explain the Ten Commandments to the children of Israel, a moody teenaged future King Solomon having to explain his "love poetry" to his parents, David and Bathsheba, or priests in the Temple who enjoy getting fat off the best offerings Israelites can bring them for sacrifice while not really wanting to deal with the sins of their people—and other sketches dealing with great moments in Jewish history, the history of Zionism, and the state of Israel, the show also offers satirical looks at World War II and the Holocaust. To what extent do the show's writers and performers seek to "laugh off the trauma of history"? How much prior knowledge must the audience have to "get the joke"? Does humor function as a political tool to criticize contemporary manipulations of the past or to reinforce the centrality of a dominant (Ashkenazi) collective memory? The show very clearly situates Israeli humor within the broader traditions of Jewish humor, while also playing for an insular audience expected to be well versed in Jewish and Zionist history. Such jokes for "insiders" enable the show to perform sketches that would be considered taboo in a broader context. (Even the show's title, *The Jews Are Coming / HaYehudim Ba'im / Di Yidn Komen*, is an insider reference to a slogan that Jewish Brigade soldiers serving with the British Army emblazoned across their trucks as they entered Nazi-occupied territory at the end of World War II: "The Jews Are Coming!")

The show first premiered in 2015, not without a fair bit of controversy. Marcus and Beiser, cocreators of the show, first aroused the ire of the right wing in Israel, with a nineteen-second promo clip in 2013 that "featured three actors portraying murderers Baruch Goldstein (who killed 29 and wounded 125 Palestinian worshipers in Hebron, in 1994), Yigal Amir (who assassinated prime minister Yitzhak Rabin in 1995); and Yona Avrushmi (who killed one person and wounded nine, in 1983). The trio, smiling and dancing, sang, 'sometimes I assassinate and sometimes I butcher, but I am a right-wing murderer.' . . . The backlash was immediate, with comments on YouTube and Facebook denouncing Channel 1 and creators Natalie Marcus and Asaf Beiser, calling them 'Nazis,' and accusing them of painting all religious settlers as murderers." In an interview with Esther Kustanowitz for *The Forward* after the original controversy delayed the launch of the show, Marcus explained that *The Jews Are Coming* is "a different look at Jewish history from Abraham until the 1990s. . . . We have a range of opinions, ways of looking at history from different angles, giving our interpretations of different stories." Marcus sees the show as drawing on a long well of Jewish humor: "Maybe compared to the U.S., we have a mentality of making jokes very quickly. . . . In the history of the Jewish people, we take it to a humorous perspective and this is how we survived. Humor was always embedded in our DNA." And indeed, the show does tackle more recent difficult subjects, such as the case of Baruch Goldstein or the assassination of Rabin.[4]

Marcus and Beiser have also argued that they see this format as a secular reclaiming of religious texts, part of a broader project in Israel to wrest control of the Jewish canon from Orthodox gatekeepers. Marcus and Beiser are both acclaimed screenwriters with multiple awards (for shows like *Fauda* and *Eretz Nehederet*), and *The Jews Are Coming* won the Israeli equivalent of an Emmy for best comedy show. And as much as the show is Jewish humor, it is almost certainly not Jewish humor written for a non-Jewish audience. What distinguishes *The Jews Are Coming* from most of the Jewish humor we would encounter in the United States is the fact that it has *very* high expectations of its audience. To get the joke, the audience must possess a rather sophisticated understanding of Jewish history. And if they don't, it stands to reason they would indeed be motivated to learn after watching the show, if only to get the jokes. Marcus and Beiser have said as much:

> When we write "The Jews are coming," we always think about it as an inner thing. It's a thing which is, for us, it's our thing. . . . It's an inside humor. We never stop and think, how would it look like from the outside? We know that once we would stop and think how does it look from the outside, we will be in a problem. So we just eliminate this.[5]

They have also described their approach to analyzing Jewish history as "Jewish family therapy." The comedic impulse, they argue, is "deep in Jewish DNA." So, of course, sketches about Abraham as a bad father attempting to sacrifice Isaac or Abraham circumcising Isaac and Ishmael together can take a traumatic text and reread it as a humorous midrash, turning biblical commentary into sketch comedy, especially when the writer chooses an unconventional view to tell the story. As Marcus explained in an interview with me from November 2020, "Choosing point of view means silencing the voice of God."[6] Retelling the "bris," or ritual circumcisions, of Isaac/Ishmael from the children's point of view offers another perspective and makes it funny. And a major goal of the show is to "always take larger than life figures and bring them back to normal (Abraham and Moses, for example)." At the same time, the historical midrashim, both biblical and modern, present opportunities to offer commentary on current events by projecting onto history (again, both biblical and modern). Sometimes the sketches do not necessarily try to solve the contradictions in Jewish text through midrash but actually often emphasize absurdity of the text for humor:

> We feel that we can relate to everything that is "Jewish"—by Jewish we mean: Jewish history, Jewish religion, Jewish state, and Jewish people. In other words: Jews. Every famous and non-famous Jew from the last 2000 years is fair game for us.[7]

Above all, for the show as satire, Marcus and Beiser argue, "the most important goal is to maintain freedom of speech." A television show may not directly influence political behavior by "changing anyone's mind in terms of voting," but it can get people to think another way.

There is also something deeply subversive about this approach to Jewish history from a Zionist perspective, for while the show does focus primarily on biblical and Israeli history, it also integrates Israeli history into the broader scope of Jewish history—essentially refuting the famous claim of Yudka in the story of Haim Hazaz ("The Sermon") that there is nothing to be learned from studying Jewish diaspora history, that Israeli youth could cut themselves off from a lachrymose Jewish history and start anew. Just as the show reintegrates Jewish diaspora history into Israeli history, it then also subversively reintegrates the history of the Shoah into that Israeli history. And if laughing at Jewish history and Jewish religion is a birthright bestowed upon every Jew "in their DNA," what can the comedy about the Shoah by Israeli descendants of survivors and the Holocaust humor on *The Jews Are Coming* tell us about the place of the Shoah in Israeli society?

Most clips from the show seek to critically analyze mythological figures in Jewish history, offering humorous midrashim on what may actually have happened in well-known incidents. These satires reflect both critiques of top-down collective memory projects engaged in national mythologizing and critical analyses of Jewish behavior in times of crisis. One episode from the first season (season 1, episode 12) includes a skeptical Hannah Senesh worrying about her fate before she is deployed as a parachutist. Senesh, the famous Hungarian-born member of the Haganah who parachuted into Yugoslavia in 1944 in an ill-fated plan meant to rescue Hungarian Jews (including her mother) from transport to Auschwitz, is among the heroes of Jewish resistance to the Nazis subjected to reinterpretation on the show. Senesh, a poet, was captured attempting to cross into Hungary, where she was imprisoned, tortured, and eventually executed in November 1944. Her poems "The Walk to Caesarea (Eli, Eli)" and "Blessed Is the Match" are among her most well-known works, and she has been mythologized by the Zionist leadership of the Yishuv and the state of Israel as a symbol of Jewish resistance to Nazism. *The Jews Are Coming*, however, asks serious historical questions through its signature satirical midrashic form: Why was the operation to parachute Senesh into occupied Europe so poorly planned? Why were Jewish military leaders so comfortable placing the young, enthusiastic recent Hungarian immigrant (eager to rescue her mother) into harm's way? What did the mythological Hannah actually think of the plan? As her commander (played by Moni Moshonov) offers a rousing speech to encourage the parachutists before their departure, Hannah (played by Yael Sharoni) asks a serious question:

"The Nazis have hundreds of thousands of soldiers in Hungary and we have . . . one." As the camera pans to Hannah, sitting alone on a bench in the operations room, she asks, "What can I do against a whole army?"

"We have a plan," her commander responds. "You will fly and fly and fly, then you jump, and hopefully . . . land."

"What worries me: what do I do after I land?" Hannah asks.

"Aha," her commander explains with satisfaction, "then you will attack the Nazi army from three sides."

As she suggests, the plan—to parachute one woman behind enemy lines in Hungary where hundreds of thousands of German soldiers will be waiting—doesn't sound like a great idea. But at least her commander offers her a warm drink before she goes. A voice-over concludes the sketch: "Senesh parachuted into Europe in March 1944 and never returned."[8]

In the same episode, in the sketch "Art Academy in Vienna" an admissions committee for the art school (chaired by a Jewish representative named Mr. Weiss) rejects Adolf Schickelgruber's artwork as having "old-age home chic." "My son can paint better work than you and he has no arms," Weiss ridicules a young Hitler, while berating him for accepting rejection so easily and without anger. "Don't you have any work with anger in it?" Weiss asks, explaining to Adolf that his work must have some emotion in it. The young Schickelgruber is encouraged by the Jewish committee members to change his name "to something more catchy," stop painting fanciful portraits of cats, and channel his inner rage into something productive. As the sounds of a Wagner opera overture rise in the background, Weiss yells at Adolf: "Get angry! I am ruining your future! Get angry! You have no talent! Your work is shit! . . . Say: 'Weiss, I hate you!' I am pissing on your dream! Do you hate me? My family?" As the camera zooms in on his face, the transformed Adolf Hitler reaches a frenzy of channeled rage: "I will burn you! I will destroy all of your faces!" Weiss concludes: "Good. Now take the anger and do something with it." The sketch, which absurdly imagines Adolf Schickelgruber as a harmless illustrator of cats and flowers who never really gets angry about anything, is also a critique of psychohistory, of the tendency to play "what if" with history. If only Hitler had been accepted to art school, some may suggest, perhaps the Holocaust would have never happened. The sketch renders this idea completely absurd, while also reversing the historical narrative. What if Hitler's inner rage at his rejection from art school was motivated by a Jewish committee member who "pissed on his dream"? In its first season, the show made it clear it would not hesitate to tackle any historical subject, from Adolf Hitler, to Yigal Amir, to Adolf Eichmann.

The first episode of the first season—an episode that examines various manifestations of the commandment *lo tirtzach* ("thou shall not murder"), including a sketch in which Moses explains repeatedly the meaning of "thou shall not murder" to a group of questioning Israelites able to find multiple loopholes; another sketch that pictures the family of Yigal Amir sitting around the dinner table willing to murder anyone for the slightest infraction; and more—concludes with a sketch that imagines the first state-sanctioned execution in Israeli history: the hanging of Adolf Eichmann in Ramle prison in 1962. Eichmann (played by Moshonov) offers his last words: "I regret nothing." But the bumbling and inept guards are incapable of executing Eichmann, incapable of stooping to the depths of evil represented by Eichmann himself. They have Eichmann, they have a noose, and they have the gallows, but they have no idea how to actually kill him. After several failed attempts, Eichmann's supposed last words become: "Why don't you get it over with, amateurs?"

In the end, the head guard (played by Yossi Marshak), in recounting the previous fifty-three attempts over six months to execute Eichmann, having gotten to really know the prisoner and feel even closer to him, concludes: "You should know, I learned so much from you. The whole thing with the door [in the floor]." Eichmann gets impatient and finally places the noose around his own neck, concluding that "if you want something done right, you have to do it yourself." While the trial may have been meant as a manifestation of Jewish power, the sketch ends up perpetuating a sense of (perhaps self-righteous) Jewish weakness or at least questions whether the state of Israel was capable of stooping to the same level as the Nazis. At the same time, the sketch may also be a subtle reflection on how Jews in Israel must deal with exercising power and the responsibility that comes along with it.[9]

Very few sketches from *The Jews Are Coming* actually reimagine historical events from the period of World War II, but one sketch from season 3 does critique the inability of the two fighting organizations in the Warsaw Ghetto, the Revisionist-Zionist Jewish Military Union (ZZW) and the Socialist-Zionist Jewish Fighting Organization (ZOB), to join forces and fight together against the common enemy, the Nazis. Alas, the differences between the ZOB's Mordecai Anielewicz (played by Moshonov) and the ZZW's Pawel Frenkel (played by Marshak) are simply too great. The sketch is a critique of the inability of the two ideological enemies, the Hashomer Hatzair and the Revisionists, to unite and fight the Nazis and a not so subtle jab at collective mythmaking and so-called Jewish heroism. A narrator explains that by the end of the revolt, the two groups managed to kill a total of seventeen Nazis.

In another sketch from season 2 that tries to situate the Shoah within the broader scope of Jewish history, the show brings *Night at the Museum* to the (old) Diaspora Museum (Beit Hatfutsot), where historical actors from the Shoah (Moshonov) and the expulsion from Spain (Sharoni) engage in a debate of competitive historical suffering that comes straight out of Salo Baron's lachrymose theory of Jewish historical woe. The Polish Jew from the Shoah warns the ancient Jew, "You have no idea what is waiting for you," which prompts a response from Sharoni's exiled Sephardic Jew accusing Moshonov's character of always bringing up the Shoah. The Polish Jew responds, "What do you want from me? I am from the Shoah exhibit. I wear clothes from the Shoah, eat the food of the Shoah, live the Shoah, am forced to watch films on TV from the Shoah." Responding to the Jewish Spaniard's complaint that "you think you are the only one who suffers here?" as she brings up the expulsion from Spain—"How can one compare 'expulsion' to 'mass murder'?"—Moshonov's character asks, "One time they had a temporary exhibit here about *ma'abarot* [transit camps] and now all I hear about is Mizrahi suffering in the transit camps?"

Suddenly a tough Sabra in a nearby display (played by Yossi Marshak) shuts up the debate of "weak" Diaspora Jews, first by calling the Holocaust character "*saboni*" (i.e., soap, a derogatory reference to the cruel name native-born Israelis used to refer to Holocaust survivors after their arrival in Israel) and then by referring to him as "sheep to the slaughter." The biblical character stops the fight, reminding them they are all historical actors—biblical, modern, medieval, Ashkenazi, and Sephardi—but above all, they are all Jews. They are all on the same page, until they are stumped by the appearance of a Jew they cannot explain: an Ethiopian. The sketch reminds us that despite a long Jewish history of suffering and persecution, contemporary Israeli society has a long way to go in overcoming racism and developing a pluralistic Jewish state. In the end, the group lets the Ethiopian cleaning man get back to work, with the biblical character telling him, "Work sets you free!" (Arbeit macht frei!), which only sets off another quarrel.[10]

Other sketches critique the politicization of Holocaust museums and memory, asking whether the mantra of "never again" actually applies to Israeli foreign policy. A sketch from season 3, episode 2, imagines a tour of Yad Vashem with a Rwandan general before the genocide of the Tutsi. After learning about German brutality in the Holocaust, the general places an order for machine guns, bombs, and electrified fence ("like from the camps")—"the Tutsi will never know what hit them."

In other cases, the tendency to see every slight against Israel as antisemitism and continued Nazi persecution is carried to its most absurd ends. In the sketch "Final Solution 2.0," situated in 1956, the last surviving Nazis in Europe (dressed in full SS uniform) are meeting in a bunker to discuss the ultimate Final Solution. This time the final plan is to scatter Nazi sympathizers among all of the media enterprises in Europe and guarantee that Israel does not receive one point in the Eurovision Song Contest. The plan is greeted with enthusiasm by all in the bunker, and one of the Nazis announces in a German-accented Hebrew: "Zeh yaharog otam" (That will kill them)! The sketch concludes with the Nazis gathered around the table singing the West German entry to the 1979 Eurovision Song Contest, "Dschinghis Khan" (Genghis Khan).[11] A seemingly farcical addition to the end of the sketch, singing this song is by itself meaningful on multiple levels: the 1979 Eurovision Song Contest in Jerusalem marked the first time Israel hosted the contest, as well as the first time Eurovision was held outside of geographic Europe. The performance by the West German group was groundbreaking, as they performed in German, in Israel, for the first time. The irony is that although the sketch parodies the Israeli tendency to perceive every slight against Israel as antisemitic, Israel in fact won Eurovision in back-to-back years in 1978 and 1979 for the songs "A-Ba-Ni-Bi" and "Hallelujah" (Israel would triumph again in 1998 with Dana International's "Diva" and in 2018 with Netta Barzilai's "Toy"). This is, of course, very "insider humor." To get the multiple jokes embedded in the sketch, one must know Israel's Eurovision history and understand how ridiculous it is to imagine every Israeli loss in the kitschy song contest as part of an antisemitic plot against the Jewish state (although, objectively, Eden Alene's "Set Me Free" in 2021 should have finished higher than seventeenth place). The sketch also asks both literally and figuratively: Are Jews capable of "acting like Nazis"?

In "Don't Say Nazi" (season 3), two friends sitting in an outdoor café in Berlin recognize Adolf Hitler sitting across the way. Hans (Moni Moshonov) recognizes him: "I know him, he's that Nazi . . . Hitler!" He is reprimanded by his friend, Fritz (Yossi Marshak): "Stop saying that word! Nazi." Hans retorts: "But he is a Nazi. He is the head of the Nazi party. He's a Nazi." Fritz explains, "You cannot call every person who opposes your political viewpoint a Nazi. . . . It demeans the level of discussion." Hans responds, "But this guy stripped Jews of their citizenship, put them in ghettos, that's as Nazi as it can get!" The waitress (Yael Sharoni) comes over and berates Hans for so casually using the word "Nazi": "My grandmother is a Holocaust survivor," she says, "at least, so far" (implying she has the right to judge proper use of the word and on a meta-level both playing with the audience's knowledge of what was to come and critiquing descendants of survivors who claim the moral high ground simply on the basis of their lineage). Fritz explains to Hans that the "casual use of such terms is exactly what is dividing the nation today" (a reference to debates in contemporary Israeli society about labeling political opponents as "Nazis"). As they watch Hitler actively murder someone across the café, Fritz and the waitress caution Hans not to jump to conclusions and label Hitler a Nazi without understanding the broader context, until they end up accusing Hans of being a Nazi himself for labeling everyone else Nazis, accusing him of being someone who perhaps deserves to be murdered by Hitler for his judgmental nature, before leaving him in disgust. Hitler walks over and tells Hans not to worry about Fritz and the waitress, because they're just "fascists." The sketch ends with Hitler offering Hans a plate of nachos (a play on the word "Nazis"). The word "Nazi" is used at least twenty times in the three-minute sketch, as if reinforcing the casual manner in which the term has come to be thrown around in current political discourse. It has become so trivialized, the writers seem to suggest, that when an actual Nazi appears, it becomes impossible to actually label them a Nazi without questioning whether the appellation fits. Marcus and Beiser were themselves labeled Nazis by opponents of the show who saw the satire of Jewish history as an attack on Jews and Judaism.[12]

A similar sketch satirizes German Jews who voted for Hitler in 1932, with the same actors sitting in a Berlin café, explaining why they have decided to vote for Hitler in the upcoming elections: "He's a patriot, a hero, he speaks well, he looks good, he wrote a book. . . . It's an obvious choice. . . . And you know what, Greenberg, worst case, no good, maximum four years we will replace him." "Exactly. We will replace him. Long live the people and the democracy. Long live Germany." Asaf Beiser explained, "We wrote this sketch after discovering that several thousand Jews actually voted for Hitler in 1933. This is satire aimed not only at government but also at the people; in this case as voters in a democratic system. How do we decide for whom to vote? Not in cafés but through misleading news on Twitter and Facebook. Democracy is in trouble."[13] In this case, we have an even more direct comparison to contemporary politics in both Israel and America, where superficial factors will lead voters (even Jewish voters) to elect a Donald Trump or a Benjamin Netanyahu based on what they hear from their friends, without actual consideration for whether the candidate is qualified for office or is a danger to the nation. While Beiser and Marcus may not have known that 2023 would see a massive wave of protests in Israel over the very nature of its continued "democracy," with each side labeling their opponents "Nazis," their remarks from 2020 seem especially prescient.

Beyond critiquing the place of the Shoah in Israeli society, the show also occasionally takes aim at the place of the Holocaust in American Jewish memory and identity, with several references to Spielberg and *Schindler's List* over the course of four seasons. In one sketch from the third season (episode 6), Spielberg (played by Ma'ayan Blum, speaking Hebrew with a very American accent) meets with Hollywood film producers (Yossi Marshak and Yael Sharoni) to discuss his next film, "a very heavy film, even difficult to watch, but there is really no other way to make this film differently, that is, when dealing with the murder of millions."

"We know, Steven, we know. We just have a few suggestions for improvement. . . ."

"We felt the film was not scary enough."

Spielberg responds: "Not frightening? It's a film about mass murder, entire families destroyed, what's scarier than that?" The producers explain they want shock value, something that will make the audience really scream when they watch the film. "What about special effects? Robotic dolls?" they ask.

Spielberg is flabbergasted: "Effects? What kind of special effects? This is a historically realistic film."

"But children are not going to come to a film without special effects."

SPIELBERG: This is not a film for children!

FEMALE PRODUCER: But how are we going to sell all of the dolls and toys?

SPIELBERG: We are talking about millions killed! Nothing is left from them. You want to make merchandise? Bones, that's all that's left!

FEMALE PRODUCER: Bones? That's great. Children can build the skeletons by themselves!

SPIELBERG: I understand you are trying to run a business, but this is not a film that is made to sell merchandise. It is a film about millions who disappeared in an instant. It is the most traumatic moment in the history of my people.

MALE PRODUCER: Steven, they are not your people.

SPIELBERG: Of course, it is my people.

MALE PRODUCER: Steven, I have told you a hundred times: you are not a dinosaur.

SPIELBERG: Gerald, you will not erase my identity. You have your narrative, I have my own.

MALE PRODUCER: Jurassic Park can be an amazing film but you are ruining it with your heaviness and your stubborn obsession to make it so artistic and historical.

FEMALE PRODUCER: Historical? Steven, you know there are many people who don't even believe dinosaurs existed, so seriously, come on.

SPIELBERG: I'm very sorry, I had no idea you had a meteor denier here. What happened to you? You don't believe that dinosaurs lived here millions of years ago? . . . I may have to make a little "ET Phone Home" and call my friends from the T. rex anti-defamation league!

Finally, the producers relent, but not before asking Spielberg to remove all of the "slapstick" moments from *Schindler's List*: "It's not appropriate." The sketch, beyond playing with our associations of Spielberg with *Schindler's List*, also joins the genre of comedy that critiques Hollywood's efforts to turn serious topics into entertainment. In *Seinfeld*, Jerry can be accosted by his parents for "making out during *Schindler's List*" ("The Raincoats," season 5, episode 18); here the joke is on us: How are we to know whether a film about mass extinction by Spielberg refers to the Holocaust or large dinosaurs that supposedly once roamed the earth? Once historical fact becomes entertainment, the writers suggest, the path to distortion and denial is not far away.

Another sketch, from the fourth season of the show, tackles *Schindler's List* even more directly, imagining Oskar Schindler as Michael Scott (Steve Carell's character) from *The Office*.[14] The sketch portrays Schindler (Yossi Marshak) as a "horrible boss" who likes to play jokes on his employees, slapping "Kick me, I'm stupid" stickers on an employee's back, tricking employees into believing they have been selected for deportation, and, in a direct reference to an episode of *The Office*, bringing male strippers into his factory to surprise one gay employee for his birthday. The opening theme song of the sketch overlays the theme from *The Office* with scenes of Krakow, Schindler's factory, and Auschwitz (instead of Scranton, Pennsylvania, and Dunder Mifflin paper company). Herr Schindler is very proud of his "best boss" coffee mug and is always the only one amused by the many gags he pulls on his captive laborers.

Modeling the mockumentary format, the sketch interviews Herr Schindler, who explains: "Everyone says: Schindler the hero, the angel, the guardian, very successful, very attractive, but all of this is not important; first, I want everyone to see me as a friend, and a hero, and successful. And that's it . . . and funny! Mwahaha!"

The camera cuts to one of his female employees, Rachel (Yael Sharoni): "Of course everyone wants to say something to him, but it's not like we have a lot of options. We can either stay here or play dead in a pit somewhere." Yitzhak, the accountant (Moni Moshonov, modeled on Ben Kingsley's Yitzhak Stern), says: "I'm still thinking about leaving." Schindler loves to surprise his employees, for example, sneaking up from behind while yelling at them in German wearing a clown nose: "Before this whole thing with the prisoners and the war, I was a pretty well-known comedian, performing a lot . . . for free. For this reason, it's important to me that people enjoy themselves. That in the end they will say [in English]: 'I had a good time at Schindler's (factory).'"

In a dramatic moment, two German guards enter the factory to arrest a female employee (Esther, modeled on Pam from *The Office*), but Schindler intervenes, offering them his watch—and Josef, the pot maker—in her place. Of course, this all turns out to be another one of Schindler's gags in honor of Josef's birthday, and the two guards turn into male strippers grinding to techno music in the factory. Josef is crying on the ground, too traumatized to enjoy the moment. In fact, only Schindler seems to be enjoying the strippers and the champagne, while the rest of his factory workers gaze on, continuing their work in bewilderment and shock.

Marshak's Schindler reflects in an interview, "Even if we didn't have a war right now and even if all of these people were not my workers, you know where we would be right now? Drinking a beer together. I really love these people, and they love me." And then he emerges from his office with a cake to celebrate the end of the war; but his factory is empty, everyone is gone, no one remains to celebrate with him. He responds, "I have had the thought, 'Maybe they don't really love me? Maybe they just stayed here to survive?' But then you see this [holding up his 'best boss' mug] and you remember. I made this mug [for myself]."

The sketch, of course, questions Schindler's motivations as a "rescuer" who exploited free labor during the war. It questions true love and adoration for Schindler versus begrudging gratitude for rescue (not based in real love). Michael/Oskar is desperate for approval but also tries way too hard to gain the love and respect of his employees. By juxtaposing *Schindler's List* and *The Office*, the sketch is also a commentary on the boundaries of humor and the Holocaust. Can you situate a sitcom in *Schindler's List*? What questions does humor allow you to ask that other forms do not? Are Oskar/Michael's motivations pure? Is rescue truly an altruistic act? How much did Spielberg construct a Hollywood fantasy version of the Christian savior who rescues his Jewish subjects?[15] The sketch is also an implicit critique of how Americans remember the Holocaust, with the assistance of Hollywood archetypes and commercialized market-driven considerations.

Another sketch from the fourth season tackles American Jewish responses to the Holocaust even more directly, imagining the moment when Ruth Handler, the inventor of the Barbie doll in 1959, first presented the doll to her daughter Barbara as a combined Chrismukkah gift.[16] The asthmatic, bespectacled, dorky Barbara is very disappointed by her gift doll, hoping to have received a big dreidel or a shofar instead, not a skinny blond doll who looks nothing like her (and more like the "ladies from Dad's magazine").

RUTH: No, no . . . it's a beautiful doll for you to play with, and her name is Barbie, just like you.

BARBARA: My name is Barbara.

RUTH: Fine, we just improved the name slightly, but it's you. . . . Sweetie, she looks just like you, we have just improved her slightly.

ELLIOTT (father): Sweetie, it's you . . . just that she's blond, tanned, skinny, with a distracting bosom . . . and a flirty smile.

BARBARA: It doesn't look like me.

RUTH: Sweetie, what matters isn't that Barbie looks like you but that you look like Barbie.

BARBARA: What's wrong with the way I look?

ELLIOTT: Honey, you are perfect in our eyes . . .

RUTH: But in antisemitic eyes, you are easy prey.

BARBARA: What's wrong with the way I look?

RUTH: Sweetie, you look more Jewish than a knaidel.

ELLIOTT: Just by looking at you, people get charged interest.

RUTH: You look like you just came back from attacking Jesus.

ELLIOTT: You look like you could be holding the globe in your hand. . . . You are an antisemitic caricature.

BARBARA: Fine, fine. I look Jewish. What's wrong with looking Jewish?

RUTH: Nothing. You like showers . . . with one hundred people and no water?

ELLIOTT: Look, my little trash receptacle for allergies, if our people has learned anything, it's that it is best not to look like our people.

Barbara's parents then show her Barbie's dream house: "Wow, surprise! Not some miserable attic to write a diary and die in, a big house, like the goyim have. . . . And it's made out of plastic, so you can take it from place to place in case of relocation or a pogrom." Her father then playacts for her with Nazi soldiers who discover Barbie in her house: "Danger! Mean Nazis on patrol. . . . Dear Goya [non-Jewish woman], have you seen any miserable stinking Jews? 'Not in this house, maybe next door. . . . Here there are only blond people.'"

ELLIOTT: Thank you! In this house we won't rape anyone . . . even though you turn me on!

RUTH: Bye-bye, says Barbie. Merry Christmas, officer!

Barbara gets excited, imagining that her Barbie can grow up to be a banker, just like she wants to be. Ruth smacks her on the forehead: "What? Maybe you just write Jew on your forehead! You have no calculator, just a bikini and vacant eyes. Understood? Now go play with your friends, and show them you are exactly like them, while I look out the window and worry." In the interview from November 2020, Natalie Marcus noted that "while a lot has been written about Barbie from a feminist stand-point questioning whether she is a good role model for girls, we tried to understand just why a few years after WWII an American Jew whose family came from Europe decided to invent a doll who looks non-Jewish. To be frank, a doll that looks Aryan . . . we wanted to ask a historical or philosophical question."

The sketch, while a satirizing critique of American Jewish responses to the Holocaust, does raise serious questions: Did American Jews in the 1950s consider assimilation to be a strategic response to antisemitism? While most critiques of the Barbie doll have questioned her physique and its impossible human proportions, this sketch represents one of the few analyses of Barbie from a Jewish Israeli perspective. Can American Jews actually pass as non-Jews? Or have American Jews in fact attempted to construct an identity that still responds to avoiding the Holocaust? Is this a critique of American Jews in the 1950s or 2000s? The sketch directly invokes Holocaust symbols: antisemitic stereotypes, Anne Frank, a joke about "showers," and more, but the target of the jokes is clearly the American Jewish belief that assimilation and "passing" might shield them from annihilation. Will this sketch translate to a non-Jewish audience? Beiser and Marcus argue that they write for "multiple Jewish audiences." This is certainly "insider humor" meant for a Jewish audience who will "get the jokes"; whether it translates out of Hebrew to a non-Jewish audience without sounding antisemitic is up for debate.

As distance from World War II grows, the Shoah continues to assume a central role in both Israeli and American Jewish identity. A show like *The Jews Are Coming* highlights the profound differences in how Jews in Israel and Jews in America relate to the event. In the United States, the historical specificity of the Shoah is reduced to a number of "Holocaust icons." American sketch comedy about the Holocaust makes fun not of specific historical events but of symbols and terms the audience will be able to identify—survivors (think of the *Curb Your Enthusiasm* survivor episode; the Anne Frank "game" as in Nathan Englander's short story or in a historical roast of Anne Frank on Comedy Central), as well as jokes that relativize Spielberg, Schindler, and a vague sense of collective suffering.[17] While humor in America may reflect an anxiety over forgetting, over the ways in which "remembering the Holocaust" has become a stand-in for Jewish identity, it would seem that Holocaust humor in Israel—where the Shoah is too central to Israeli national identity to be forgotten—can function in multiple ways: as a political tool to criticize the centrality of Holocaust memory in the culture and as a part of Jewish history that has become normalized in a way that its historical aspects, the heroic, the historical, and the mythological are no longer off-limits for comedic reinterpretation. *The Jews Are Coming* still tends to use the Shoah to critique the state for constructing national heroes, but as part of a broader critique of the ways in which history and historical education become politicized; it critiques trivialization and the slippage that occurs when terms like "Nazi" and "fascist" are overused, and, above all, it continues a tradition of self-deprecating Jewish humor that asks Jews not to take themselves too seriously. *The Jews Are Coming* makes the Holocaust part of Jewish history equally subject to satire and fair game for critique and reexamination. The twelve examples discussed in this chapter tackle sacred cows like the mythology of Hannah Senesh, the Warsaw Ghetto Uprising, Oskar Schindler, and the place of Eichmann in Israeli history. At the same time, the show uses the backdrop of the Shoah for contemporary critiques of Israeli society and politics, along with a foreign policy that allows for cozying up to genocidal dictators in Africa in the decades after the creation of the state. In other cases, the sketches satirize trends in Israeli and especially American Holocaust memorial culture and the Hollywoodization of memory, while also critiquing American responses to the Holocaust through assimilation and commercialization. What is clear is that the Holocaust humor on *The Jews Are Coming*, while certainly representing the "insider humor" of descendants of survivors, confirms Liat Steir-Livny's thesis that the Shoah has become so central in Israeli culture and society that Holocaust humor stands right at the center of Israeli society and culture. By making symbols of the Shoah fair game for Israel's best sketch comedy show, *The Jews Are Coming* returns the Holocaust to the broader scope of Jewish history, not only integrating Israeli humor into the best traditions of Jewish humor but using humor to do what it does best: produce material where nothing is sacred or off-limits. We can ask questions about every aspect of Jewish history, even the Holocaust.

*   *   *

This chapter was written before October 7, 2023. In this regard, it is worth noting that it is entirely unclear what impact this traumatic day, along with the ongoing trauma of the war in Gaza, the hostage crisis, and the war with Hezbollah and Iran, will have on Israeli comedy in general or how the creators of *The Jews Are Coming* will wrestle with the impact of this catastrophe on their work specifically.

Approximately six months after October 7, 2023, *The Jews Are Coming* aired a clip called "Never Again All Over Again." The short sketch includes actors sharing their testimonies from traumatic events throughout Jewish history—the burning of the Second Temple in Jerusalem by the Romans in 70 CE; the First Crusade in Cologne in 1096; the Kishinev pogrom in 1903; the Hebron massacre of 1929; Kristallnacht in 1938 in Berlin; the 1943 Farhud massacre in Baghdad; and, finally, October 7, 2023, in Kfar Aza, which lost over one hundred people when Hamas attacked that day. The testimonies intentionally evoke echoes of October 7—cries for help, loved ones murdered, feelings of helplessness, people who were once neighbors turning into vicious attackers. Moni Moshonov's character from Kristallnacht in 1938, after describing the destruction of stores and synagogues, says, "It was just like looking at human evil in the eye." The sketch is purposely not funny. Instead, the writers situate October 7 within a much longer history of Jewish suffering and conclude with the faith that the Jewish people are resilient, that "we will rebuild, we will not leave, we will continue to live here." While situating October 7, and especially the sense of Jewish powerlessness, within the much broader spectrum of Jewish history, the show's writers and actors suggest that Israelis will be able to overcome this trauma as they have done so often in the past. But they also seem to suggest that it is too soon to laugh.[18]

Notes

1 Avinoam Patt, " 'Laughter Through Tears': Jewish Humor in the Aftermath of the Holocaust," in *A Club of Their Own: Jewish Humorists and the Contemporary World*, ed. Eli Lederhendler and Gabriel N. Finder (Studies in Contemporary Jewry 29) (New York: Oxford University Press, 2016), 113–31.

2 See Avinoam Patt, "Yad Vashem You So Fine: The Place of the Shoah in Contemporary Israeli and American Comedy," *Laughter After: Humor and the Holocaust* (Detroit: Wayne State University Press, 2020), 261–84.

3 In an email correspondence from March 4, 2020, with Natalie Marcus
and Asaf Beiser, Marcus explains: "About your first question—my grandparents are Holocaust survivors from both sides, we have some crazy
stories from my father's side but basically everybody died in the war and
my grandparents are pretty much the only survivors. Asaf's father was
himself a survivor. A big part of his mother's side died in
the war. If it matters? Well, we have more sketches about Rabin's assassination, which is the big trauma of our generation."

4 Esther D. Kustanowitz, "Will Israel Yank Satire over 'Murderers' Promo"?
The Forward, September 26, 2013, accessed February 18, 2020, https://
forward.com/schmooze/184439/will-israel-yank-satire-over-murderers
-promo/.

5 "Natalie Marcus and Asaf Beiser, Humor Across the Divide," Hebrew
Union College, https://collegecommons.huc.edu/bully_pulpit/natalie
-marcus-asaf-beiser/.

6 See "The Jews Are Coming to UConn! A Jewish Humor Program with
the Creators of *HaYehudim Ba'im*, November 11, 2020," https://www
.youtube.com/watch?v=rNxQbTGMqQ8.

7 "The Jews Are Coming to UConn!"

8 *The Jews Are Coming*, "Hannah Senesh," season 1, episode 12. All translations from Hebrew to English are my own.

9 Another sketch from season 5, episode 2, imagines two Mossad agents
in Argentina (played by Marshak and Yaniv Biton) who stumble upon a
German with a tiny mustache hiding out, who has been "expecting the
guests we always thought would come." While he almost gives himself
away as "the Fuhrer," it turns out the Mossad agents have been searching
for another Adolf, to whom he is more than happy to lead them.

10 *The Jews Are Coming*, "The Diaspora Museum," season 2, episode 14.

11 *The Jews Are Coming*, "Final Solution 2.0," season 2, episode 13, https://
www.youtube.com/watch?v=Pp3Qi07nJK4. "Dschinghis Khan" became
the basis for several popular covers of the song, including the Hasidic hit
song "Yidden" by Mordecai Ben-David.

12 See Raz Shechnik, "We Have Done More Than Any Rabbi in Israel to
Bring the Israeli Public Closer to the Bible," *Yediot Ahronot*, March 1,
2022. As the headline of the interview notes, "They threatened them with
murder, called them Nazis, wished them to be raped and also went on a

demonstration against them. But the creators of 'The Jews Are Coming,' Natalie Marcus and Asaf Beiser, were not surprised by the storm around them but by the fact that it took time to explode," accessed July 21, 2023, https://www.ynet.co.il/entertainment/article/ry7tqfje5.

13 Asaf Beiser, November 11, 2020, interview with Avinoam Patt.

14 *The Jews Are Coming*, "*Schindler's List* meets *The Office*," season 4, episode 7, https://youtu.be/M5ke37xDVLg?t=162.

15 See, for example, Sara Horowitz, "But Is It Good for the Jews? Spielberg's Schindler and the Aesthetics of Atrocity," in *Spielberg's Holocaust*, ed. Yosefa Loshitzky (Bloomington: Indiana University Press, 1997).

16 *The Jews Are Coming*, "Barbie," season 4, episode 1, https://youtu.be/3BYWOhuSKoM?t=1150.

17 The term "Holocaust icons" comes from Oren Baruch Stier, *Holocaust Icons: Symbolizing the Shoah in History and Memory* (New Brunswick, NJ: Rutgers University Press, 2015). Nathan Englander plays with the idea of the "Anne Frank game" in his short story "What We Talk About When We Talk About Anne Frank," in which the characters examine the meaning of living a Jewish life predicated on remembering the Holocaust while also grappling with the question of whether they would have sheltered one another during the war.

18 *The Jews Are Coming*, "Never Again All Over Again," special release, May 21, 2024, https://www.youtube.com/watch?v=KjwrV0wG9E0&list=PLLttfoK87AdV6BZt7uEgffNyEcfk3GLBT&t=1s.

Selected Bibliography

Lipman, Steve. *Laughter in Hell: The Use of Humor During the Holocaust.* Northvale, NJ: Aronson, 1993.

Slucki, David, Gabriel N. Finder, and Avinoam Patt. *Laughter After: Humor and the Holocaust.* Detroit: Wayne State University Press, 2020.

Steir-Livny, Liat. *Is It OK to Laugh About It? Holocaust Humour, Satire, and Parody in Israeli Culture.* London: Valentine Mitchell, 2017.

Wisse, Ruth. *No Joke: Making Jewish Humor.* Princeton: Princeton, 2015.

Ziv, Avner, ed. *Jewish Humor.* Abingdon, UK: Taylor and Francis, 1998.

11

THE TRAVAILS OF BEING A SOVIET JEWISH COMEDIAN
Michael Idov's The Humorist (2019)

Marat Grinberg

When visiting the exhibit "Let There Be Laughter—Jewish Humor Around the World" at the Tel-Aviv Museum of the Jewish Diaspora (now ANU) in 2019, I was pleased to see that it included a segment on Soviet Jewish comedians. The segment's heading, however, "Laughter Behind Bars," struck me as an overt simplification and a cliché. Many of the most popular Soviet comedians showcased in the exhibit, such as Arkady Raikin (1911–87), were indeed Jewish. Beloved by millions and enjoying the protection of some Party higher-ups, including at times even Leonid Brezhnev, they were quite daring in satirizing the inadequacies of Soviet life. Always at the mercy of censorship and on occasion the object of antisemitic attacks, they were, nevertheless, hardly behind bars. The preponderance of Jews among Soviet satirical writers, performers, and humorists should be seen as one of the many paradoxes of post-Stalinist Soviet culture: the culture of a closed off society that was nonetheless vibrant in many explicit and covert ways, where Jews occupied a center stage despite continuous waves of persecution. It is impossible to understand the nature of Soviet Jewishness without taking these contradictions into account.[1]

Thus, while the notion of "laughter behind bars" is not entirely incorrect, it tells only part of the story. The main question at hand is, To what extent did these comedians' Jewish identity inform their art? Was their humor a Jewish humor, or would such a definition only essentialize and decontextualize the phenomenon? And if indeed it was a Jewish humor, are there parallels between the Soviet Jewish and American Jewish comedic traditions, for instance? The 2019 film *The Humorist*, directed by Michael Idov, brings an authentic, fresh, and provocative insight to these questions. As Idov explained to me in an interview in 2020 shortly after the film's release, he sees a close connection between the American and Soviet cases: both schools of humor came from the same "shtetl," as he puts it. In his film, Idov foregrounds the link between Jewishness and humor and provides a somber view of the place of Jews in Soviet and post-Soviet society. However subtly, the film would agree that in Russia, to laugh for a Jew is to laugh from behind bars.

The Humorist is Michael Idov's first film. Born and raised in Soviet Riga, Idov immigrated with his family to the United States at the age of sixteen in 1992. Ostensibly, he belongs to what Adam Rovner has somewhat pejoratively called "the new immigrant chic": the American writers of Soviet Jewish lineage, such as Garry Shteyngart, David Bezmozgis, and Larisa Vapnyar, among others, who often capitalize in their texts and personas on their Soviet past.[2] Yet, Idov is different from this cohort in that he has a much firmer foot in both the contemporary American and Russian worlds: his satirical novel *Ground Up* was critically acclaimed in the United States and became a bestseller in Russia, which led to his work as an editor in chief of the Russian *GQ* and a screenwriter for several popular Russian films and TV series. There's very little discussion of or allusions to Jewishness in Idov's work prior to *The Humorist*. As he explains in his memoir, *Dressed Up for a Riot: Misadventures in Putin's Moscow*, "Being Jewish [in the Soviet Union] meant zip in the way of religion: it meant a funny last name (Zilberman—check), and funnier nose and/or hair (check and check), and the stigma of 'rootless cosmopolitanism,' a sticky Stalin-era formulation guaranteeing that no Jew would ever be considered fully Russian."[3] While ostensibly true, this definition deliberately eschews the many paradoxes and complications of the Soviet Jewish condition—that is, how Jewishly "thin" or "thick" it was. If in the "thick" category, "knowledge of . . . ethnoreligious tradition/culture" is crucial; in the "thin" one, the identity is much more essentialized, nominal, and, hence, not "sufficiently substantive and sustainable to preserve a group's distinctiveness on more than a symbolic level."[4] As pointed out by Anna Shternshis, "Studying . . . humor will aid in dismantling the false dichotomy of thin versus thick culture as well as allowing for the study of Soviet Jewish culture as an example of 'subjectivity' . . . an internalized code of mutual recognition and self-awareness."[5] The fact that in his first feature film, Idov devotes much attention to Jewishness suggests that he always knew or suspected that there was more to it than the shape of a nose or the thickness of hair.

The Humorist is filled with the codes of Jewish subjectivity. It takes place in 1984, in the senile stage of the stagnation epoch, on the eve of Mikhail Gorbachev's ascent to power and the reforms he would undertake. The protagonist is Boris Arkadiev (Alexei Agranovich), a popular satirical writer who delivers his routines onstage to mass audiences. Arkadiev's character is an amalgamation of many Soviet Jewish comedians and performers, most notably Mikhail Zhvanetsky but also Arkady Arkanov, Gennady Khazanov, Semen Altov, and Efim Smolin, to name a few of the most prominent ones. Their sketches were usually published on page 16 of the main literary periodical, *Literaturnaia gazeta* (Literary Newspaper), and were enormously popular with the intelligentsia readers. A hit TV program, *Vokrug smekha* (Around Laughter), featured their recitals of these routines, a Soviet version of stand-up.

Idov recreates Zhvanetsky's persona in Arkadiev: Like the legendary writer (1934–2020), Arkadiev comes onstage with a bag over his shoulders and extracts out of it the crumpled pages of his arabesques. His quick idiosyncratic delivery is similar to Zhvanetsky's as well. Throughout the film, Arkadiev recites the same monologue about a photographer with a monkey on a beach in a touristy town, most likely Odessa, evocative of Efim Smolin's sketch, famously performed by Gennady Khazanov. This also links Arkadiev to Zhvanetsky, who, according to Jarrod Tanny, "emerged as the emblematic Odessit of the post-Stalin era" (the film begins on an Odessan beach with the child Arkadiev telling a joke about Reagan and Brezhnev).[6] Besprinkled with sexist and racist innuendos and slight jabs at the Soviet reality, Arkadiev's satire is largely innocuous, revealing his caution and self-censorship. The photographer, for instance, refers to his monkey by the patronymic "Ivanovich," whereas originally it was supposed to be Ilich, clearly alluding to both Lenin's and Brezhnev's patronymics.

Despite the many similarities between the fictional Arkadiev and the actual Soviet Jewish comedians, Arkadiev is his own character, despondent and disgusted with himself for the compromises he's made to lead the life of a celebrity. Creatively and sexually impotent and a drunkard, he sees his life and career as one irredeemable failure. Constantly at the mercy of the authorities and the KGB, his laughter, which is hardly a laughter at all, indeed symbolically emanates from behind bars. The matter of Jewishness appears early on in the film, when at a party after Arkadiev's performance, a question is brought up whether the cosmonaut Malkin, who is currently part of a space mission, is in fact Jewish. Thus, while never publicly discussed or acknowledged, Jewishness is presented as the main topic of "kitchen" conversations—the proverbial space of subterranean Soviet privacy.

At the party, Arkadiev and his friend/rival Semion Greenberg start a challenge: Who will tell a funnier joke about why no Jews are accepted into space programs? With all jokes alluding to Soviet antisemitism and containing the Jewish "internalized code[s] of mutual recognition and self-awareness,"[7] Arkadiev's last and winning joke verges on tragic: No Jews are admitted because they might not want to come back to Earth; they have too much experience of living without air. Greenberg, who does not mask his Jewishness—as we later learn, Arkadiev's surname is a pseudonym—accuses his frenemy of cowardice and sycophancy. Arkadiev retorts by disavowing the label of a humorist, insisting that what he writes is part of a grand Russian literary tradition, from Nikolai Gogol to Anton Chekhov. His pronouncements are hollow, desperate, and simultaneously honest: Jewishness underpins his creative and existential condition, as does his belonging to Russian culture and language. Unwilling to immigrate, he chooses to remain in the airless Soviet atmosphere, creatively, emotionally, and spiritually moribund. At the same time, the least convincing part of the film is the fact that Arkadiev never succeeded as a serious writer; his first and only novel was a flop. This element is central to Idov's conception of why humor was a Jewish profession in the USSR: as he told this author, the Jews "escaped" into humor because they could not publish in any other genre. Factually incorrect (there were a number of prominent Jewish writers and poets), it also seems to erroneously suppose that one can easily turn into a humorist. The contrary, however, is true—Zhvanetsky wrote what he wrote because he couldn't do it in any other way.

Where *The Humorist* succeeds is in recreating the atmosphere of the pre-Perestroika Soviet 1980s, with its rebelliousness, on the one hand—Arkadiev's teenage son listens to rock music while he watches a VHS tape of Eddie Murphy's stand-up—and the pervasiveness of the authorities' control, on the other. Ideology here is a sham, and everyone, including those in power, is fully aware of it. To survive, one must obey the rules of the game and the shifting limits of what can be said and where and how. Throughout the film, Arkadiev verges on the brink of stepping outside these limits. For instance, right before his performance in honor of the Day of the Railroad Worker, another Soviet absurdity, he is approached by a KGB officer who informs Arkadiev that he and his wife will be in the audience. Disgusted, Arkadiev first refuses to go up onstage, but then he contemplates reading a new monologue about the cosmonaut Rabinovich, the stand-in for the Jew in the Soviet psyche. We don't know what the monologue is actually about, but it's safe to presume that it satirizes antisemitism. Yet, once onstage, Arkadiev chickens out and once again recites the routine about the photographer and his monkey, which he finds insufferable.

The idea of the impossibility of a Soviet Jewish cosmonaut is the film's main thrust. It is Arkadiev's idée fixe and his futile desire for freedom and transcendence. In the film's pivotal scene, Arkadiev is awoken in the middle of the night by KGB officers who order him to accompany them. Depressed and resigned to his world collapsing all around him, he is convinced that he is either being arrested or being taken to the house of yet another Party boss to perform his routines. Instead, Arkadiev is put on a plane and flown to what is ostensibly the Soviet NASA headquarters. Alone in a decrepit cell-like room—Idov has flair for the surreal—he's connected to a spaceship in orbit because its crew demanded to hear his monologues. Unsurprisingly, they request the photographer routine. Arkadiev acquiesces but this time dares to say that the monkey's patronymic is Ilich. His listener-cosmonaut naturally recognizes this reference to Lenin and finds it hilarious. With no one around, Arkadiev crosses the line of the permitted. The monkey is the epitome of the Soviet system—dirty, stupid, and sneaky—which can bite and kill at any moment.

The cosmonaut stops Arkadiev, perhaps fearing that he might say something too out of bounds, but their conversation continues. He directly asks Arkadiev whether he's a Jew. Arkadiev confirms and reports that his actual name is Boris Moiseevich Aronson. Earlier, Arkadiev asked the cosmonaut whether hopefully there was indeed no God in space—"hopefully" alludes ironically to Soviet atheism—and now the cosmonaut asks him if he at least believes in the Jewish God. Arkadiev responds that he doesn't, although he cannot say with certainty. The cosmonaut persists and asks Arkadiev, if he met God, what he would say to the Almighty. "Am I truly worthy of love?" is Arkadiev's desperate response.

The scene is noteworthy in many respects and is purportedly based on what actually happened to Mikhail Zhvanetsky (whose estranged son, who happens to be Idov's friend and collaborator, relayed this story to him). It is especially striking in terms of what it suggests about Arkadiev's Jewishness. On the one hand, the idea of the "Jewish God" is simplistic; it betrays both Arkadiev's and the cosmonaut's ignorance about the monotheistic premise of both Judaism and Christianity. There's also an antisemitic subtext to the cosmonaut's supposition as well as the recognition that Jews are fundamentally different—Arkadiev acknowledges and embraces this difference. While Arkadiev is by no means an observant or knowledgeable Jew, his Jewishness does include a transcendent element. It is intuitive, aspirational, and ironic and does sum up for Idov the idea of Soviet Jewishness.

Obsessed with the cosmonauts and fearing that they might have died in a crash, Arkadiev is at the end of his rope by the end of the film. All hell breaks loose in the final segment, which offers Idov's most scathing portrayal of the Soviet attitude toward Jews. In it, Arkadiev is invited or rather forced to come to the birthday party of the spouse of an important KGB general who prides herself on having access to the stars. The party is a Satan's ball, where the attendants gather around the television set to watch an American pornographic flick while gorging on delicacies no ordinary Soviet citizens could either obtain or afford. The joke, as Arkadiev's actor friend, who is also at the party, whispers to him, is that they believe that this bacchanalia is a regular occurrence in average American homes. This privileged Soviet class possesses no understanding of the moral difference between what is permitted and what one ought to do. Arkadiev is nauseated by his hosts and their tastes but gives an honorary toast and tells a few cheap jokes. He turns himself into a groveling servile puppet.

The debauchery continues in a bathhouse where the general gathers the men from the party, including Arkadiev. As Idov explained, he deliberately set up the bathhouse scene as a parody of a Greek symposium. Sitting in a circle, everyone here is wrapped in towels, resembling togas. Instead of reaching for purification or philosophical heights, they, however, like the depraved ancient Romans, crave more cheap entertain-ment and order Arkadiev to perform his act: tell jokes. Rather than the usual monkey sketch, he proposes to deliver new material. It is his tour de force and a final fatal act. He throws all care to the wind and speaks with his "jokes" truth to power. The audience tolerates this at first, when he mocks the current Party leader, Chernenko, but they grow weary once he touches Lenin. To deliver his pièce de résistance, which he knows will enrage his host, he goes after the general's wife, ridiculing her generous proportions. Outraged, the general orders his goons to attack Arkadiev, which they happily do. He also throws himself at Arkadiev, calling him a "huge kike" (*zhidyara*), but suddenly collapses on the floor and dies from a heart attack. No one helps the general; Arkadiev is the only one begging to save a fellow human being. In fact, Arkadiev the Jew is the only human being among these fascistic animals.[8]

The film's final message is offered in the conversation that occurs out-side the bathhouse between another general from the scene and a KGB officer who was earlier keeping his eye on Arkadiev. The general cannot figure out why Arkadiev, who had everything one could desire, would decide to throw it all away. He wonders if there's something about *them* that makes them act this way; perhaps *they* should be allowed to tell jokes once in a while to not go berserk, the general concludes. The "they" here means Jews, and, thus, an intrinsic connection is established between Jew-ishness and comedy as a venue of resistance. The general's plan is that rather than crush Jews, they should be allowed to occasionally let out steam. This is, however, a plan for the future—for now, this "little kike" (*zhidok*) Arkadiev should be disposed of.

Arkadiev returns home and, we think, is about to die by suicide. Yet, this does not happen. The film's final image, in the manner of Marvel movies, comes out after the credits have already begun to roll: it is now 2018, and the aged Arkadiev, with visibly trembling hands, comes out onstage and begins to recite the monkey routine. His life and career have been spared while the general's plan has worked. "They" are allowed to tell jokes, old and new ones, and let out steam in a new Russian society where censorship is ostensibly gone, but in reality, the same power structures have stayed in place and even grown stronger. Idov's own film, produced with funds from the Russian Ministry of Culture and offering a clear cri-tique of Putinism, is the confirmation of this ironic situation.

Thus, *The Humorist* is ultimately much more concerned with the contemporary Russian condition than going down the Soviet memory path, although it also posits that one cannot be understood without the other. Idov essentially sees the post-Soviet as the continuation of the Soviet. And while such a view might have seemed out of place when the film was released, in the wake of Russia's aggression against Ukraine, which has led to a severe crackdown on opposition and even the resurgence of occasional Soviet-style state-sponsored antisemitism, Idov's film has acquired a prescient quality. As the result of the war, Idov foreswore any relations with Russia and even the use of Russian language for himself.

His film ultimately suggests that to be a Soviet or post-Soviet Jew is to tell jokes and to do so perennially from behind bars. As a song in the film's soundtrack, "I'm a Humorist," written by the popular Russian rapper Face, puts it, "Gold on my wrist, I'm a humorist / If you tell a wrong joke—you'll get on the black list / Why the tsar's disfavour if I'm kind of clean / sky is for the planes and censorship is for the artist."

Notes

1 For the analysis of Soviet Jewishness, see Marat Grinberg, *The Soviet Jewish Bookshelf: Jewish Culture and Identity Between the Lines* (Waltham, MA: Brandeis University Press, 2023).

2 Adam Rovner, "So Easily Assimilated: The New Immigrant Chic," *AJS Review* 30, no. 2 (2006): 313–24.

3 Michael Idov, *Dressed Up for a Riot: Misadventures in Putin's Moscow* (New York: Farrar, Straus and Giroux, 2018), 6.

4 Zvi Gitelman, *A Century of Ambivalence: The Jews of Russia and the Soviet Union, 1881 to the Present* (Bloomington: Indiana University Press, 2001), 266.

5 Anna Shternshis, "Humor and Russian Jewish Identity," in *A Club of Their Own: Jewish Humorists and the Contemporary World*, ed. Eli Lederhendler (Oxford: Oxford University Press, 2016), 102.

6 Jarrod Tanny, *City of Rogues and Schnorrers: Russia's Jews and the Myth of Old Odessa* (Bloomington: Indiana University Press, 2018), 138.

7 Shternshis, "Humor and Russian Jewish Identity," 102.

8 The shot of Arkadiev's bloodied face held by his tormentors is evocative of a similar scene in Pier Palo Pasolini's *Salo, or the 120 Days of Sodom* (1975).

Selected Bibliography

Gitelman, Zvi. *A Century of Ambivalence: The Jews of Russia and the Soviet Union, 1881 to the Present.* Bloomington: Indiana University Press, 2001.

Grinberg, Marat. *The Soviet Jewish Bookshelf: Jewish Culture and Identity Between the Lines.* Waltham, MA: Brandeis University Press, 2023.

Idov, Michael. *Dressed Up for a Riot: Misadventures in Putin's Moscow.* New York: Farrar, Straus and Giroux, 2018.

Idov, Michael. *Ground Up.* New York: Farrar, Straus and Giroux, 2009.

Krasuska, Karolina. *Soviet-Born: The Afterlives of Migration in Jewish American Fiction.* New Brunswick, NJ: Rutgers University Press, 2024.

Rovner, Adam. "So Easily Assimilated: The New Immigrant Chic." *AJS Review* 30, no. 2 (November 2006): 313–24.

Shternshis, Anna. "Humor and Russian Jewish Identity." In *A Club of Their Own: Jewish Humorists and the Contemporary World,* edited by Eli Lederhendler, 101–12. Oxford: Oxford University Press, 2016.

Tanny, Jarrod. *City of Rogues and Schnorrers: Russia's Jews and the Myth of Old Odessa.* Bloomington: Indiana University Press, 2018.

12

SAMSON KOLETKAR, AKA MAHATMA MOSES
The Cultural Politics of Indian Jewish Humor

Daniel Heifetz

You know, I don't know if I have a thick skin or if I'm stupid, but . . .
I sometimes feel people yell out discrimination at the smallest thing.
And that irks me a little bit. It's like people are curious and yes, they're
ignorant because they haven't encountered somebody, but it doesn't
make them racist or bigoted or anything, right? They're just curious
people who don't know and they're asking you questions, and twenty-
five other people might have asked you that question in the last week,
but the twenty-sixth person hasn't spoken to the twenty-five people,
so they don't know those answers, so they're going to ask you those
same questions—why do you get irritated, right? So, to me I don't
think I felt any discrimination here. Or even back in India, growing
up Jewish was like people are just curious and they ask you questions,
and you get tired of answering the same questions over and over—
I don't.[1]

This chapter is about a Jew of Color who has never experienced any discrimination. More specifically, it is about how humor enables Samson
Koletkar, a Mumbai-born Jewish American comedian, to render questions about the legitimacy of his Jewish identity too absurd to be offensive. Through his assertion that disbelief in his Jewishness is not offensive
or discriminatory, Koletkar defied my expectations about the experiences
of Jews of Color. My expectations are rooted in my own attraction to the
idea of the academic as killjoy, in Sara Ahmed's sense of a person who

disrupts contentment with a problematic status quo.[2] By making it difficult for people to be content with the status quo, the killjoy incentivizes
social change. Koletkar aims to produce radically different feelings with
his comedy, easing social tensions through good feeling, rendering them
innocuous, and moving past them. His rejection of killjoy sensibilities
about the implications of his experiences does not mean his comedy is
socially aloof or accepts Ashkenazi normativity.

To understand what Koletkar means when he says he has never experienced discrimination, this chapter will offer a brief historical introduction to Koletkar's community, the Bene Israel of India. It will then examine
some scholarship that is helpful for interpreting Koletkar's work, focusing
on themes of dignity, legibility, and resilience in humor and other forms of
discourse from Jews of Color and other marginalized people. It will then
discuss some key moments in a personal conversation with Koletkar that
shed light on his experiences as a minority and immigrant as well as his
beginnings in stand-up comedy. This conversation is also the source of the
epigraphs that open each section.[3] Finally, the chapter will examine three
of Koletkar's routines that are available on YouTube.

The Bene Israel of India

> But I really think about it now the history goes two thousand years
> back when Jews arrived on the shores of India, and to imagine that
> they have maintained the "purity" per se for two thousand years, it's
> like—I don't know, it's a little hard to trace that far back especially
> when only seven couples survived the shipwreck according to the
> story. So how do you go from seven couples to seventy thousand Jews
> and maintain your "purity" like I say in double quotes.[4]

This section provides a brief overview of Indian Jewish communities to
provide context for our discussion of Koletkar's life and work. In particular,
I will focus on Koletkar's own community, the Bene Israel. I will also discuss the Cochin and Baghdadi communities, both of which have inter-
acted with the Bene Israel in significant ways over the course of history.[5]

The most popular Bene Israel account of their arrival in India holds
that their ancestors were members of one of the Ten Lost Tribes who were

able to remain in the Levant after 722 BCE but later fled the persecution of Antiochus IV in the Levant around 175 BCE.[6] They were shipwrecked off the western coast of India, not far from what is now Mumbai. With the intervention of the prophet Elijah, seven men and seven women survived the shipwreck and made their new home in the area.[7]

Historians have not been able to corroborate this story or document the history of the Bene Israel before the eighteenth century. A major turning point for the community and our historical knowledge of it came in 1768, when Ezekiel Rahabi, a Jew from the less isolated community in Cochin, sent a report to a contact in Amsterdam detailing his efforts to educate the Bene Israel.[8] Documents from this period indicate that prior to their reconnection with other Jewish communities, the Bene Israel did not know Hebrew or have access to Jewish texts but observed Shabbat and the major holidays, recited the Shema, revered Elijah, and observed dietary prohibitions like avoiding fish without scales.[9]

Life changed dramatically for the Bene Israel as a result of contact with other Jewish communities and encroaching British colonialism. With the growth of the city of Bombay nearby, many Bene Israel left behind their traditional occupation as oil pressers in search of better opportunities in the city. In Bombay, they had a close relationship with India's third Jewish community, the Baghdadis. The Baghdadis arrived with the British in pursuit of lucrative international trade opportunities. The Bene Israel initially welcomed these newcomers into their synagogues.[10]

The Bene Israel increased their conformity to normative Judaism to a certain extent but retained some of their distinctive customs and rejected norms that were impractical for a community with their difficult economic position. Consequently, despite the warm welcome, the more economically privileged and culturally hegemonic Baghdadis were skeptical of the authenticity of Bene Israel Jewish identity. This is demonstrated most dramatically by their efforts to partition their cemetery and frequent inquiries to rabbinical authorities about the suitability of the Bene Israel for marriage.[11]

With Indian independence in 1947 and the founding of Israel in 1948, a substantial portion of the Bene Israel and Cochin communities moved to Israel (the Baghdadis, who identified strongly with the British, tended to move to the United Kingdom instead). In Israel, the Bene Israel faced discrimination and financial hardships. The Sephardic chief rabbi renewed

Baghdadi skepticism of the Jewishness of the Bene Israel, demanding that they prove their marriages were legitimate going back ten generations or undergo conversion if they wanted to wed non–Bene Israel Jews. This resulted in large-scale protests in 1964 that prompted the Knesset to intervene, affirming the legal status of the Bene Israel as Jews.[12]

Outside of Israel and India, Indian Jewish communities are relatively small and have received less scholarly attention. Kelly Amanda Train's study of Congregation BINA (Bene Israel North America) in Toronto is a helpful exception. Train outlines the forms of discrimination that Bene Israel immigrants to Toronto experienced not only on the basis of their conformity with normative Judaism but also due to their cultural and phenotypical divergence from Ashkenazis. For example, while Bene Israel immigrants were served by the Jewish Immigrant Aid Society, these services did not extend to determining if the new arrivals needed kosher food or to live within walking distance of synagogues. Despite attempts to integrate with the Jewish community in Toronto, the Bene Israel were frequently othered, with many Ashkenazi community members questioning their Jewishness or assuming they were converts. Children at religious schools were subject to racism from students and teachers alike and had to endure curricula in which Ashkenazi history and culture were taught as the definitive Jewish experience.[13]

Dignity, Legibility, and Resilience

> The thing about comedy, right—most comedians, I think, come from sort of like, they're almost like social rejects who are rebellious against the norms of the society. That's the DNA of a comedian.[14]

Literature on Indian Jewish humor is in short supply, so to a large extent I am looking to scholarship from several adjacent areas to inform my analysis of Koletkar. Although literature on Indian Jewish immigrants does not tend to engage with humor in a direct and sustained way, it is clear enough that humor can play a role in helping Indian Jews cope with the forms of discrimination they encounter in the wider Jewish community. For example, in Train's work on Congregation BINA, several of the community members she interviews use humor to call attention to the limited

Ashkenazi normativity they often encounter. For example, when Ruby Benjamin's coworkers at the Canadian Jewish Congress gave her a hard time for wearing saris to work, she wittily retorted: "What you're wearing is Anglo-Saxon. If I met you on the street [in India] I would never think that you're Jewish because you don't look Jewish. You look Anglo-Saxon. If you want to dress Jewish, you should be wearing a kurta down to your feet."[15] Along similar lines, Ari Kala recounts a time when he was applying to work at a Jewish summer camp. During the interview, the director claimed he could tell Ari wasn't Jewish. Ari acerbically replied, "This is what Jews looked like before we went to Europe and became white."[16]

In both of these situations, Ruby's and Ari's Jewish identities are not being taken seriously because they do not conform to Ashkenazi expectations about how Jews look. And both Ruby and Ari respond to these situations by mocking the inherent absurdity of questioning a person's knowledge of their own identity. To accomplish this, they reverse the Ashkenazi gaze, suggesting that Ashkenazim, who are used to going about with their Jewishness unquestioned, are in fact the ones who ought to be treated as suspect. One would hope that in getting a dose of their own medicine, Ruby's coworkers and Ari's interviewer might have learned something about the complexity of Jewish identity. But more importantly, by calling attention to the absurdity of Ashkenazi normativity, Rubi and Ari used humor to protect their dignity and the legitimacy of their own Jewish identities.

To some extent, these strategies bear similarities to those used by other Jews of Color who work to affirm that different aspects of their identities form a cohesive whole. For example, Sarah Bunin Benor's "Jews of Color: Performing Black Jewishness Through the Creative Use of Two Ethnolinguistic Repertoires" highlights the way Black Jews juxtapose linguistic features and cultural referents of African American English and Jewish English when they talk about their identities. For example, Benor describes the comedy music video "Black and Jewish" on *Funny or Die*, in which Kali Hawk and Katerina Graham present their audience with a series of humorous juxtapositions that evoke Black and Jewish language and culture such as "pouring hot sauce on lox and bagels." Benor asserts that the humor in this video lies in presenting things that seem to belong to one cultural context only and that are therefore surprising when they appear in combination. She goes on to suggest that this parody breaks down racial essentialism for audiences and confronts them with the complexities of transcultural and multiracial identities.[17] We might see Ruby's assertion that Jewish women wear kurtas and saris rather than Anglo-Saxon clothing as a kind of linguistic play in the same vein, and we will see similar juxtapositions in Koletkar's routines later in this chapter.

According to Eitan Shahar and Maya Lavie-Ajayi, juxtaposition is a key feature of the way Indian Jews from Cochin narrativize their experiences in Israel as well. This is well illustrated by an interview the authors share with a man named Yehuda. Unlike Cochin Jews who arrived in Israel as adults and lived in monoethnic communities, Yehuda arrived as a child and therefore had substantial contact with the wider community through boarding school and through his subsequent military training. After recounting hurtful colorist remarks his peers would make, he notes that he'd complain to his teachers and other leaders. These authority figures then tried to "compensate" by becoming a reliable support network for Yehuda. While he gives no indication that the bullying stopped, he suggests that this support network compensated adequately for the problem and made him feel like he could enjoy his new life in Israel. Shahar and Lavie-Ajayi suggest that like Yehuda, many Indian Jewish immigrants in Israel juxtapose these negative and positive experiences in their life narratives in order to render them into a single, balanced whole. This integration allows Yehuda to say that he now laughs when he hears the phrases with which he was once bullied.[18] The authors suggest that juxtaposition and integration through narrative produces resilience—a process of dealing with difficult situations using available resources within a specific cultural framework.[19] While this process *does not* dismantle the structural problems that create adversity, it does make adversity bearable—even laughable, for Yehuda—while those structures persist.

There is also a growing literature on South Asian American humor. One helpful piece is Samah Choudhury's "What Makes Humor Muslim?" Choudhury works to interpret the recent success of Muslim American comedians like Hasan Minhaj, Kumail Nanjiani, and Aziz Ansari, all of whom are also of South Asian descent. Their success represents a striking break from a long history of American and European stereotypes of Muslims as humorless religious fanatics. These stereotypes preclude Muslim involvement in secular civil society because a sense of humor is a prerequisite for such involvement.[20] This has changed due to increasing public perceptions that Islamophobia is a form of racism and that Muslims are a racialized group. Whereas outwardly religious articulations of Muslim identity have an uneasy place in the secular fold of American humor, racial identities are a much easier fit.[21]

The most obvious disjuncture between Koletkar and these Muslim American comedians is that Jews haven't exactly been stereotyped as humorless in the United States. Nevertheless, there are some points of comparison to be made here. Jews have long been viewed as a group that is ambiguously religious, ethnic, racial, and/or national at the same time. Consequently, Koletkar has an extant template for presenting a secular Jewish identity in his humor. In Choudhury's analysis, she also makes reference to how Muslim American comedians exhibit what W. E. B. Du Bois called a "double consciousness," in which marginalized people perceive themselves through the eyes of more privileged people.[22] Just as Minhaj, Nanjiani, and Ansari present their Muslimness in a way that reflects external perceptions in order to resonate with audiences, we will see that Koletkar presents his Indian Jewishness along similar lines.

Finally, Rebecca Krefting's *All Joking Aside: American Humor and Its Discontents* provides useful tools for thinking about the political (or apolitical) valences and identity work in Koletkar's humor. Krefting is interested in what she terms "charged humor," which she describes as a type of humor that undermines an unjust and exclusionary status quo by drawing upon often personal experiences of exclusion and illustrating audience complicity.[23] One of the significant functions of charged humor is to create "cultural citizenship," which insists on the belonging, importance, and dignity of marginalized people in a society that is structured to exclude them. It operates by demonstrating the absurdity of existing stereotypes while advancing new, alternative representations that subvert social hierarchies.[24]

Krefting contrasts charged humor with "modern-day minstrelsy," in which comedians from marginalized groups reinforce stereotypes that will evoke easy laughter from audiences due to their familiarity. In particular, she explores this contrast through the transformation of Hari Kondabolu. While comedy functions as a kind of identity work for Kondabolu from early on, his early material as a college student played heavily on the reproduction of Indian stereotypes that audiences would find familiar. Later, once he felt more secure in his status as a comedian, he began a shift to comedy that drew upon these same stereotypes at times, but for the sake of undermining them.[25] Krefting's analysis here has implications for interpreting Koletkar's work. As Koletkar works to render intelligible an identity that audiences may find confusing, what relation do his representations of Indianness and Jewishness hold to the dominant social order?

While the social and political resonances of Koletkar's comedy may seem inconsistent at times, I would suggest that it serves three closely interrelated purposes that are significant for his experiences as an Indian Jewish American. First, he debunks bogus questions about the legitimacy of his Jewish identity and affirms his dignity as an Indian Jew in ways that reflect Krefting's "charged humor" and has clear resonances with the ad hoc humor that Ruby and Ari produce in response to incredulity about their Jewish identities. In a more conciliatory, less subversive mood, he works within the framework of extant audience expectations to make his identity as an Indian Jew legible for audience members. Both of these approaches have an external function of making the audience question their assumptions and getting them to understand an identity they find confusing. Koletkar's comedy at times also has an internal function of cultivating resilience so that, like Yehuda, he can laugh at Ashkenazi normativity. Taking these three components of Koletkar's comedy as a whole, we can observe that comedy allows him to simultaneously work to undermine problematic social structures while also making life bearable as long as those social structures persist.

Minority Experiences, Immigration, and Comedy

Growing up Jewish [in Mumbai] was tricky, because the majority of people didn't know what that meant. Folks who were around me when I told them, "I'm a Jew," they're like, "I don't get it; what's that?" Right, they had to find some correlation. And the only correlation I could give them was two things. One was Israel the country. So a lot of people are like "Oh like Israel, like Palestine." And I was like, "Yeah, it's like India and Pakistan, it's the same thing." And then the other was there was one old Bollywood movie which had gotten very popular called *Yahudi*, which is the Hindi word for Jews. And so that was the other reference that they had, "Oh, *Yahudi* the movie, oh you're those people." So that was the hard part of trying to explain to people who you were.[26]

In December 2020, I had the good fortune to be able to speak with Koletkar in order to gain a better sense of context for the experiences that inform his comedy. This fascinating conversation is the basis for the basic question that this chapter looks to solve: What does it mean for Koletkar to say he has never faced discrimination as a Jew of Color? Working from this conversation, this section provides further discussion of the experiences that inform Koletkar's routines and of Koletkar's activities in the Bay Area comedy scene.

Samson Koletkar was born in the mid-1970s and grew up in and around Mumbai. During his early childhood, he lived in the suburbs of Mumbai, where there were very few Jews, and his identity was a mystery to almost everyone he met. Explaining what a Jew was seemed to be a matter of routine for him during this stage of life, as the epigraph suggests. This is a significant experience in its own way as it suggests that having to explain his identity was not an entirely novel problem for him later in life, when he arrived in the United States. The difference for him was that in the United States, there was a set of normative preconceptions for what a Jew was, whereas in India there was simply a dearth of knowledge and experience. Despite this contextual difference, the notion that his identity would be confusing and in need of explanation was established for Koletkar well before coming to the United States.

During his later school years, Koletkar moved with his family to south Mumbai, where there was a much larger Jewish population—roughly eight of the ten synagogues in the area were in this part of the city. During this time, he attended a Jewish school where he was able to study Hebrew alongside English, Marathi, and Hindi. He recalls that his mother, who converted upon marrying his father, was quite invested in Jewish tradition but that other festivals were also a part of their home life. His father was less interested in religion personally but was nonetheless invested in having his son's regular participation in Torah study and Saturday morning services. Koletkar resented being given these obligations by someone who did not keep them himself and became fairly skeptical about Jewish tradition. That said, he also notes that his "question everything" attitude toward religion was itself a Jewish attitude. Despite his skepticism, he has fond memories of some observances, particularly tashlich and Simchat Torah.

After receiving his master's degree and working in India for three years, Koletkar moved to Silicon Valley on an H-1B visa in October 2000. As with many immigrants, the transition was challenging for him, and he struggled with feelings of isolation as a result of the relative social insularity of American culture:

> If you think New York is 24/7, you should go to Bombay. New York feels quiet. And coming from there into a suburb of San Francisco where everything shuts down at 10:00 p.m.? And you're in your apartment, you don't know who your neighbors are, nobody speaks to anybody. You show up at work, people are in their cubicles, they'll come say hi, ask you the question they need for work and then they disappear at 5:00 p.m., you never see them until the next day at 8:00 a.m.

Within the first year, it was so difficult that he considered returning to India, but during a quick visit home he was rapidly disabused of his nostalgia and recognized that there were some definite advantages to remaining in the United States.

Resolving to make it work here, Koletkar joined a Bollywood dance troupe, and this played a significant role in establishing the missing feeling of community and contributed to his resilience as an immigrant. Dance had been an interest of his as a young adult, although as he noted during his interview, he had some prior performance experiences that were more harrowing: during kindergarten, his mother taught him to balance a hat on a stick and had him set to perform in costume as Charlie Chaplin. But when they announced his name, he started crying and refused to go onstage.

Although Koletkar says he "always" liked comedy and (at some point after kindergarten) was comfortable being onstage, it had not occurred to him to try stand-up until he saw a clip of Indian Canadian comedian Russell Peters performing. Remembering this moment, Koletkar said, "And that for the first time made me feel that, 'Oh, there's an Indian person doing this!' I had never seen an Indian comedian. I had always seen Black comics and White comics and maybe Latino comics, but an Indian comedian? And so that piqued my interest a little bit." This epiphany is important for understanding the relationship between Koletkar's comedy and his identity. The underrepresentation of South Asians in North American comedy had created limitations in Koletkar's sense of what kinds of cultural spaces might be open to him in his new home. Within the multicultural tapestry of the United States—indicated by the Black, white, and Latino comics he'd come to expect to see—there was room for the distinctive perspectives that the South Asian diaspora could bring. Through his comedy, Russell Peters created public visibility and cultural legibility for diaspora South Asians that Koletkar would soon work to produce himself.

After asking for suggestions from friends in his dance troupe, Koletkar took classes at San Francisco Comedy College in early 2006 and had quit dancing before the end of the year. Although this likely had to do with limitations of time to some extent, when Koletkar described this transition from comedy to dance, the implication was that comedy had taken the place of dance for him—it was providing so much more fulfillment that dance was just no longer worth the time. Since dance had provided him with the sense of connection that allowed him to be resilient in his new environment, the implication would seem to be that comedy now provided resilience in an even more powerful way.

While Koletkar noted in our conversation that comedy is more individual than dance as a performance art, he told me he still found that it fostered important social connections for him and helped him find a place in the multicultural society he now lived in:

> One of the beauties of doing stand-up for me was I wouldn't be half the man I am today if I had not gotten into stand-up. Cause it opened up such a wide area of humanity to me, right? We think about comics by race, we think about comics by gender, we think about comics by sexuality, we think about comics by political beliefs and every possible checkbox under the sun, and you'll find a comedian who has checked that box. Comedians come from a wide spectrum of life. And to be able to hear everybody and to be able to understand their stories has made me way more mature than I would have ever been. And I know

what I was before doing stand-up and I know what I am now, right? It's a huge leap that I made. And that's one of the things about comedy; I don't see anybody prejudiced against anybody for who they are, but the problem starts based upon what you say. . . . Comics are very, like, approachable; you can reach out to anybody. Especially when you are starting out there's a very like "Hey you are one of us, 'cause nobody else likes you. Come, we'll support you."

Whereas Bollywood dance may have been useful primarily as a way to affirm his identity as a South Asian American and build community with others with similar experiences, comedy creates a much wider network of connections for Koletkar, suddenly making people from all walks of life legible to him *and* showing them that they can contribute to his resilience through their distinctive forms of support.

This is not to say that suddenly Koletkar's newfound identity as a comedian somehow fully displaced his Indian American identity. After all, this started with that Russell Peters clip demonstrating possibilities for South Asian diaspora comedy. After a series of terrorist attacks that took place in Mumbai in 2008, Koletkar came to be troubled by the growing Hindu-Muslim enmity he saw in India:

In 2013, I was feeling helpless, sitting here in America looking at all the vitriol happening in India. So like what's the one thing I can do? I can bring together Indians and Pakistanis in a room and make them laugh together. So in 2013 I put together a show called "United We Stand Up." I had two Pakistani and three Indian comics. . . . And I call that thing, it's like a glass half full/glass half empty sort of thing cause we sold half the capacity of tickets. People appreciated that hey, Indians and Pakistanis can sit together and laugh as well.

For Koletkar, bringing Indians and Pakistanis together to laugh was a political act. Just as comedy provided Koletkar with a form of social integration that extended beyond his personal identity, he envisioned it doing the same for Indians and Pakistanis—perhaps making both groups more mutually legible and helping them forge bonds of solidarity that would make them all more resilient.

By 2014, the vision for this event became more expansive:

The other idea I had in my head was there was an African American comedy festival, a Latino comedy festival, a Jewish comedy festival, an LGBT comedy festival, why is there not a Desi [South Asian] comedy festival? There's more . . . Desis in the world than all those other demographics put together. We have 1.3 billion people, we can have a festival.

This reworked event, now called the Desi Comedy Festival, brought in progressively larger audiences each year. In the rationale Koletkar provides for this festival, we can hear an echo of his epiphany on seeing that Russell Peters clip—Koletkar is correcting the problem of underrepresentation and creating a world in which Desi comedy can become more legible.

"Preparing for an Indian Jewish Baby"

What I find most interesting is, a lot of people expect me to say things because I'm an immigrant. And then I say something completely opposite. And I tend to look at things, like I said, I don't get annoyed by people asking me the same questions over and over, right? So, a lot of people would expect me to say mostly anti Donald Trump jokes. I don't have any! I don't have any against him, to be honest. My only anti Donald Trump joke used to be, "I don't like him because he has put too many Indian people in the government. And if I wanted to live in a country run by Indian people, I wouldn't have left the country I left behind, right? So that's the only reason I don't like Donald Trump." And that sort of messes with people's heads 'cause they're all expecting me to say something and that doesn't fit their idea of what I should be saying.[27]

Koletkar identifies two different relations between his humor, on the one hand, and his identity and experiences as an Indian Jewish immigrant, on the other hand. One involves defying expectations about what an immigrant "should" say, while the other is about a minority "punching up." In this section, I will be exploring the former motif through one of his routines that deals with Indian and to a lesser extent Jewish stereotypes, at times in conjunction. By trafficking in these stereotypes, Koletkar works with audience expectations and renders himself legible for them. At the same time, because Koletkar feels that audiences expect him to reject and criticize these stereotypes, Koletkar is demonstrating a refusal to conform to these expectations.

> I'm doing great right now in my life. I'm really happy. [*audience laughs*] Apparently that's a joke for some people. I know I'm brown in America, I shouldn't be happy, but I am. I am happy right now because my wife and I are having our first baby! [*audience cheers*] Again, some of you clap, you're happy for me, the others are like, "Whoa, whoa, why are you encouraging him? It's not like we need more of them, there's like a billion of them already. It's not like he's doing something no one's ever done before." I get it, OK?

This opening establishes context that is important for understanding the rest of the routine. He calls to mind what he sees as an expectation that as a brown comedian in America, he should have a bone to pick. Having reminded the audience of this fact, he sets it aside. What is particularly interesting about this opening is the way he uses audience reactions to attribute views to them—the notion that brown people in American shouldn't be happy or that there's no need for more of them.

Koletkar continues:

> But let me clarify one thing first, because the minute I say my wife and I, some people say, "Dude, where's your ring?" And now I had a ring, and unfortunately, I lost it. [*audience groans*] Better the ring than the wife, you know? But then I bought another ring, and unfortunately, I lost that too. And look people, I am Indian and Jewish. There's no way I'm buying a third ring.

Here Koletkar invokes a similar stereotype that persists about Jews and Indians. This does some interesting things. At the surface level, it may come across as modern-day minstrelsy, as Krefting would describe it. He makes his material relatable and accessible by invoking and reinforcing stereotypes about Indians and Jews being cheap. But due to its context, there are other significant dimensions here. Koletkar has already opened the routine in a way that calls attention to the fact that he is defying expectations. Given that framing, this isn't a joke about Indians and Jews being cheap; it's a joke about the audience expectation that Koletkar would not say such a thing.

Koletkar's implicit observation that Jews and Indians are subject to the same stereotype is also significant in relation to his identity as an Indian Jew. To some extent, what Koletkar is doing here resembles the juxtaposition that Benor describes in her analysis of Black Jewish linguistic repertoires. In the cases that Benor described, the imagery was often striking because the items she described did not seem to go together. But in this case, Koletkar seems to be invoking this stereotype in a way that suggests that Indianness and Jewishness are not so incompatible—his Indian Jewish identity should be legible enough, in that case.

Sticking with this theme, he goes on to say, "And it's also a mixed marriage, my wife and I, it's a mixed marriage. My wife is Hindu, I'm Jewish, so I thought I should name my firstborn 'Mahatma Moses . . . dot com.'" Here again we have the juxtaposition of Jewish and Indian, or more specifically Hindu, elements. Although in this routine Koletkar proposes this name for his unborn child as a way to synthesize his Jewish heritage with his wife's Hindu heritage, he also at times "brands" himself as Mahatma Moses. Modern Anglophone audiences like Koletkar's associate "Mahatma" with Gandhi. Gandhi and Moses each serve as widely recognizable tokens for their people. Koletkar thus makes himself legible as an Indian Jew by invoking the two figures with whom his audience is most likely to be familiar.

Koletkar concludes the routine with two more stereotypes: a reprisal of the cheap Jew followed by the sexually repressive Indian parent. As with his previous invocation of stereotypes, it's easy to dismiss this as a kind of modern-day minstrelsy. Nevertheless, it is worth recognizing the double bind in which Koletkar finds himself. If Koletkar rejects his routines and consistently places American white supremacy and xenophobia in his crosshairs, he feels as though he is embodying a stereotype himself. In the very pursuit of dignity as a racialized minority, he risks becoming what he perceives as an undignified caricature—the unhappy brown man. There is, therefore, a sense in which Koletkar resists one stereotype by invoking these others. Of course, invoking these stereotypes, even ironically, can still confirm them. But for someone in Koletkar's position as a comedian, perhaps the unhappy brown man stereotype poses more immediate personal danger and therefore must be dealt with.

"There Are No Jews in This World"

> Sometimes it's the approach of a minority punching up, right? Which is the whole idea behind the Jewish bit, about "Are you really Jewish? Were you born Jewish?" And it's like wait, you are trying to invalidate me, let me invalidate your entire existence. If you go by the actual logic, there are no Jews in the world. So that's the other one, where if it's an established and tried and tested tradition that people are like, "This is how it is," I'm like, "No it is not! How can I poke holes in the things that you're not supposed to poke holes in?"[28]

While Koletkar may take some steps to defy expectations about his politics, he has no shortage of acerbic observations about his experiences as an Indian Jewish immigrant. The remainder of this chapter will explore two such routines. First, I will examine a routine in which he addresses the inevitable questions that arise about the legitimacy of his identity as an Indian Jew. Like the ad hoc humor in the examples of Ruby and Ari from Congregation BINA, Koletkar's approach in his routine "There Are No Jews in This World" involves making those who would question the legitimacy of his identity feel what it is to have the legitimacy of their identities questioned instead.

He begins by introducing three questions he gets, typically from other Jews looking to "validate" him: "Are you really Jewish? Were you born Jewish? Are both your parents Jewish?" Each of these questions gets its own sarcastic answer, suggesting the fruitlessness of the line of inquiry, the implausibility that he would be making it up, and the unlikeliness that such skepticism can really be satisfied. He wants the audience to understand at the outset that such questions are ridiculous and do not deserve to be dignified with a serious answer. In doing so, he makes it possible for him to go on to explain his identity in a way that will be legible for the audience without accepting the indignity that it should be necessary for him to do so. He makes this explicit by stating that he won't explain the story of his family "except onstage."

Koletkar then tells the audience that while his father was born a Jew, his mother was born a Hindu. This raises the specter of patrilineality for his skeptical questioner, who is still unsatisfied when Koletkar explains that his mother converted before marriage: "Eh, I dunno. She wasn't born Jewish. I don't know if you're Jewish enough." What follows is a reflection on what makes a person Jewish via the story of Abraham:

> And I'm like, really? Let's think about this for a minute. Now, do you guys know who was the first Jew? [*audience member: "Abraham!"*] Abraham. See, this is why I like Sunnyvale. Smart crowd. Elsewhere, people scream, "Jesus!" Just to remind me which country I'm in, "Hey, welcome to America!" No, Abraham, right? And how was Abraham the first Jew? According to the story, one day he heard this voice that said, "Abraham, from now on, you are a Jew."

After this jab at Christian normativity in the United States, he goes on a brief digression about God's voice before continuing:

> And Abraham was like, "Uh, who are you?" "I am God." "Really? Are you really God? Were you born a God? Are both your parents Gods?" And I guess God must've been happy. He's like, "Hey look, I chose the right Jew! He's asking me all the questions! Hey Vishnu, Rama, Krishna, come on, let's do the 'Hava Nagila'!"

Abraham is questioning God's identity with the same three questions that Koletkar's identity is being questioned. This reinforces for the audience the absurdity of questioning a person's self-identification: Just as it's ridiculous to suggest that God could only *really* be God if he was that way from birth and has the right parentage, it's ridiculous to suggest that about Koletkar. At the same time, just like Koletkar says he doesn't get angry when people question his identity, God doesn't get angry when Abraham questions him here. Instead, Koletkar leans into the stereotype that Jews ask a lot of questions or perhaps the religiously normative value that we are supposed to. Regardless, this creates some legibility and perhaps even promotes a bit of sympathy for the person who is questioning Koletkar's identity. We also get legibility out of the Hava Nagila in its juxtaposition with Hindu deities, who function as a token for Indianness that can be reconciled with Jewishness.

Now he comes to the central point of the routine:

> So OK, let's say Abraham was the first Jew, but he married Sarah. Not born Jewish, no Jewish parents, so obviously not a Jew. And in Judaism, the mother has to be a Jew for the son to be a Jew, therefore Isaac isn't a Jew either. So pretty much, Abraham was the first and the last Jew! The rest of us? The rest of us, just bluffing. How 'bout that for validation?
>
> And see usually at this point, I can differentiate between people of faith and people of common sense. Because people of common sense laugh through the joke, come up to me after the show and say things like, "Dude, that was funny, that was good, that was smart, I like you." People of faith come up to me after the show and say things like, "You are right, Sarah wasn't born Jewish. But you don't know, maybe she converted." And I'm like, "Dude, that's the whole bloody point of my story." So, you're telling me that you're OK with the hypothetical possibility that Sarah might have converted, but you have a problem with the *fact* that my mom did convert.[29]

Koletkar spells things out clearly here by completing his story and then stepping back to describe the audience member who misses the point. If Koletkar's identity isn't legitimate, no Jew's identity is. In making this point, Koletkar affirms his dignity even as he makes himself more legible for the audience—his Jewishness is no stranger than that of Isaac or any other Jew who has come since.

"Airport Security and School Shootings"

> Didn't happen overnight, took me a while, but I'm completely comfortable being onstage saying things that don't elicit laughter. And yet I see people saying, "Hmmm . . . that's a good point," right? Like I'll give you a very basic example. I don't have a ha-ha punchline for

this joke yet, but I talk about how, during this whole demonstration against police brutality one of the excuses given was "a few bad apples." Right, there's always a few bad apples. And I'm like dude for a group of people that are hired, trained, and paid every single day to find the bad apples in the society, a few bad apples is a bad excuse to make. You guys are the experts at finding the bad apples. Find them and throw them out; it's not that hard. Again, I don't have a joke as such. It's more of a statement that I'm making. I'm okay making that statement and not getting a laugh.[30]

In describing his process for developing routines, Koletkar says he starts with a point or idea he wants to get across and then lets the punchlines come later. In the epigraph above, he describes what this process can look like. Although Koletkar is looking for a punchline as he tries out these new ideas on audiences, the comfort he describes with getting no laughter but instead provoking thought in his audience is significant for the political work his humor does. This willingness to deprioritize laughter in favor of a politically salient point like Koletkar's observation here about hypocritical deflections of the systemic nature of police brutality is a key feature—and challenge—of Krefting's charged humor. Krefting notes that such humor often entertains a limited audience and that it can be difficult to achieve commercial success that way. Uncontroversial comedians who are focused on drawing laughs from everyone tend to find their way into the mainstream much more readily. As a consequence, very few comedians are able to perform charged humor exclusively, aside from a few who have already made it big.[31]

Koletkar is no exception, as his "Preparing for an Indian Jewish Baby" routine demonstrated, but he does have some routines that demonstrate his capacity for charged humor, including a very self-aware willingness to be polarizing. To some extent, this was evident in his "There Are No Jews in This World" routine, but it is even clearer in a YouTube clip called "Airport Security & School Shootings: 2 Problems 1 Solution." Koletkar begins this routine by joking that sometimes airport security screenings seem less random than they are supposed to be. He then goes on to defy audience expectations by suggesting that this doesn't bother him, because "it's for the safety and security of all Americans." Although in this case the defiance of expectations is a pretense for setting up the rest of the joke, it continues to demonstrate his unwillingness to be stereotyped as having a particular viewpoint just because of his identity, in this case as a South Asian immigrant.

He goes on to offer the first part of his suggestion:

> See, why not have two lines of security checks at every American airport. One line for all Americans, they just walk in, no checking, nothing, just go. 'Cause let's face it, Americans don't carry bombs on passenger planes, right? They don't. They have separate planes for that. So, they just walk in. The other line for all brown people. Check us for knives, guns, bombs, drugs. I am OK going through that separate line of security check at every American airport.

There are several eye-catching elements to this joke. First is likely the dichotomy he constructs between "Americans" and "brown people." It will eventually become clear that by "Americans" he means white people. His initial phrasing here may be a mis-delivery, or it may be an attempt to soften or obfuscate the racial dimensions of this joke. The goal here might be to keep up the charade of being OK with being racially profiled, so an appeal to a "racially neutral" (white) American as distinct from a racialized, brown person would help to uphold that charade. Through this charade, Koletkar creates appeals to stereotypes about potentially dangerous brown people and creates a kind of legibility for himself by invoking stereotypes. This process of racialization is analogous to what Choudhury describes in her discussion of Minhaj, Ansari, and Nanjiani: Like Koletkar, they operate within frameworks given by audience stereotypes in order to achieve legibility and to draw humor from their out-of-place-ness as racialized others.[32]

Of course, despite the pretense that this is a joke about it being OK to profile brown people, the reality is that white people are the butt of this joke. The audience's reaction to his line about "Americans" having other planes for bombs only elicits a little laughter from the audience at first, with the rest of the audience joining in as Koletkar pauses to let them process what he has said. Having invoked a stereotype about violent brown men, Koletkar subverts audience expectations by highlighting white violence. And, of course, Koletkar only reinforces this point as he continues to describe how this same system would work just as well at schools: "One line for all the brown kids, they just walk in, no checking, nothing, just go [*audience laughs and cheers*]. And just in case somebody missed it, the other line is for the white kids, right?"

Koletkar concludes this routine with a reflexive moment about how this joke lands differently depending on who hears it:

> And see, this is why I like California. You guys laughed at the right time. I told that same joke at a show in Dallas, Texas, a while ago? They also cheered and clapped way too hard at the first half. And then I didn't have the heart to disappoint them, so I did not finish the joke. I'm like why ruin the special moment, right? You guys look happy, I got my applause break, let's just leave it as it is. This is beautiful. Besides, how often are you going to see cowboys cheering an Indian?

Here Koletkar articulates the polarization problem of charged comedy but also hints at how this routine solves that problem: listeners who are unwilling to grapple with the problem of white violence will hear what they want to hear in this routine. And in doing so, they make themselves the butt of the joke for a third time—audience members who laugh at the wrong time make fools of themselves, even if they don't know it. Along similar lines, in our conversation, Koletkar noted that sympathetic audience members don't laugh at this joke so much as they cheer—a reaction he is more than happy to elicit.

Conclusion

> And it was, it was more of—and I talk about this in my stand-up—a lot of my stand-up comes from like, from something that has really happened, its source of truth, but what I did find was this disbelief that I could be Jewish. So, I don't know if it was discriminatory or anything, but it was more of some people just unwilling to imagine that there's a Jew coming out of India because they had never heard of Jews in India, right? So, if anything it would take just sitting down and telling them the whole story of what we've been told, and then leaving it up to them whether they accept it or not and they can do their own research, but I don't know, I don't feel discrimination. There's a

lot of disbelief, but I don't equal disbelief to discrimination. Nobody ever stopped me from walking into anyplace or doing anything, so totally fine.[33]

This chapter has attempted to understand what it means when Samson Koletkar says he has never experienced discrimination as a Jew of Color. It would be easy to interpret this as a mere desensitization via comedy to the structural problems faced by Jews of Color and other minority communities. Koletkar is simply aligning himself with the dominant social order through smiles and laughter, the argument would go. Such an analysis might be appealing in light of routines that invoke stereotypes, like "Preparing for an Indian Jewish Baby." But it would not adequately account for the charged humor in his other routines.

Sara Ahmed may call for us to be killjoys, but she also argues that for marginalized people, self-care is a radical and revolutionary challenge to a society that tells certain people that they don't deserve to be happy. Moreover, she notes that to criticize marginalized people for their coping strategies only furthers their marginalization:

> Sometimes, "coping with" or "getting by" or "making do" might appear as a way of not attending to structural inequalities, as benefiting from a system by adapting to it, even if you are not privileged by that system, even if you are damaged by that system. . . . But to assume people's ordinary ways of coping with injustices implies some sort of failure on their part—or even an identification with the system—is another injustice they have to cope with.[34]

Ahmed's analysis here is crucial for understanding Koletkar, especially his occasional tendency to defy expectations that immigrant comedians have a perpetual duty to perform the exhausting emotional labor of challenging the social structures that marginalize them. To refuse that duty in order to maintain his own resilience is itself a liberatory act.

Although the resilience Koletkar finds through comedy allows him to characterize "discrimination" as too strong a term for his experiences, his comedy does not desensitize him to structural inequities but allows him to address them on his own terms. To treat white supremacy, xenophobia, and Ashkenazi normativity as serious threats would be to acknowledge

that they have power over him. To treat them instead as rooted in ignorance and laughably absurd is to deny their power and insist that they are
beneath his dignity. Not only does such an approach extend the value of
comedy as a form of self-care for Koletkar, but it also inverts the social
order and in doing so challenges it.

Finally, comedy builds social connections for Koletkar that readily
provide a reprieve from potential feelings of discrimination. The comedy
scene, including both comedians and audiences, constitutes a community bound together by laughter. In connecting with other comedians,
Koletkar felt understood in a way he had not before. The unifying force of
laughter was significant not only for helping Koletkar find his own sense
of belonging in the United States but also in bridging social divides such
as that between India and Pakistan. By providing an ability to connect
with audiences, humor allows Koletkar to ensure that he and other South
Asian Americans have opportunities to speak to the public about their
experiences and render themselves legible.

Notes

1 Samson Koletkar, personal communication, December 10, 2020.
2 Sara Ahmed, *The Promise of Happiness* (Durham, NC: Duke University
   Press, 2010), 65–66.
3 This conversation was conducted in collaboration with Maria Carson,
   who also contributed invaluable insights to this project during its early
   stages.
4 Samson Koletkar, personal communication, December 10, 2020.
5 As I do not intend this section to be a comprehensive overview of Indian
   Jewish communities, I am omitting Jewish communities in India that
   have not had many interactions with the Bene Israel, such as the Bene
   Ephraim and Bnei Menashe. For a broader overview, see Nathan Katz,
   Indo-Judaic Studies in the Twenty-First Century: A View from the Margin
   (New York: Palgrave Macmillan, 2007).
6 There is some disagreement about the date, location, and circumstances
   of their ancestors' departure, with some suggesting they were merchants
   during Solomon's reign, others citing the destruction of the First or Second Temple, and others suggesting Yemen or Persia in the fifth or sixth

century CE (Joan Roland, "Bene Israel," *Encyclopedia of Indian Religions: Islam, Zoroastrianism, and Judaism* [New York: Springer, 2018], 126; Shalva Weil, "The Bene Israel Indian Jewish Family in Transnational Context," *Journal of Comparative Family Studies* 43, no. 1 [February 2012]: 72).

7 Jacoba Kuikman, "The Bene Israel of India and the Politics of Identity," *Studies in Religion* 41, no. 1 (2014): 105–6; Roland "Bene Israel," 126; Weil, "Transnational Context," 72.

8 The Cochin Jews had been present in India since at least the early eleventh century, with an additional group of Inquisition refugees arriving around 1511 (Katz, *Indo-Judaic Studies*, 33–38).

9 Kuikman, "Politics of Identity," 107; Roland, "Bene Israel," 128.

10 Joan Roland, *The Jewish Communities of India: Identity in a Colonial Era* (New York: Routledge, 1998), 16–19.

11 Kuikman, "Politics of Identity," 108–10; Roland, *The Jewish Communities of India*, 19–21.

12 Kuikman, "Politics of Identity," 110; Roland, "Bene Israel," 131–32.

13 Kelly Amanda Train, "'Well, How Can You Be Jewish and European?' Indian-Jewish Experiences in the Toronto Jewish Community and the Creation of Congregation BINA," *American Jewish History* 100, no. 1 (January 2016): 4–8.

14 Samson Koletkar, personal communication, December 10, 2020.

15 Train, "Jewish and European," 4.

16 Train, "Jewish and European," 7.

17 Sarah Bunin Benor, "Jews of Color: Performing Black Jewishness Through the Creative Use of Two Ethnolinguistic Repertoires." In *Raciolinguistics: How Language Shapes Our Ideas About Race*, ed. H. Samy Alim, John R. Rickford, and Arnetha F. Ball (New York: Oxford University Press, 2016), 178–79.

18 Eitan Shahar and Maya Lavie-Ajayi, "Using Narratives to Understand the Adaptation Process of an Ethnic Migrant Group from a Resilience Perspective—A Case Study of Cochin Jews in Israel," *International Migration & Integration* 19 (October 2017): 85.

19 Shahar and Lavie-Ajayi, "Using Narratives," 77.

20 Samah Choudhury, "What Makes Humor Muslim?," in *American Examples: New Conversations About Religion*, ed. Michael J. Altman, vol. 1 (Tuscaloosa: University of Alabama Press, 2021), 109, 112–14.

21 Choudhury, "What Makes Humor Muslim?" 119–21

22 Choudhury, "What Makes Humor Muslim?" 118

23 Rebecca Krefting, *All Joking Aside: American Humor and Its Discontents* (Baltimore: Johns Hopkins University Press, 2014), 2–3, 25.

24 Krefting, *All Joking Aside*, 17–24.

25 Krefting, *All Joking Aside*, 199–205.

26 Samson Koletkar, personal communication, December 10, 2020.

27 Samson Koletkar, personal communication, December 10, 2020.

28 Samson Koletkar, personal communication, December 10, 2020.

29 The version of this routine that appears on YouTube continues with a final joke that uses the R-word, which I do not reproduce here. Not only does it not expand upon the observations the joke has already made, but Koletkar has also indicated that he has since become aware of the problems with the term and dropped it from the joke.

30 Samson Koletkar, personal communication, December 10, 2020.

31 Krefting, *All Joking Aside*, 31–32.

32 Choudhury, "What Makes Humor Muslim?" 118–19.

33 Samson Koletkar, personal communication, December 10, 2020.

34 Sara Ahmed, "Selfcare as Warfare," *feministkilljoys*, August 25, 2014, accessed July 31, 2023, https://feministkilljoys.com/2014/08/25/selfcare -as-warfare/.

Selected Bibliography

Ahmed, Sara. *The Promise of Happiness*. Durham, NC: Duke University Press, 2010.

Ahmed, Sara. "Selfcare as Warfare." *feministkilljoys*, August 25, 2014. Accessed July 31, 2023. https://feministkilljoys.com/2014/08/25/selfcare-as-warfare/.

Benor, Sarah Bunin. "Jews of Color: Performing Black Jewishness Through the Creative Use of Two Ethnolinguistic Repertoires." In *Raciolinguistics: How Language Shapes Our Ideas About Race*, edited by H. Samy Alim, John R. Rickford, and Arnetha F. Ball, 171–84. New York: Oxford University Press, 2016.

Choudhury, Samah. "What Makes Humor Muslim?" In *American Examples: New Conversations About Religion*, vol. 1, edited by Michael J. Altman, 106–24. Tuscaloosa: University of Alabama Press, 2021.

Katz, Nathan. *Indo-Judaic Studies in the Twenty-First Century: A View from the Margin.* New York: Palgrave Macmillan, 2007.

Koletkar, Samson. "Airport Security & School Shootings—2 Problems 1 Solution." YouTube video, 6:14, November 22, 2018. Accessed July 31, 2023. https://www.youtube.com/watch?v=MI1MuDKpgbM.

Koletkar, Samson. "Preparing for an Indian Jewish Baby." YouTube video, 3:10, August 22, 2011. Accessed July 31, 2023. https://www.youtube.com/watch?v=ViEymSgVBu0.

Koletkar, Samson. "There Are No Jews in This World!" YouTube video, 5:42, November 10, 2010. Accessed July 31, 2023. https://www.youtube.com/watch?v=sUAEbEsQjUQ.

Krefting, Rebecca. *All Joking Aside: American Humor and Its Discontents.* Baltimore: Johns Hopkins University Press, 2014.

Kuikman, Jacoba. "The Bene Israel of India and the Politics of Identity." *Studies in Religion* 41, no. 1 (2014): 102–15.

Roland, Joan. "Bene Israel." In *Encyclopedia of Indian Religions: Islam, Zoroastrianism, and Judaism,* 126–133. New York: Springer, 2018.

Roland, Joan. *The Jewish Communities of India: Identity in a Colonial Era.* New York: Routledge, 1998.

Shahar, Eitan, and Maya Lavie-Ajayi. "Using Narratives to Understand the Adaptation Process of an Ethnic Migrant Group from a Resilience Perspective—A Case Study of Cochin Jews in Israel." *International Migration & Integration* 19 (October 2017): 75–90.

Train, Kelly Amanda. "'Well, How Can You Be Jewish and European?' Indian-Jewish Experiences in the Toronto Jewish Community and the Creation of Congregation BINA." *American Jewish History* 100, no. 1 (January 2016).

Weil, Shalva. "The Bene Israel Indian Jewish Family in Transnational Context." *Journal of Comparative Family Studies.* 43, no. 1 (February 2012): 71–80.

CONTRIBUTORS

JONATHAN A. ABEL is professor of comparative literature and Asian studies at Penn State University and the author of *Redacted: The Archives of Censorship in Transwar Japan* (2012) and *The New Real: Media and Mimesis in Japan from Stereographs to Emoji* (2023), as well as the co-translator of Azuma Hiroki's *Otaku: Japan's Database Animals* (2008) and Karatani Kōjin's *Nation and Aesthetics: On Kant and Freud* (2017). He edited the special issue of *Japan Forum* entitled "Beyond Fukushima: The Ethics of Cultural Production in a Post-Disaster Japan" (2015) and of *Verge: Studies in Global Asias* entitled "Digital Asias" (2021).

LAUREN BROOKS, PhD, Pennsylvania State University, is associate teaching professor at North Carolina State University. Her research focuses on decentering authority in German language pedagogy by empowering students through project-based learning and on rethinking traditional methods of assessment. She has also written on Kafka and his absurdist treatment of authority across his corpus by analyzing his humor through the US situation comedy *Seinfeld*, a topic she also enjoys incorporating into her teaching. Since 2010, she has taught a range of German language curriculum from novice to advanced, including writing-intensive, conversation, film and media, and literature and cultural studies courses. She was a US Fulbright Scholar at the University of Münster in 2024–25, investigating Germany's colonial past and how its ongoing struggles with racism shape contemporary understandings of national identity and historical memory.

JENNIFER CAPLAN is associate professor and the Jewish Foundation of Cincinnati Chair in Judaic Studies at the University of Cincinnati. She is the author of *Funny, You Don't Look Funny: Judaism and Humor from the Silent*

Generation to Millennials (Wayne State University Press, 2023) as well as numerous articles and book chapters on Jewish humor.

Mᴀʀᴀᴛ Gʀɪɴʙᴇʀɢ is professor of Russian and humanities at Reed College. He is a specialist in twentieth-century Russian literature and culture; modern Jewish literature, culture, and politics; and global Jewish and Holocaust cinema and television. His most recent book is *The Soviet Jewish Bookshelf: Jewish Culture and Identity Between the Lines* (2023). He is also the coeditor of *Woody on Rye: Jewishness in the Films and Plays of Woody Allen* (2013) and the translator and editor of Mikhail Goldis, *Memoirs of a Jewish District Attorney from Soviet Ukraine* (2024).

Dᴀɴɪᴇʟ Hᴇɪꜰᴇᴛᴢ is assistant teaching professor in the Religious Studies Department at the University of Pittsburgh. His research focuses on modern South Asia in relation to themes of transnationalism, mass culture, emotion, and scientific rationality. He is the author of *The Science of Satyug: Class, Charisma, and Vedic Revivalism in the All World Gayatri Pariwar* (2021).

Bᴇʀ Kᴏᴛʟᴇʀᴍᴀɴ is professor of Yiddish studies in the Department of Literature of the Jewish People at Bar Ilan University, Israel, where he is the Yitzhak and Clara Sznajderman Chair in Yiddish Culture and Hasidism and head of the Rena Costa Center for Yiddish Studies. He served as scholar-in-residence and visiting professor at the Yeshiva University, Kokushikan University in Tokyo, the University of Cape Town, Vytautas Magnus University in Kaunas, Lithuania, and recently the Tohoku University in Sendai, Japan. He is the author of a number of monographs in the field of Yiddish culture, among them *Broken Heart / Broken Wholeness: The Post-Holocaust Plea for Jewish Reconstruction of the Soviet Yiddish Writer Der Nister* (2017); *Disenchanted Tailor in "Illusion": Sholem Aleichem Behind the Scenes of Early Jewish Cinema, 1913–16* (2014); and *In Search of Milk and Honey: The Theater of "Soviet Jewish Statehood" (1934–49)* (2009).

Mᴀʀᴋ Lᴇᴜᴄʜᴛᴇʀ's field of research is ancient Judaism. His work includes the study of mythology in ancient Israel and Second Temple Judaism, the phenomenon of prophecy in the ancient Near East, the formation of the Hebrew Bible, and the history of the Israelite priesthood. He earned his PhD from the University of Toronto and currently serves as director of Jewish studies at Temple University. He has previously served as coordinator of biblical studies at the University of Sydney, Australia, and visiting professor of Hebrew Bible at the University of Pennsylvania. His favorite band is Rush.

Grace Kessler Overbeke is assistant professor in the Theater Department of Columbia College Chicago with a focus on comedy writing and performance. Previously, she served as the Perilman Postdoctoral Fellow in Jewish Studies at Duke University. Her monograph, *Jean Carroll: The First Lady of Laughs* was published in 2024. Other recent scholarship appears in *Shofar: An Interdisciplinary Journal of Jewish Studies*, *Theatre Topics*, *Theatre Annual*, *The New England Theatre Journal*, *Theatre Survey*, *Studies in American Humor*, and *The Jewish Forward*. She received her BA in theater and English from Wesleyan University and her MA and PhD from Northwestern University's Interdisciplinary PhD in Theatre and Drama program.

Avinoam Patt is the Maurice and Corinne Greenberg Professor of Holocaust Studies at New York University and the Ingeborg H. and Ira Leon Rennert Director, NYU Center for the Study of Antisemitism. He previously held the Doris and Simon Konover Chair of Judaic Studies and was the director of the Center for Judaic Studies and Contemporary Jewish Life at the University of Connecticut. He is the author of multiple books on Jewish responses to the Holocaust, including *Finding Home and Homeland: Jewish Youth and Zionism in the Aftermath of the Holocaust* (Wayne State University Press, 2009); the coeditor (with Michael Berkowitz) of a collected volume on Jewish displaced persons, *"We Are Here": New Approaches to Jewish Displaced Persons in Postwar Germany* (Wayne State University Press, 2010); and a contributor to several projects at the United States Holocaust Memorial Museum, including *Jewish Responses to Persecution, 1938–1940* (2011). He is also the author of *The Jewish Heroes of Warsaw: The Afterlife of the Revolt* (Wayne State University Press, 2021). Together with David Slucki and Gabriel Finder, he is the coeditor of *Laughter After: Humor and the Holocaust* (Wayne State University Press, 2020), and with Laura Hilton he is the coeditor of *Understanding and Teaching the Holocaust* (2020). His most recent works include the book

Israel and the Holocaust (2024) and the coedited volume *The Surviving Remnant: Documents on Jewish Displaced Persons in Postwar Germany, 1945–1950* (2024).

ARIANE SANTERRE is professor of French literature at Collège Jean-de-Brébeuf in Montreal, Canada, and a researcher affiliated with the Canada Research Chair in Music and Politics at the University of Montreal. She is the author of *La Littérature inouïe: Témoigner des camps dans l'après-guerre* (2022). With Marie-Hélène Benoit-Otis, she co-commissioned the multimedia exhibit "Sur l'air de la liberté: Chansons de résistantes dans les prisons nazies" on songs written by French female Resistance fighters in Nazi prisons, presented in Montreal in spring 2025 and touring in France in 2025–27. A virtual exhibit is also accessible online.

LIAT STEIR-LIVNY is full professor at Sapir Academic College and the Open University of Israel. She teaches in the Department of Culture at Sapir Academic College, the Cultural Studies MA program, and the Department of Literature, Language, and the Arts at the Open University of Israel. Her research focuses on Holocaust commemoration in Israel from the 1940s until the present. It combines Holocaust studies, memory studies, cultural studies, trauma studies, and film studies. She is the author of many articles and six books.

JARROD TANNY is professor of history and the Charles and Hannah Block Distinguished Scholar in Jewish History at the University of North Carolina Wilmington. His first book, *City of Rogues and Schnorrers: Russia's Jews and the Myth of Old Odessa* (2011), examines how the city of Odessa was mythologized as a Jewish city of sin, celebrated and vilified for its Jewish gangsters, pimps, bawdy musicians, and comedians. Odessa's Yiddish-inflected humor drew him further into humor studies, and he has published numerous essays on the subject, such as "Curb Your Orgasm: Larry David and the Schlimazel as Sexual Deviant" in *Jewish Film & New Media: An International Journal*, and "Decoding *Seinfeld*'s Jewishness" in *Studies in Contemporary Jewry*. Tanny's obsession with *Seinfeld* yielded his second book, *The "Seinfeld" Talmud: A Jewish Guide to a Show About Nothing* (2023). Tanny also frequently publishes opinion pieces on antisemitism and Jewish identity in *The Forward*, *Tablet Magazine*, *The Times of Israel*, *The Jewish Journal*, and *The Jewish Review of Books*.

INDEX

Note: Page numbers appearing in *italics* refer to photographs.